THE TASTE FOR BEAUTY

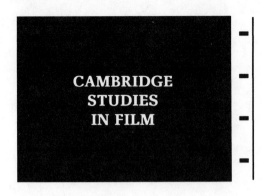

**CAMBRIDGE
STUDIES
IN FILM**

OTHER BOOKS IN THE SERIES

THE TASTE FOR BEAUTY

ERIC ROHMER

Translated by
CAROL VOLK

Compiled for *Cahiers du cinéma* by Jean Narboni

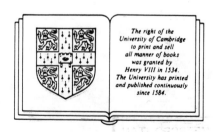

The right of the
University of Cambridge
to print and sell
all manner of books
was granted by
Henry VIII in 1534.
The University has printed
and published continuously
since 1584.

CAMBRIDGE UNIVERSITY PRESS
CAMBRIDGE
NEW YORK   PORT CHESTER   MELBOURNE   SYDNEY

Published by the Press Syndicate of the University of Cambridge
The Pitt Building, Trumpington Street, Cambridge CB2 1RP
40 West 20th Street, New York, NY 10011, USA
10 Stamford Road, Oakleigh, Melbourne 3166, Australia

First published 1989

Printed in the United States of America

Library of Congress Cataloging-in-Publication Data
Rohmer, Eric, *1920–*
[Goût de la beauté. English]
The taste for beauty / Eric Rohmer ; translated by Carol Volk.
    p.   cm. – (Cambridge studies in film)
Compiled for *Cahiers du cinéma* by Jean Narboni.
Translation of : Le goût de la beauté.
ISBN 0-521-35152-9 (hard covers)
ISBN 0-521-38592-X (paperback)
1. Motion picture plays – History and criticism.
I. Narboni, Jean.   II. Title.   III. Series.
PN1995.R63513   1989
791.43'75 – dc20   89–22229

British Library Cataloguing-in-Publication Data
Rohmer, Eric, *1920–*
The taste for beauty. – (Cambridge studies in film)
1. Cinema films
I. Title   II. *Cahiers du cinéma*
791.43

ISBN 0-521-35152-9 (hard covers)
ISBN 0-521-38592-X (paperback)

Contents

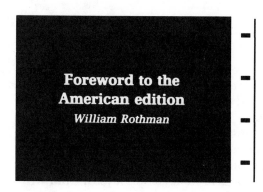

My films, you say, are literary: The things I
say could be said in a novel. Yes, but what
do I *say*? My characters' discourse is not
necessarily my film's discourse.... What I
say, I do not say with words. I do not say it
with images either, with all due respect to
the partisans of pure cinema, who would
speak with images as a deaf-mute does with
his hands. After all, I do not say, I show. I
show people who move and speak. That is
all I know how to do, but that is my true
subject.*

In recent years, the advent of what is called "theory" in academic film
study has led the field to turn away from the study of authorship in
film, both from critical studies of individual authorships and from reflection on the implications of the *fact* of authorship in film, on the conditions that make authorship in this singular medium possible.
Historically, this turning away occurred at the precise moment rigorous practices of film criticism, responsible to the films and to the critic's experience, were being instituted in the university, and film study
was claiming – and beginning to earn – its rightful place in the university's intellectual life.

When the field turned away from "author criticism," it turned away
from criticism as such. Instead of critical acts grounded in experience,
it turned to a succession of "isms" that shared a common understanding of the role of theory: Theory was to be primary, and was to be applied to films from the outside, seeking neither inspiration nor evidence from the films themselves or from the theorist's experience of
them. Predictably, these theorists discovered in the films only what the
theories they were applying had already determined, a priori, to be
there. As a consequence, the achievements of the masters of the art of

* From "Letter to a Critic: Concerning my *Contes Moraux* (*Moral Tales*)."

film – that is, the films themselves – and the achievements of those critics who defied fashion and never abandoned criticism remain substantially unacknowledged by a field that nonetheless possesses the means to acknowledge them. In other words, this "turning away" was – and is – also a repression.

For film study to undo this repression, to come to itself in the wilderness of theory, it must attain a new perspective on itself: on its own history; on its subject, film; and on film's history. I view the publication in English of this collection of Eric Rohmer's essays on film written between 1948 and 1979 as an important step toward this goal.

Love them or hate them (and all film lovers seem to do one or the other), no one would deny that Eric Rohmer's films bear his personal signature. Rohmer has his own unique style, method, and thematic concerns and his unique vision of the power and limits of the film medium. Rohmer is an *auteur* if ever there was one. And as the essays in this volume abundantly demonstrate, when it comes to film criticism, too, Rohmer is an author who must be taken seriously.

"I don't believe there is one good critic who isn't inspired by an *idea*, whether of art, of man, or of society," Rohmer writes.* It is clear that Rohmer is indeed inspired by such an idea, around which all his critical writing revolves: It is Bazin's seminal insight that the key to film lies not in the realm of language but in the realm of ontology, in film's unique, unprecedented relationship to reality – a relationship that is radically different from that of literature, theater, or painting.

Until film, one had either to paint a painting or describe something. Being able to photograph, to film, brings us a fundamentally different knowledge of the world, a knowledge that causes an upheaval of values.†

Film doesn't say, it shows. For Rohmer, this principle has fundamental implications on the nature of the *art* of film.

Painting, poetry, music, and so forth try to translate truth by the intermediary of beauty that is their domain, with which they cannot leave without ceasing to exist. Film, on the other hand, uses techniques that are instruments of reproduction or, one might say, of knowledge. In a sense, it possesses the truth right from the beginning and aims to make beauty its supreme end. A beauty, then, and this is the essential point, that is not its own, but that of nature. A beauty that it has the mission of discovering, and not of inventing, of capturing like a prey, of almost abstracting from things.... But although it is true that the cinema manufactures nothing, it doesn't deliver things to us in a neat package either: It arouses this beauty, gives birth to it.... If it gave us nothing

* From "Of Three Films and a Certain School."
† From the interview with Jean Narboni.

but things that were known in advance, in principle if not in detail, all it would capture would be the *picturesque*.*

In turn, what film is has fundamental implications for the direction the history of the art of film has taken. .

Ever since the cinema attained the dignity of an art, I see only one great theme that it proposed to develop: the opposition of two orders – one natural, the other human; one material, the other spiritual; one mechanical, the other free; one of the appetite, the other of heroism or of grace – a classical opposition, but one that our art is privileged to be able to translate so well that the intermediary of the sign is replaced by immediate evidence. A universe of relationships therefore appeared that the other arts may have illuminated or designated but could not show: the relationship between man and nature and between man and objects – directly perceptible relationships that are quite beautiful – but also, since the age of the talkies, the less visible relationship between the individual and society.†

I have quoted these passages at length because they are so characteristic. Reading the essays in this volume, so profoundly insightful, so cogently and eloquently expressed, it continually strikes me that Rohmer is very much a figure from a bygone age, an age these pages bring vividly to life – the postwar age when the best minds of a generation (at least in France) fervently believed in cinema, believed that making films, and also viewing and thinking about them, was a heroic enterprise. It was the age of André Bazin's pioneering investigations of the ontology of film, the age of the founding of *Cahiers du cinéma*, the age of the triumphant emergence of the "Nouvelle Vague." And it was also the age that immediately preceded film study's turning away from criticism. It is no accident that it was the thinking of this postwar age, and specifically thinking like Rohmer's, that film study repressed above all when the field turned away from criticism.

Nor is it an accident that the essays in this volume, which speak to us from a bygone age, are nonetheless so stunningly contemporary. I do not mean by this that they resemble current writing about film, which of course they do not. Rather, Rohmer's questions and ideas are fresh and alive today precisely because they have been repressed, not addressed, by film study. The vibrant life in Rohmer's writing gives it the power of making most of today's academic writing about film seem obviously repressed and repressive, dead from the neck up and the neck down, and specifically *dated* – dated because it is clearly past time for such denial of life to end.

As a filmmaker, Rohmer is not only still active but at the peak of his powers, continuing to make films that are at once classical and

* From "The Taste for Beauty."
† From "Of Three Films and a Certain School."

astonishingly modern. In his films as in his critical writing, Rohmer strikes me as a figure out of the past. Yet his films, old and new, also have the power of making most other films seem dated. These films about contemporary life, pulsing with life themselves, are decisive demonstrations of the undiminished power of the ideas that are worked out in this volume – ideas about humanity, freedom, history, space, time, language, art, beauty, and, of course, about the medium, the art, and the history of film.

The ideas that stand behind Rohmer's films are also those that stand behind his critical writing, enabling it to penetrate to the heart of the films made by the masters he most admires, such as Renoir, Murnau, Hitchcock, Hawks, and Rossellini. Rohmer's own films cry out for criticism that is equally penetrating, honest, responsible, and philosophical. I hope that the publication of this volume will help spur the field to undertake to acknowledge Rohmer's exemplary authorship. That is a challenge fit to awaken film study from its dogmatic slumbers.

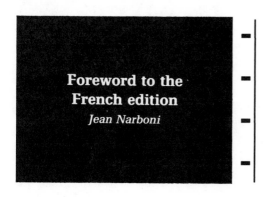

Foreword to the French edition
Jean Narboni

This four-part collection of articles written between 1948 and 1979 contains the most important of Eric Rohmer's essays on film. The articles appeared in various publications, primarily *Les Cahiers du cinéma*.

"The classical age of film" treats both fundamental and theoretical questions from different angles, but from a single theoretical viewpoint: questions of space and development, dogma and re-creation, different levels of discourse, classicism and the avant-garde, ontology and language.

The title of the second part refers to the famous injunction ("For an impure cinema") by André Bazin, whose closest disciple is still Eric Rohmer. It opens with the analysis in the form of homage that Rohmer paid to *What Is Cinema?*, discusses the problems of literary adaptation, and points out the (at times involuntary) beauty that sprang from "marginal" films: those in which the idea of mise-en-scène – an accepted notion today but that was newly adopted at the time – came to life.

The third part is dedicated to these "marginal" films. Because it discusses directors such as Hawks, Rossellini, Hitchcock, and Ray, it needed a title like "The *politique des auteurs*" to indicate its diversity. Last but not least is the section entitled "Jean Renoir," because for Rohmer and a few others, he is still the greatest of them all.

The author of these articles did not wish to see them republished in their original state, nor did he wish to modify or annotate them. "The critical years," a recent and unedited interview, provides the distance necessary to put them in perspective.

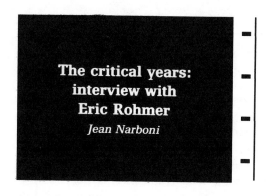

The critical years: interview with Eric Rohmer

Jean Narboni

NARBONI: I offered to publish your essays on film: You didn't want them to appear as they were (even annotated), and you didn't want to update them with a preface; you wanted instead to talk about them. I'd like to know why.

ROHMER: You were the one who wanted to publish them, not I. Under the circumstances, the choice had to be yours, not mine. And since I had no desire to publish these essays, I didn't really want to write a preface, either. I don't want to publish them, but I'm not opposed to it. Many books by journalists are published. Sometimes they're posthumous works, and so the author isn't there. But when he is there, it's normal for him to indicate the distance between his current thoughts – his thoughts at the moment of publication – and his thoughts at the time he was writing. But if I had to write down all the differences, I'd never finish. It therefore is up to you to ask me questions, because I don't know what I'd say, except for this very vague and general thought: There are many things that I wrote at the time that I would no longer write. There are other things that I wrote that I would still write today. But is that at all interesting for the readers?

NARBONI: I think that for the readers, one thing may seem to be missing: a certain piece that was very important to many film enthusiasts. It appeared in *Cahiers* in five parts, entitled "Le Celluloïd et le marbre," and was almost an essay in itself. In it you began by noting that film generally was analyzed in terms of the other arts. In response to this, therefore, you wrote some articles on the modern novel, painting, architecture, music, poetry, and so on. But now you don't want to publish them.

ROHMER: That is, in fact, the only restriction I made. Why? Because, as you said, it's practically an essay in itself, and so I might want to publish it as a separate piece, if at all. But I don't want it published as it is now because there are too many things that I no longer believe and that now seem horribly naive to me – so much so that I'd have to write

1

notes that would be longer than the essay. And since I haven't the least desire to address this question, or even to write film theory, let's just say that I'm putting it all off for the moment, perhaps forever.

In any case, this is how I'd define "Le Celluloïd et le marbre": I introduce myself as a film buff. That is, I speak in the name of this film buff, not in my own. The film buff seems to judge the other arts a bit too hastily. In fact, as a film buff, he recognizes that he lacks the cultural background necessary to judge the other arts. So he judges them from the point of view of a film buff, with a knowledge only of film. It's obvious that his judgments are extremely naive, unpolished, and reactionary. He doesn't know anything about modern art, because the aesthetics of film date back to before modern art, before impressionism – impressionism having been a reaction to photography. The film buff doesn't ask that the other arts return to the past; he's not quite that pretentious; he believes they must follow their own path, which is – in any case according to him – a dead end. He thinks that they're going to die at any minute and that another, younger art will take their place: film.

Now, in retrospect, many things have become apparent. I will say – quickly – that this return to the past, which seemed impossible in the fifties, has happened in the other arts. The international style in architecture and functionalism has been thrown into question. Likewise, painting has returned to the figurative style. In literature, it seems as if traditional forms are no longer ignored as they were before. Here I'm talking about the novel, poetry, and theater. As for music, it's more difficult to say. The greatest phenomenon of the twentieth century, I believe, is that there are two types of music: on the one hand, concert music and, on the other, popular music. Right now, owing to new techniques, especially electronic ones, it seems as if there's a bit more exchange between the two than there was in the fifties. Music is the most mysterious art. The things I wrote about music are what would have to be explained the most. But on the other hand, film has entered a decadent period – I'm not using this word in a pejorative sense – it's gone beyond its classical era. My theory, which I outlined in an article for *Combat,* called "L'Age classique du cinema," was that film's classical period was not behind us, but ahead. Now I'm not so sure. What I'm saying now might be just as open to criticism as what I said then. I therefore don't want to address the question. The only thing I can say for sure is that I no longer consider film to be the savior of all other arts, an art that could begin a new era, just as Jesus Christ began the Christian era. This idea may be more pessimistic in regard to film but may be more optimistic in regard to the other arts.

In addition, there are two "Celluloïd et le marbre." There's the series of articles published in *Cahiers* in 1955. And ten years later in 1965, there's the television program that was completely different but that had the same title. I was no longer the film buff questioning himself about other arts; I was instead asking the contemporary artist about film. I spoke to artists who seemed to me to be at the forefront of art at that time: people like Xennakis in music, Vasarely in painting, Parent and Virilio in architecture, Claude Simon and Klossowski in literature, Planchon for the theater, and so forth. One day Claude-Jean Philippe gave me the idea for the program. He asked me: "Why don't you do something on 'Le Celluloïd et le marbre'?" The program is part of a series called "Cinéastes de notre temps" ["Filmmakers of our times"], produced by Janine Bazin and André Labarthe. Labarthe's collaboration was important, especially for the selection of the artists. Labarthe knows contemporary art very well. My way of questioning the artists no longer was critical of the other contemporary arts; I tried to be very open. I was the opposite of what I was in the articles. It's no longer a question of a film buff who thinks that in order to love film, he has to be closed to contemporary art; it's a film buff who believes that loving film doesn't prevent him from being open to contemporary art. Oddly enough, at that time I found myself agreeing with *Cahiers*'s new viewpoint, when Rivette had interviews with people like Barthes, Lévi-Strauss, Boulez, and so forth. Today, with a new generation of artists, things would be different still.

NARBONI: You've written for several publications, as different as *Les Temps modernes, La Gazette du cinéma* (which you founded), *La Revue du cinéma, Cahiers*...Could you give us a history of your criticism, and tell us what it was at each time? Who were you fighting against before *Cahiers* became the champion of the *politique des auteurs,* the Hitchcocko–Hawksians, and so on? What was the climate like, and who was your adversary? Even the articles you wrote before the ones in *Cahiers* were always rather polemic.

ROHMER: I think it comes from *L'Ecran français*. There was a disagreement among the staff of *L'Ecran français,* which was a very popular weekly review at the time of the liberation. There was one group, Bazin–Astruc, that had its roots in *La Revue du cinéma,* which unfortunately appeared very infrequently and disappeared, I think, in 1949. The *Revue* was directed by Jean George Auriol, and that's where I wrote my first article, "Le cinéma, art de l'espace." That group represented the aesthetic wing. And then there was the political wing. Bazin and Astruc were, for example, the only ones who said good things about American film. During the cold war it was not acceptable to say anything good about American film. Little by little, all the people from Bazin's group – which we could call the noncommunist wing – left, and *L'Ecran français* became communist and finally teamed up with

Les Lettres françaises. The spirit of opposition is still around from those years.

NARBONI: What about you, weren't you writing then?

ROHMER: I wrote something in 1948 for the last edition of *La Revue du cinéma,* while *L'Ecran français* was still in existence. I had given Astruc an article that had appeared in *Les Temps modernes,* entitled "Pour un cinéma parlant." I asked him if he could publish it in *L'Ecran français,* and he told me that he'd broken off with *L'Ecran français,* that it had become communist, but that he could give the article to Merleau-Ponty at *Les Temps modernes.* I left *Les Temps modernes* a few months later, because of a review of the Biarritz festival. I had done it on purpose – it was quite a feat, in fact – I had written something like: "If it's true that history is dialectic, at some moment conservative values will be more modern than progressive values." Jean Kanapa picked up on this and wrote in *Les Lettres françaises:* "You see, *Les Temps modernes* is reactionary." I don't think that Merleau-Ponty had read my article, and my collaboration stopped there.

NARBONI: What was your first occupation?

ROHMER: I was a teacher, I taught in Parisian high schools.

NARBONI: After your break with *Les Temps modernes,* how did you come to write for other publications, *Gazette du cinéma, Cahiers,* and so on?

ROHMER: I presented films at the Latin Quarter film club, which is where I met Rivette. Rivette wrote a remarkable article criticizing film editing, for the film club's bulletin. We transformed the bulletin with the help of Francis Bouchet, a television producer, into *Gazette du cinéma,* which published some of Rivette's articles and some of Godard's articles signed Hans Lucas. Truffaut didn't work on the *Gazette;* I met him at the Festival du film maudit sponsored by Objectif 49.

NARBONI: Did the film club have any specific orientation?

ROHMER: It had been founded by one of my former students, who was very resourceful. He was able to show copies of films that were going to be destroyed. We saw an enormous number of films there, especially American films from the thirties. The good thing about this film club was that it was for film buffs, and they showed the most films possible, without picking and choosing. It was different from the university film club which had its own theory, which showed film masterpieces, as judged by critics, by Moussinac, for example. But our film club showed everything, and that allowed us and our audience to say: "This is a masterpiece, this isn't."

NARBONI: How did *Gazette du cinéma* evolve?

ROHMER: The *Gazette* had the support of the film club. We had wanted to change the film club bulletin into a paper, but we never managed to sell it at kiosks. It was very naive to try to get into all of that; I had financed a part of it, and some friends had given money as well. But we were lucky: We had readers from the film club, and *La Gazette's* first issues were profitable. But the last issues were unprofitable, and the *Gazette* disappeared. We thought of replacing *L'Ecran français,* but no one ever succeeded. There was never another film weekly. The weekly papers that came later were television weeklies, like *Telerama.*

NARBONI: Later on, there was *Cahiers?*

ROHMER: No, *Cahiers* is something entirely different. *La Gazette du cinéma* was the work of my film club friends, that is, Rivette, Godard, and me. Our film club was considered to be very amateurish. The people at *Cahiers* came from a different film club made up of professional critics, former collaborators from *La Revue du cinéma* – whose director, Jean George Auriol, had just died in an accident – as well as Doniol, Bazin, Kast, Astruc, Dabat, and so forth. The mentors of the group were Jean Cocteau, René Clément, and Robert Bresson. It had been founded at the end of 1948 and was called Objectif 49. It was a film club that, unlike ours, had a definite philosophy and debates that were held by all of these people. I joined them sometimes myself. Having begun to write for *La Revue du cinéma,* I could speak like a critic or even, I might say, like a film announcer and not just like a member of the audience, but I was really just a newcomer. Objectif 49 was led primarily by Doniol-Valcroze, who had decided after Jean George Auriol's death – and even when he was alive – to continue the *Revue du cinéma.* Because he couldn't get Gallimard's name, he took another one, *Les Cahiers du cinéma.* The first editions of *Cahiers* were very eclectic, written by people like Chalais, Mauriac, and so on. Even I was invited to write. My friends at *La Gazette du cinéma* came into it later. Truffaut, for example – I'm talking about this as if it were a political plot – had connections on both sides. He had a place in Objectif 49 because of his friendship with Bazin, and it was as Bazin's friend that I met him, rather than from the film club. Rivette, though, was connected only through *La Gazette du cinéma.* Rivette and Godard came from the *Gazette* side, Truffaut from the Bazin side. In the end, we all became friends; we went to films together and formed a small group, thereby creating a nucleus at *Cahiers du cinéma* that grew and grew, until the publication of the famous thirty-first issue which marked the first attack on "French quality cinema."

NARBONI: Thirty issues, that means the group had been in existence for over two years. But you and your group had had very definite ideas way before that, through the Festival du film maudit, the *Gazette,* your

Eric Rohmer and Jean-Luc Godard celebrating the thirtieth anniversary of *Cahiers du cinéma*.

taste for American films, and so on. Why did this statement appear so late?

ROHMER: You have to separate my situation from my friends': Each one has his own story. In Truffaut's case it was a bit different; his article had been written one year earlier. It was put aside because of his attack on René Clément. As for me, Doniol had asked me to write something, and so I did. But Godard and Rivette waited a year before agreeing to write something.

NARBONI: You say that there were two sides in criticism, an aesthetic one and a political one, more or less identified with the Communist party. When I reread the entire batch of articles, I noticed there was a great deal of criticism that focused on content. You and your New Wave friends considered yourselves to be advocates of the idea of mise-en-scène. But political and even religious and ethical ideas also seemed to have contributed to your philosophy. In rereading Truffaut's article "Une certaine tendance du cinéma français," which everyone saw as the most violent attack on "quality" film, I was struck by the fact that Truffaut also attacked these films on the grounds that they were blasphemous, childishly anarchist, and antireligious. You also wrote political criticism. You didn't like "decadence" . . .

ROHMER: Yes, that's true. It's difficult to talk about. I could say that that's the most outdated part of what we wrote. But in fact, I'm not quite sure. Let's just say that at the present time, I wouldn't get involved in politics – no one does anymore, not even *Cahiers du cinéma*. Having said that, there are many ideas today that I consider right leaning but that the left claims: For example, the idea of specifics – which extends to regionalism and nationalism – was considered extremely reactionary. Today, that's no longer the case. Criticism of industrial progress was considered to be a purely rightist idea, but now it's more or less a leftist theme. While reading these articles you have to make an allowance for the right wing's provocation, which I was not necessarily consciously aware of. It came from the polemic we had with *Positif,* which was, at the time, very political.

NARBONI: If we take away the part played by circumstances or provocation, there still remain some fundamental ideas. You were often charged with being a conservative, but I noticed that your articles continually advance the idea of modernity – you cited Rimbaud's famous injunction several times. I'd like you to talk about the relationship between the modern side, which you have always championed, and your desire to preserve a classical side. How could you both attack what you called decadence and refuse to look toward the past?

ROHMER: My idea is very simple, and I still believe it. It's the idea that in the evolution of art there are cycles, and so it returns to the past.

There was Antiquity and the Middle Ages, then the Renaissance, then once again we returned to the Middle Ages with romanticism. It's as simple as that. When I say, "We have to be absolutely modern," I mean that to be modern sometimes means being backward looking, although right now I'm against such "retro" tendencies. I'll use a simple example: In the past, if an architect had been told that he could design a house with a roof, he would have fallen into a horrible rage, it was unthinkable. Now, a modern architect does design houses with roofs. To lock oneself into a so-called modern form, and to want it to remain fixed, represents a conservatism worse than saying "Classical values are permanent." I thought that modern art was somewhat deceptive. It could be just as tyrannical as classical art, and as tyrannies go, we may as well have classical tyranny! But I was careful to indicate that I was speaking in the name of modernity.

NARBONI: Yes, in fact, everyone was surprised when you finished making your film for educational television, on the changes in industrial landscapes. Some people were expecting a nostalgic film, but you insisted on the true beauty of modern architecture.

ROHMER: In an article that is the introduction to an interview that Michel Mardore and I had with Henri Langlois, I said that the preservation of the past ensures the possibility of modern art. If museums were to disappear, we would have to start painting like Raphaël again, but as long as Raphaël's paintings still exist, why bother imitating him? We can do other things. So we should preserve the past. It's the same for film. Maintaining links with the past, with the works of the past, doesn't prevent our moving forward — quite the opposite. In other words, in my opinion — and if I reread this sentence later on I don't think I'll be ashamed of it — I've always been against destruction. I think that in order to build, we mustn't destroy. Many people think the opposite, that destruction is necessary. I don't agree at all: New structures must take their place next to old ones. There's plenty of room in the universe; destruction is not a prerequisite for construction. That's why, politically, I'm a reformist more than a revolutionary. It's true that in the seventies, the word *revolutionary* was so revered that to say "I'm a reformist" seemed incredibly vulgar — but I think that now it's OK to say it.

NARBONI: At the time, there was a certain kind of film content that you didn't like: It was the opposite of films that glorified ideas of grandeur and nobility, heroic acts, and equilibrium between man and nature.

ROHMER: In this, I think that Rossellini had a great influence. If you want to retrace my aesthetic and ideological itinerary, you'd have to start with the existentialism of Jean-Paul Sartre, which made its mark on me in the beginning. I never talk about Sartre, but he was still my starting point. The articles that appeared in *Situations I,* which discovered Faulkner, Dos Passos, and even Husserl, contributed a great deal to my thinking. I went through an existentialist period before I began thinking about film, but the influence remained, I think, and continued to affect me in my first films. Rossellini is the one who turned me away from existentialism. It happened in the middle of *Stromboli.* During the first few minutes of the screening, I felt the limits of this Sartrian realism, to which I thought the film was going to be confined. I hated the way it invited me to look at the world, until I understood that it was *also* inviting me to look beyond that. Right then and there, I converted. That's what's so great about *Stromboli.* It was my road to Damascus: In the middle of the film, I converted, and I changed my perspective.

NARBONI: You went through the same changes as Ingrid Bergman did in the film.

ROHMER: Yes, it's extraordinary! That's what I tried to show in my article for the *Gazette,* to show that these values of grandeur, values that were completely rejected at that time, the resolution to create greatness using great means was able to exist through film, whereas the ideology at the time was to create something from nothing.

NARBONI: In talking about *Pauline at the Beach (Pauline à la plage),* you once said that you'd always been in favor of the optimistic film, in the tradition of Renoir – even if it led to sad, cruel films and might include death – rather than existential films like – as you mentioned – Wim Wenders's films, for example.

ROHMER: That's right. I'm very sensitive to the existential charm of film, which we see, for example, in Antonioni or Wim Wenders. That's the way I feel at the moment. In fact, I recently saw *Alice in the Cities (Alice dans les villes)* again, and I found it wonderful, yet I'm still as in favor of optimistic films as I was then.

NARBONI: For you, then, the source of film's greatest current is "the boss," Jean Renoir?

ROHMER: Renoir is something else, he represents another current. Renoir is no longer at all existentialist. But he's modern. More expressionist than impressionist, closer to Cézanne than to his father. There's a Brechtian side to him as well, a certain didacticism, but much more deeply buried. I might have been opposed to Brecht as a film critic, and none of Brecht's ideas, in fact, has come to the cinema, except perhaps through Renoir. You mustn't look for Renoir's modernism in the same place you find it in Antonioni or Wenders: It's completely different, it's unique, inimitable. Renoir is the least theatrical of all the filmmakers, the one who goes the furthest in his criticism of the theater and, at the same time, the one who is closest to the theater. It's a total paradox. It's the paradox of film, which is an art without being an art, performance without being performance, theater without being theater, which rejects theater, in fact. For me, in this sense, Renoir is the greatest of them all; I can see his films over and over and always find something new, and just the fact that his importance has not yet been recognized proves to me that he is in fact the greatest.

NARBONI: Greater than Hawks, for example, who is another of your favorite filmmakers?

ROHMER: Hawks's importance has not yet been recognized either, it's the same thing. It is recognized, they say, but in my opinion, Hawks is way above the place they've assigned him. Hawks is different from Ford, different from Walsh. I think people who admire Hawks generally admire him as an American filmmaker. At the moment, I'm rather anti-American, but that doesn't prevent me from liking Hawks, because there's a paradox in him, just as there is in Renoir. As far as I'm concerned, Hawks and Renoir are not so different, but I can't talk about that here. I can only say again what I said about Hawks in a little article on his filmography: He is not the filmmaker of appearances but the filmmaker of being.[*] What does that mean? I can't say. I can't explain it, but that's what it is: There's no difference in his films between being and appearing. It's not being and nothingness, either. It's being opposed to being, I could say.

NARBONI: Rivette ended his article "Génie de Howard Hawks" ("The Genius of Howard Hawks") with this sentence: "What is, is." [†]

ROHMER: Yes, in the end what I'm saying isn't original, since Rivette has already said it, but I agree with him.

NARBONI: Your articles are based on the idea that film isn't an art that says the same things that the other arts say, but just in a different manner. Instead, it's an art that says things that are fundamentally different.

ROHMER: Yes, and that's an idea that I still believe in very much.

NARBONI: It was very strange at the time to say things like that.

ROHMER: That's why I was opposed to all the sixties' structuralist and linguistic ideas. For me, the important thing in film – to repeat what Bazin said – is ontology and not language. Ontologically, film says something that the other arts don't say. In the end, its language resembles the language of the other arts. If one studies the language of film, one finds the same rhetoric as in other arts, but in a rougher, less re-

---

[*] *Cahiers du cinéma* 139, January 1963 (Howard Hawks special issue), p. 39 (JN).
[†] *Cahiers du cinéma* 23, May 1953, p. 23 (JN).

fined, and less complex style, an idea that leads nowhere except to say that film is able to imitate the other arts, that it does so with great difficulty, but that it isn't always bad. There's a nice metaphor for you, it's almost Victor Hugo!

NARBONI: It would mean taking note of the rhetoric and letting the essential part go unnoticed.

ROHMER: The essential part is not in the realm of language but in the realm of ontology.

NARBONI: That's the theoretical foundation of your collected articles.

ROHMER: Yes, but all I'm doing is organizing Bazin's ideas. He said, with regard to *Monde du silence (The Silent World):* "To show the bottom of the ocean, to show it and not describe it, that's film." Now, literature describes it; painting paints it; and by freezing it, by interpreting it, film shows it – for example, Nanook the Eskimo harpooning the walrus. It's like nothing else, it has no equivalent. Until film, one had either to paint a painting or describe something. Being able to photograph, to film, brings us a fundamentally different knowledge of the world, a knowledge that causes an upheaval of values. That is what I tried to prove, rather awkwardly, but I can't say it any better, it's very difficult to explain.

NARBONI: When you say that, one has the impression that the most important thing is in the realm of becoming, of time – in *Nanook of the North,* for example – and yet you wrote an article called "Cinema, the Art of Space."

ROHMER: There is a cinematic space, different from pictorial space – although some believe it can be reduced to pictorial space – that is the source of aestheticism. You have to be careful about space. The cinematic being reveals himself in space as well as in time. To tell the truth, he reveals himself in space-time, since in film one cannot dissociate one from the other. All I can say here is that this idea is very important to me, as you can see from what I've written. Perhaps today I would express it differently.

NARBONI: I've heard that you claim to write your film critiques after having seen the film only once. Yet you often write from the perspective of an enlightened amateur, and concerning some of the actors' nuances, gestures, and postures, or the lighting, you say that these things require two or three showings. You wrote, for example, that the first time one sees *Eléna et les hommes (Paris Does Strange Things),* one thinks that the actors are marionettes jumping around but that at a closer glance, the acting and gestures are infinitely varied.

ROHMER: That's true, but I wrote several kinds of articles. There are those that I wrote for *Arts* after seeing the film once. For *Cahiers,* I often saw the film twice. But I really believe in the first showing. It often happens that I see films again and don't change my opinion or even that I see fewer things the second time, but there are some films that I couldn't appreciate until I had seen them several times – Jean Renoir's films, for example. In general, my dedication to a film doesn't come after the second or third showing, but in the middle of the first, as was the case with *Stromboli.* At that time, maybe, I believed less in the subjectivity of judgment; now I believe in it entirely and consider myself to have been quite obstinate at the time. Yet I was not alone. It was rare that the point of view I chose was a purely personal one, opposed to the opinions of my friends at *Cahiers du cinéma.* Everyone agreed with the opinion we were defending. We all pretty much liked a film, or we were worked up over a film, but I don't think it ever happened that someone at *Cahiers du cinéma* would say good things about a film that everybody else hated. When I say *us,* I'm talking about the Hitchcocko–Hawksian wing. On the other hand, there was a little battle between Pierre Kast, in particular, and us.

NARBONI: The first time I spoke to you about the idea for this book, you told me: "My most personal articles are not in *Cahiers,* indeed, some of my articles in *Cahiers* were contaminated by the group."

ROHMER: I agree. Having a group is good – you know that yourself – because it tears you away from your subjective judgment and opens horizons for you. There's no question we enlightened one another. Some people bring in one kind of writer, some bring in others, but at the same time there is the danger that the sensitivity of the group will mask personal sensitivity, and one will feel obliged to defend things that one doesn't really care about deeply. Some filmmakers didn't influence me, and I haven't thought about them since; they didn't affect me in any way. I don't even know, in fact, if I wrote about them. The mannerists, the stylists, Ophyls, Minnelli, and Preminger, for other reasons, are people I never was spontaneously attracted to; I merely went along with other people. In the same way, it seems to me that Truffaut wasn't very affected by Dreyer. We each had our own taste, but in the end there was a great harmony of tastes and ideas among our team, a great sincerity.

NARBONI: In rereading today the list of filmmakers whom you defended at the time – Renoir, Rossellini, Hawks, Dreyer, Nicholas Ray – not to mention the older ones, Murnau, Eisenstein. One feels that you were right. But do you have the feeling that you were unjust toward some filmmakers whom you, Eric Rohmer, find more interesting today? It seems to me, for example, that your evaluation of Buñuel has changed.

ROHMER: Yes, I've changed. But even then, I wasn't too hard on Buñuel. I violently attacked one of his films that I haven't seen since, but I don't think it was very good: *Cela s'appelle l'aurore.* I generalized, perhaps too much. On the other hand, I said good things about *Archibaldo de la Cruz.* About Chaplin? It was crazy to say bad things about Chaplin and then to say good things about Buster Keaton. Chaplin is extraordinary, that's clear. I saw his last films again on television. I wonder how I could not have liked *A King in New York* before. It's very close to *The Testament of Dr. Cordelier (Le testament du Dr. Cordelier)* and to *The Elusive Corporal (Le Caporal épinglé).* The very type of film I should have defended. But in the fifties, Chaplin was still considered as the one and only genius of cinema. Fortunately, there are others.

NARBONI: You were one of the first to have talked about Chaplin in terms of his mise-en-scène at a time when one spoke primarily about the content of his films, of the comical side, or, as Bazin so magnificently did, of his mythology.

ROHMER: That's true. The Cinémathèque was the great generator of values. Murnau had been completely forgotten. I wrote: "Murnau is the greatest of all filmmakers," and I don't think I was wrong. Pabst was considered the greatest at that time. I was rather hostile toward Sjöström, and I don't know whether I was right or not. I maintained that *L'Aurore,* which was shown at the Cinémathèque one week after *The Wind,* was far superior. Renoir's *Grand Illusion (La Grande illusion)* and *A Day in the Country (Une Partie de campagne)* were admired at the time, but many people, even then, considered Feyder to be even better.

NARBONI: From time to time we witness attempts to revive filmmakers who may have been unfairly overlooked because of Renoir's presence. Duvivier or others. Very quickly, the difference becomes apparent. But you surprised me before by saying that you like Carné and Clair a great deal. Your critical works certainly don't reveal this appreciation.

ROHMER: We were very hard on filmmakers like Feyder and Duvivier. On the other hand, I was influenced by Carné. I had two epiphanies. One from *Stromboli* and, ten years earlier, one from *Port of Shadows (Quai des brumes),* a surrealist-existentialist *tour de force.* All the tendencies of the years immediately preceding the war are seen in this film. I find that Gabin's metaphysical dimension appears the most distinctly, especially in the scene at Panama's in which he doesn't want anyone to speak: There is a fundamental opposition to language as language. I say Carné, not only Prévert, because Carné was influenced quite a bit by the German Kammerspiel films. Carné was a great admirer of Murnau, and he paid homage to him in a scene in *The Cheaters (Tricheurs),* I think, where some young people go to the Cinémathèque to a projection of *Tabu.* All of Carné's films are made in the

Kammerspiel form; that is, they take place in a single location. In my *Comédies et proverbes (Comedies and Proverbs)*, I pay homage to Carné by ending my films in the same way they begin. *Pauline,* for example, begins at the gate and ends at the gate. In *Hôtel du nord,* it's the bridge on the canal; in *Port of Shadows,* the road; in *Daybreak (Le Jour se lève),* the besieged house, and so on. I saw Carné's films from this period again. I don't want to say anything about his recent films, which I haven't had a chance to see again – for better or worse. I'd rather limit myself to the older ones. *The Gates of the Night (Les Portes de la nuit)* may be a failure, but it is one of the most ambitious works in the history of film. You have to wait until Antonioni and Wenders to find this style again, for example, when Montand enters and says to Bussières's wife: "Your husband is dead," even though he's alive. The whole scene is based on discontent, an existential discontent, and not on comedy or tragedy, or a mix of the two. There is great precision in Carné's films, which unfortunately is coupled with a lack of imagination in the images, and yet some shots of Jouvet in *Hôtel du nord* do have a Murnauesque side.

NARBONI: You like the German side of Carné?

ROHMER: The German side from the twenties, yes. The rest of French film from between the wars lacks formal precision. There's no real link between the mise-en-scène and the image, as there is in Carné's work, no spatial precision, even though Carné's space is artificial and stiff compared with Renoir's. Some remarkable work is being done on the sets in his films. Few French films are built around the set in the way that *Hôtel du nord* or *Daybreak* is. Bazin admired Carné, in fact: He wrote an interesting article on *Daybreak* showing that each object had a particular function in the film.

And then there's René Clair. I was touched – later on and less deeply, but quite touched – by *Quatorze juillet.* There again, I liked the extremely solid construction. One finds it in Buñuel sometimes as well: its "not-a-hair-out-of-place" aspect, often coupled with a sort of dryness. I'm also crazy about *A Nous la liberté,* in which the assembly-line gag appears, a gag that Chaplin repeated in *Modern Times.* Clair said that Chaplin had given him so much that he certainly had the right to steal something! I think that French film has deep roots in Carné and in René Clair, and not just in Renoir. For my part, I'm indebted to Clair and Carné as well as to Renoir.

NARBONI: All this didn't show up in your writing.

ROHMER: That's true, aside from two allusions made in passing to *Port of Shadows* and *Quatorze juillet.* To tell the truth, my period of admiration for Clair and Carné came before I began writing.

NARBONI: On the other hand, there is a filmmaker about whom you have written a great deal – Bergman – whom at first sight one would not expect you to like. His films are the epitome of existentialist cinema, their modernity hidden by certain archaisms in the mise-en-scène.

ROHMER: First of all, you have to consider the period. At the beginning, while we were involved in all the polemics, we defended people who matched our aesthetic tastes; the acknowledged values didn't interest us. It was paradoxical to defend Hawks, Hitchcock, or Renoir. Then, when we finally became the majority at *Cahiers du cinéma,* and when I became the editor, this changed. It was no longer a question of trying to defend what we liked unconditionally but also of making the public aware of important filmmakers. It's a completely different task. Maybe we set aside our individual tastes, and the Bergman phenomenon came about. We said to ourselves, "Bergman is someone who is very important, we have to talk about him." It happened that for me, because there were things in Bergman that I felt an affinity for – there were others things I felt more distant from – it happened that I started talking about Bergman. I could have talked about Fellini just as well, but for Fellini the job was left to others.

NARBONI: There were things that touched you in Fellini's work as much as in Bergman's?

ROHMER: Fellini is a great filmmaker, I think, but I'm not quite sure why, I never knew much about him. If someone were to say to me, "Is Jean Renoir a greater filmmaker than Duvivier?" I would swear on my life that he is. But if someone asked, "Bergman or Fellini?" I'd be stumped. I like Bergman's films, I said good things about them. I liked Fellini's films less, but in the end, Fellini might be a greater filmmaker. I seem to be very unkind to Bergman. One thing is certain: I've become somewhat detached from him – perhaps I'm wrong – after a small run-in. In short, I don't think that Bergman inspired me any more than Fellini did.

NARBONI: In 1963 there was a sort of battle at *Cahiers* between the Ancients and the Moderns, in which you appeared to be the defender of classicism. In an article for *Cahiers Renaud–Barrault,* you recently stated that Marguerite Duras was a tremendous filmmaker. How did this change of heart come about concerning what was considered in the past to be the height of modernity or the avant-garde?

ROHMER: Well, I've changed, and then again I haven't changed. In my article in *Combat* I said, "In film, classicism is ahead." In 1949 when I wrote that, classicism was ahead; that is, chronologically it was to come, but in 1983 we can consider that it's behind us; Marguerite Duras was possible only because the classical age of film had already passed. Before classicism, what was the avant-garde? It was film that copied other arts, pseudopictorial film, and so on. Duras was possible because classicism went through all that, because Rivette – who is perhaps the most obvious descendant – went through that.

NARBONI: What do you like in her films?

ROHMER: Marguerite Duras is a little like Bergman; her universe doesn't touch me personally, I'm a stranger to it, it's distant. I've never written about her, and I'm not here to do so, but I think that she brings a new element to Bazin's theory, according to which theater and film are the same. But the theater she films is not the *théâtre du boulevard*. It's not avant-garde theater either, such as Ionesco or Beckett. It's a postcinema theater.

NARBONI: Oddly enough, you also wrote about the lettrist movement and Isidore Isou, and you wanted very much for us to republish this piece.

ROHMER: At the start of it all, there was a provocation. I wanted to show the people at *Cahiers du cinéma* that my point of view was very modern, that we were not only the pillars of the Cinémathèque, reactionaries admiring Hollywood, refusing the great topics, social questions, Buñuel, and so forth. Modernism for me wasn't surrealism, it was lettrism, which corresponded completely to my idea at the time that the arts were on the road to destruction. Lettrism is the absolute end of literature, since the word disappears and is replaced by the letter and noncodified sound.

NARBONI: Yet you weren't an iconoclast. You never were.

ROHMER: I wasn't iconoclastic. Besides, I didn't agree with lettrism at all. I didn't think that film's destiny was the destiny suggested by Isou, I said only that he should be taken into consideration. He was, in a certain sense, the precursor of the "happening." Whatever happened on the screen was destined only to stimulate the spectator's participation. He also said that Godard hadn't invented anything. There were in fact some of Godard's ideas in what he said – if only the idea of mistreating the film, dirtying it, stomping on it, or even just neglecting the links in editing.

NARBONI: Many of the New Wave filmmakers have used film as a point of reflection in their films, sometimes addressing it directly: Truffaut in *La Nuit américaine (Day for Night)*, Godard in *Contempt (Le Mépris)*, and so forth. You seem very far away from this. You are more wary of cinematic clichés in film than of theatrical or pictorial clichés.

ROHMER: Yes, and this is truer and truer. I believe more and more what I wrote in my last article, that is, that cinema has more to fear from its own clichés than from those of the other arts. Right now, I despise, I hate, cinephile madness, cinephile culture. In "Le Celluloïd et le marbre" I said that it was very good to be a pure cinephile, to have no culture, to be cultivated only by the cinema. Unfortunately, it has happened: There now are people whose culture is limited to the world of film, who think only through film, and when they make films, their films contain beings who exist only through film, whether the reminiscence of old films or the people in the profession. The number of short films by novices who in one way or another show only filmmakers is terrifying! I think that there are other things in the world besides film and, conversely, that film feeds on things that exist outside it. I would even say that film is the art that can feed on itself the least. It is certainly less dangerous for the other arts.

NARBONI: Does that make you want to eliminate the explicit presence of the cinema in your films, or in addition, does that make you want to look elsewhere, to the theater or painting or to conversation?

ROHMER: You mean in their contemporary form? Painting and the plastic arts mostly. The theater for *Perceval.* Music very indirectly. As for current literature, I'm not very familiar with it.

NARBONI: Do you feel there is continuity between your activities as a critic and your activities as a filmmaker?

ROHMER: I don't know. Even in the past, it was wrong to think that my criticism paved the way for my films, since I began to shoot – in 16mm – before I began to write.

NARBONI: The wariness in regard to cinematic clichés and the importance of conversation are so great in your films that often one hears the question "Where is the cinema in all this?"

ROHMER: Currently, I want to make a film with few words. In fact, I made one: *Le Signe du lion (Sign of the Lion).* That being said, I most often have been inspired by people who talk for a very simple reason: The situations I know best in life are those in which people talk. Situations in which no one talks are the exception. It has nothing to do with literature but, rather, with reality.

NARBONI: There's an article that I absolutely wanted to include, the one on *The Quiet American,* which in my opinion contains many things that later appeared in your films. You never defended psychology in *Cahiers,* and you even defended Renoir's opposition to it, yet you write that this is a great psychological film. Moreover, there are people, often specialists, who talk about themselves, who talk intelligently about why they are as they are. There is, then, this professional quality such as one finds in your films. Not to mention the taste for plots, machinations, and playing with language. In the end, it's a film that you say conjures up the muffled silence of libraries more than the ambience of a movie theater.

ROHMER: The taste for plots is part of my Balzacian side. I've been compared with many moralists, people whom I'm not particularly interested in, Laclos, Marivaux, Jacques Chardonne, and so on. All I have to say is, No, that's not it, my authors are Balzac and Victor Hugo. Balzacian, yes. That is, antiexistentialist, against the new novel, against people like Moravia, Sartre, and Beckett. In Balzac's novels one finds content in conversations. But in twentieth-century novels, there are conversations but no content. Their sense exists between the lines; the characters' sentences are flat. Second, in twentieth-century novels things occur, one is subjected to them, but there's no plot. The plot is something which is completely outdated. There's no psychology either. I personally have always been in favor of psychology. In his last films, which never cease to amaze me, Renoir claims not to have used psychology, but he shouldn't be taken literally. They're nothing like the films of Antonioni, Wenders, or Buñuel. Against psychological convention, OK. But against the psychological consistency of characters, no. I love to portray thinking people, people gifted with a psyche. I still believe that film founded on intrigue and characters is always modern – if not more modern than apsychological, dedramatized film. It's the latter, which in the eighties seems to be on its last legs.

(Interview conducted in November 1983)

CHAPTER I
**The classical age
of cinema**

Cinema, the art of space

The systematic use of the still shot, in works by directors like Orson Welles, Wyler, or Hitchcock, has recently reminded us that the art of cinema is not limited solely to the technique of changing frames. Indeed, even today, the expressive value of the interplay of dimensions, or of the displacement of lines on the screen's surface, can be the object of rigorous attention.

Up until the past few years, we could have characterized the evolution of film by the weakening of a certain *sense of space,* not to be confused with a pictorial sense or a simple visual sensibility. It is remarkable that this evolution became noticeable only about ten years after the invention of editing. If the birth of film as an art dates back to the time when "the scriptwriter imagined his story divided into shots" it is not, as André Malraux* stated, because the motion picture is a means of reproduction and not of expression, but rather because the technique of using a sequence of shots helps reinforce the expressive nature of each one. It does so, for example, by making slight movements perceptible (the batting of an eyelid, the clenching of a fist) or by allowing the viewer to follow the trajectories of movements that actually extend far beyond his visual field. Compared with theatrical space, cinematic space would thus be defined by the narrowness of its visual surface and by the breadth of its place of action. The director must therefore determine not only the interior of each shot according to a certain spatial concept but also the total space to be filmed: The coming and going of the train in Buster Keaton's *The General* depicts a very precise spatial obsession.

The concern with spatial expression, then, appeared very early in the history of film. One may wonder, after all, whether Méliès's *The Doctor's Secret (Hydrothérapie fantastique)* is not as purely cinematic

---

* *Esquisse d'une psychologie du cinéma* (Verve 1941).

Buster Keaton in *The General*.

as is one of the *"montage savant"* [intellectual montage films] of 1925–30. This concern came first historically, but also logically, in the logic of an art – the art of movement par excellence – whose duty is to organize its hierarchy of significations according to a general concept, either of time or of space, without any reason beforehand why time should play a privileged role. On the contrary, space would seem to be the general form of sensibility most essential to film, given that film is a visual art. This is why the works considered to be pure cinema – the films of the avant-garde – were especially concerned with the problems of plastic expression, with creating a "cineplastic" of gesture.* Nonetheless, we should be aware that some of these films, whether Cocteau's *Blood of a Poet* (*Sang d'un poète*) or Buñuel's *An Andalusian Dog* (*Un Chien andalou*), reveal a method of signification that is

* See *De la Cinéplastique* (Elie Faure, *L'Arbre d'Eden*), *Idées d'un peintre sur le cinéma* (Marcel Gromaire, *Le Crapouillot* 1919).

linked more to literary or pictorial concepts than to truly cinematic ones. One cannot determine the extent of a film's purity by its degree of abstraction but, rather, by the specificity of the means it uses.

It is therefore not necessary to demonstrate once again how certain directors were influenced by the aesthetics of painting – to look for a "distortion" analogous to one found in a painting by Paolo Uccello or El Greco – or by the aesthetics of dance – to see how the actor's movements resemble those of ballet dancers. Rather, it is necessary to indicate to what extent cinema can use its own means of expression in this area. The very nature of the screen – a completely filled rectangular space occupying a relatively small portion of one's visual field – encourages a plasticity of gesture very different from what we are used to seeing on the stage. For example, the arm movement common to an opera singer, which the characters in Méliès's films use, is more easily justified in theatrical space, which is at once fixed and undefined, than inside a rectangle whose edges are clearly indicated and that only provisionally circumscribes a variably wide portion of the surface where the action takes place. The film actor's gestures have become gradually more discreet and also more "compact," distorted, as it were, by the edge of the screen's proximity. The director bides his time, waiting to interrupt the actor the moment he violates the plastic equilibrium, an equilibrium that may be pursued as diligently as in a painting or a fresco. Moreover, as paradoxical as it may seem, the space of the screen was a three-dimensional space even before the systematic use of depth of field, whereas the space of the stage usually has only two dimensions. The height of the stage makes movement from front to back imperceptible for at least a part of the audience. In film, on the other hand, the great directors made a point of suggesting the depth that the screen lacks: It cannot be merely coincidental that the visual theme of the spiral is found in works like *Caligari* (the kidnapping of Lil Dagover), *Nosferatu* (the "eight" on the car in the land of the ghosts), *The General Line* (the line of carts on the winding road), and *The Lady from Shanghai* (the fall of the toboggan). Finally, spatial forms of expression must correspond to a film's general method of expressing time. That is, each spatial distortion must be accompanied by a distortion in time, a slowing down or a speeding up. By establishing its own rhythm into which the individual rhythm of each shot can be integrated, editing can remarkably change the expressive character of a particular movement.

Hence, contrary to what one might think at first, a film may run a greater risk of being accused of aestheticism while having a smaller degree of purity, such as when the director's intended style is not able to determine the content, according to the mode of expression adopted, in a sufficiently rigorous manner. Works whose subjects are richest in direct emotional impact have the hardest time avoiding visual clichés. When the expressive character of a shot seems to be merely a parasitic element, the beauty of the image will be sought on its own. From our point of view, the most valid films are not those with the most beautiful pictures, and the collaboration of a genius cameraman* cannot ensure that a film will depict an original view of the world.

A geometry of the comical

This is why our first examples will be taken from works that are least suspected of aestheticism: comic films. We have already shown how in Chaplin's films there is a perfect understanding of the demands of cinematic perspective, of the difference between the screen and scenic space. Yet his films cannot be considered examples of a spatial art of expression depicting a universe in which movements and gestures acquire meaning beyond their emotional sense, which is somehow more essential to their mobile nature. This type of research seems incompatible with the human character of Chaplin's art. Visual gags such as Charlie followed by the barrel of the carbine (*The Gold Rush*), Charlie near the freight elevator (*Pay Day*), Charlie followed by the policeman (*The Adventurer*), and so on, are sufficient proof of Chaplin's purely cinematic genius. Yet gestures, stances, and movements take on meaning only in reference to the series of states of consciousness or intentions that they reveal, one by one: Spoken language or mimicry is replaced by an "allusive" mode of expression, less conventional than the first, subtler and richer than the second, but whose value depends not on the necessary quality that gesture acquires by means of its presence in a certain space, but on the relationship we establish between the gesture and its significance. Sometimes, it is true, in the most intense emotional moments – joy or fright, adversity or triumph – the movement ends up devoid of any precise meaning and develops by following its own rhythm. These moments, which constitute the height of Chaplin's art – Charlie menaced in the store (*The Store*), Charlie fighting a duel (*Carmen*), Charlie ripping open the pillow (*The Gold Rush*) – cannot be considered the most typical examples of a pure comedy of movement, as they spring from an overflow of emotion, which in expressing, they transfigure, but from which they still derive meaning.

This is valid not only for Chaplin but also for all those who have been influenced by him. With a more rigorous logic but with less genius, René Clair was able to have his characters evolve inside a universe where their smallest intentions were immediately translated into

* Unless there is perfect agreement between the cameraman's and the director's concepts, as in the case of Toland–Wyler, Toland–Welles.

spatial language. Even the choice of a setting for *Quatorze juillet* allowed him to tell his story by simply moving the camera back and forth from one side of the street to the other. Space here is more a convenient means of signifying than it is a creator of signification. On the other hand, a less refined cinema, based on a less psychological concept of the comical, is closer to a pure art of movement: A more intense though less "intelligent" laughter is born of the simple confrontation of two dimensions, of the mechanical repetition of a gesture. One can find many examples of this in Mack Sennett's films and in the first American burlesque films. The Marx brothers' burlesque, even in its most purely cinematic moments (the curtain dropped to stop the cannon balls in *Duck Soup,* the state room full of people in *A Night at the Opera*), still refers too much to the usual signification of gesture. The absurd in their work becomes apparent only in relation to an already established code of meaning.

Though rarely noticed, it is mostly in Buster Keaton's films that we can see a spatial universe in which gestures and movements take on new meaning. Buster Keaton is not only one of the greatest comics of the screen but also one of the most authentic geniuses of film. Many people have pointed out the mechanical quality of his comic scenes, which a certain dryness renders rather disconcerting at first glance. True, he cannot be included among the burlesque, whose rich imagination he lacks, or among Chaplin's imitators, although he was strongly influenced by him. One is correct in considering the allusive style he frequently uses to be rather poor. The reason is that the psychological significance of a movement counts much less for him than does the comical aspect, which is revealed in the way the movement is etched on the space of the screen. In *Battling Butler,* for example, for almost fifteen minutes we watch the novice boxer try in vain to recreate the simple uppercut movement that his manager is trying to teach him. This comedy of failure would not be original if the awkwardness of the gesture had not been developed, so to speak, in its own right – to the extent that the gesture can finally find an aesthetic justification through repetition – but especially because it appears as a sort of questioning of space, an inquiry into the "workings" of the three dimensions – in this case ludicrous, but one that could just as well be troubled and tragic. To continue with this film, its most extraordinary moment is undoubtedly when, in spite of himself, the boxer gets tangled in the ropes as he tries to enter the ring. The impossibility of describing the humor of such a "position" to someone who has not seen the film guarantees the authenticity of its cinematic value.

Conversely, even Chaplin's most visual discoveries – Charlie juggling bricks, Charlie walking on his knees, Charlie sinking into a tub he thought was empty – make us laugh when we describe them. This is not an isolated incident: Throughout his films, Buster Keaton expresses an obsession with a certain type of clumsiness and solitude whose equivalent cannot be found in film. In a note attached to the publication of *America,* Max Brod tells us that certain passages of Kafka "irresistibly evoke Chaplin." But it is more in Buster Keaton, than in Chaplin or even in Langdon, that one should look for a vision of the world that, because of its rigorous nature and geometrical activity, would approach the inhuman world of Kafka. Solitude for Chaplin, even in the famous scenes of *The Circus* or *The Gold Rush,* is never more than man's solitude in an indifferent society. For Buster Keaton, the isolation of beings and things appears instead as intrinsic to the nature of space. Such isolation is expressed particularly by a back-and-forth movement – as if everything were continually "returned" to itself – as well as by the brutal falls, the flattening on the floor, and the awkward grasping of objects that turn or break, as if the external world were impossible to grasp. Moreover, this obsession can take on a more static nature: The relationships among the dimensions of objects or among the characters' respective heights are always carefully attended to.*

The example of Eisenstein

Eisenstein's work offers another example. Of all directors, he is certainly the one whose sense of proportion is the most intense, to the point that each of his shots respects to the millimeter the rules of the golden mean. Many have also spoken of a *distortion* comparable to that found in Grünewald, Tintoretto, or El Greco, a distortion that cannot be explained by the almost constant use of low-angle camera shots. We should emphasize that the vanishing of lines along one or two dominant directions, the swelling of diagonals, always takes place *in the direction of the movement* and organizes the principal planes along which the surfaces slide into the shot. In this way the shot is constantly saved from aestheticism. In addition, the precision of the editing makes it possible to follow the same visual obsession across a series of shots. A universe is thus constructed in which the most abstract movement has meaning. The human content of the messages expressed in Eisenstein's first films, and the realism of their subjects, has prevented us from seeing to what point his world was as arbitrary a construction as that of *The Cabinet of Dr. Caligari* or *The*

* "All gags are drawn from rules of space and timing....A good comical scene often contains more mathematical calculations than does a mechanical work" (Buster Keaton, quoted in *La Revue du cinéma,* March 1, 1930).

Que Viva Mexico! by S. M. Eisenstein.

Passion of Joan of Arc (La Passion de Jeanne d'Arc). One may find *Ivan the Terrible* or *Alexander Nevsky* less endearing than *Potemkin, The General Line,* or *Que Viva Mexico!,* but they do not in the least indicate a weakening of Eisenstein's imagination. We should cite, among other examples, the death of Ivan the Terrible and, in *Alexander Nevsky,* the closing in of the battle, in which the confrontation of the two armies is treated like a "pure" crashing and rebounding of two masses in space.

A metaphysics of space

Perhaps even more daring is German expressionism, which exerted a strong influence between 1920 and 1925 but whose intentions are not always clearly understood. It is unfortunate that today the term *expressionism* is often used simply to indicate the introduction of a certain arbitrariness in acting, a stylization in gesture. More specifically, it indicates the exploration of an exaggerated expression that is not designed to increase quantitatively the immediate power of expression but, rather, to give it a *different* meaning, a meaning that, though reinforced by its attachment to reality, does not at any moment risk being confused with it. Movements and gestures whose meaning seemed contingent are in a sense – by their insertion into a certain spatial universe – grounded in necessity: Lips spread in laughter, an arm raised in self-defense, a face convulsed in anger – all are enriched by new meaning that can deprive them even of their direct emotive powers and leave them with only their pure quality of *fascination.*

We cannot criticize the German expressionists, as we can the surrealists, for seeking inspiration in concepts outside film, on the pretext that the aesthetics to which they conformed had already been tested in painting or theater. We do not want to minimize the influence of Max Reinhardt's ideas on the modern mise-en-scène, but one must recognize that more than theater, film was the art form that lent itself best to the application of his ideas. For example, the spatial distortion created by the set of *Caligari* has a much more violent effect on the screen than it does on the stage.

It is fitting to pay special homage here to F. W. Murnau. Because his films are not shown often enough, his place – perhaps first – among the great directors is not always recognized. As rigorous as Eisenstein's universe may be, it is often not more than a setting for actions that in themselves have great beauty and grandeur. Murnau was able not only to avoid all anecdotal concessions,* but also to dehumanize those subjects richest in human emotion. Thus, *Nosferatu* is constructed entirely around visual themes corresponding to concepts that have physiological or metaphysical equivalents in us (the concepts of suction or absorption, of being held or being crushed, and so forth). All elements that draw our attention to something other than the immediate feeling of transcendence within the gesture are eliminated: all elements, for example, that could have created a scary atmosphere, because the fascinating side of horror ceases the instant it turns to fear, that is, emotion. *Tartuffe, The Last Laugh,* the admirable yet greatly debated *Faust, Sunrise,* and the "documentary novel" *Tabu* reveal, through their shots, the richest cinematic imagination possible.

Spatial expression and language

Are we witnessing a return, if not to expressionism, at least to a more systematic demand for style? In their desire to use as little as possible certain methods – already-proven methods whose existence cannot be denied – some of today's directors are beginning to follow a new sty-

---

* Most of his scripts are written by Carl Mayer.

Gösta Ekman and Emil Jannings in *Faust* by F. W. Murnau.

listic code which, though it may seem more impoverished, has been purged of certain visual clichés and permits a more rigorous organization of dramatic content according to the mode of expression adopted. If such an attempt appears more awkward than it did during the silent period, it is not only because the introduction of speech has weakened the audience's visual sensitivity or because commercial demands – which are much more tyrannical today – force the story to maintain an anecdotal quality. One must not forget that in their day (at least in Germany) *Nosferatu* and *Caligari* touched a very broad audience and that some works as popular as *Broken Blossoms, Covered Wagon,* and even Douglas Fairbanks's films contain a sense of space that many avant-garde films would envy. The modern audience (and in this connection, the principal turning point in the evolution is not marked by the date when sound began but by the moment when the allusive procedures of narration replaced the descriptive mode) has been too long accustomed to interpreting visual signals, to understanding the reason for each image, to become suddenly interested in the *reality* of what they see. The cinematic spectacle is now presented more as something to decipher than as something to view. The audience's eye is no longer naive enough to be fascinated for long by sinuous bodies intertwined in the usual brawl or by a frantic gallop across the screen.

Orson Welles is probably the only modern director who succeeded in imposing a spatial universe on us; a universe whose wealth of imagination can be compared with that of Murnau and especially with that of Eisenstein, with whom, at least from this perspective, Welles shows an affinity of temperament. We find the same spatial obsessions, characterized by a preference for low-angle shots, among other things (for instance, the low archways of *Ivan the Terrible* and the ceilings in *Citizen Kane*).

At the same time, Wyler's art seems much more in agreement with the demands of current audiences. André Bazin analyzed him in depth.* Let us just say that in the universe of *Little Foxes* or in *The Best Years of Our Lives,* the relationship between the sign and what is signified is specified. Wyler has merely created a specific language to express a predetermined psychological content, by visual as well as spatial means. Wyler's script is deliberate and allusive, in the same way that the editing of Chaplin or Pudovkin is.

The methods that the modern director uses for spatial expression are much less apparent than they were twenty years ago. As in the other arts, it is normal that the evolution of film lean toward greater economy in its means of expression. This simplification may lead to greater realism: Rossellini's success in *Paisan* is to have relied as little as possible on the editing and to have avoided breaking up his work into too many shots – though such fragmentation seems to impose itself when working with action scenes. Even in such a realistic art, simplification demands, as compensation, a certain richness in spatial expression – one very different from the distortions of the plastic arts. Even the choice of subject is primordial: The themes of the black soldier swept away by the little shoeshine boy, the crossing of the Arno, the followers wandering in the Po plain, correspond to an obsession whose mere presence brings a mythic quality to the story.

In a completely different sense, that of the search for stylization, Hitchcock's work is extremely rich in lessons, but his brilliant style is sometimes combined with an insufficiently rigorous concept of the relationship between content and expression. Bresson's art is undoubt-

* Issues no. 10 and 11 of *La Revue du cinéma:* "William Wyler ou le Janseniste de la mise en scène."

edly purer. *Les Dames du Bois de Boulogne* (*Ladies of the Park*), so unjustly condemned, represents the attempt most worthy of being compared with German expressionism. The fact that stylization in the expression of time is given more attention than is spatial construction, is a measure of the distance separating modern cinema from that of the "*grande époque*" of silent films. In learning how to understand, the modern moviegoer forgot how to see, and if film has succeeded in educating us visually, it did not do so by making us more sensitive to the pure signification of certain forms or movements. To the extent that an art of seeing still exists, we are, quite simply, more likely to understand the intentions of a language that can have the nuance and subtlety of a spoken language but that most often remains every bit as conventional.*

(*La Revue du cinéma* 14, June 1948)

For a talking cinema

Film took more than thirty years to learn to manage without speech, and so it is not surprising that after eighteen years, it still has not learned to use it. I'm talking about the distrust the best directors show toward the one power of language that is essential to it, that of *signifying.* If talking film is an art, speech much play a role in conformity with its character as a sign and not appear only as a sound element, which, though privileged as compared with others, is but of secondary importance as compared with the visual element. Even today there is too great a tendency to believe that a film is better if it can easily do without speech, and that a cinematic work worthy of this title must lose very little when seen in the original version by a foreign audience. We admire the wonderful *Lost Weekend* because with purely visual means – or with sound – Billy Wilder was able to make clear his characters' slightest intentions; eventually, however, we're sorry they speak. Speech is either superfluous or indispensable. In principle, it cannot be added without need or taken away without harm.

Without exaggerating, one can say that until now there has only been *sound* cinema. The mistake of filmmakers in 1930 was to believe that the only important problem was the cinematic treatment of sound and that the solution to the problem of speech, a secondary problem – how could one introduce the method of signifying which is language into a visual art? – could be obtained as a simple corollary to the solution of the first problem. All the ensuing efforts tended toward weakening the power of the word. It was quickly noticed that the word was

* This article is signed Maurice Scherer (JN).

a sound before it was a sign, and as an immediate consequence, it was agreed that speech had to be treated as a way of being, not of revealing. A line in film does not depend only on those that precede or follow it: It exists in time and not in the script; as a simple instant in the unfolding of the film, it needs other instants, even silent ones, to support it. "The primary problem for a film writer," wrote André Malraux in *Verve* in 1940, "is to know when his characters must speak."

Not that clever methods must be used; the problem of speech cannot be reduced to a simple question of setting. Increasing specialization, which in most cases applies to the director, is certainly one of the causes of this misconception. I know that some scriptwriters understand that one does not write for the screen as one would for the stage or the printed page. On the contrary, one could even say that they unnecessarily change the script, on the pretext that film demands special treatment. But these changes had much more effect on the mode of presentation than on the *meaning* of the dialogue. One would be correct in defining most of the dialogues written for film until now as theater dialogue in the style of a novel. The film actor's script is generally such that in its written form it would naturally call for the "he said" with which a novel assigns characters' words a predetermined place in a particular passage. But its content never reaches the neutrality of, for example, the American novel's dialogue. Moreover, experience has demonstrated that the American novel cannot be transferred as is to the screen. Its only asset, in fact, is that it brings to life the world around it. In film, this world exists: The spoken line no longer needs to evoke it, but only to reinforce it, and because of this it must have a sufficient density of meaning to save it from destruction.

It is true that the dialogue writers who have some sense of cinema have tried to make the connection between words and the filmed world in one way or another. Prévert's scripts are often a sort of poetic or humorous commentary on an image, but his mistake is in considering the image to be one of film's elements, and this has been the problem since sound films began. Griffith, Sjöström, the German expressionists, Chaplin, Gance, and Eisenstein have, in their own ways, created languages that proved to be almost as expressive, as rich, and as supple as spoken language. It is understandable that the word seemed a parasitic element that, above all, had to be kept to the side. The simultaneous presence of these two languages led to a definite weakening of each one's power to signify. Not only, as we have just seen, was the word treated as sound, but the visual element also was treated as a simple setting or set. The image was never as intrinsically beautiful and as lovingly labored on by specialists, for whom the years between 1930 and 1940, especially in France, were a true Golden Age. The director left them complete freedom concerning the placement of actors in the shot and the distribution of shadow and light.

The relationship between the visual element and speech must, in our opinion, be established in a completely different manner. Already many films permit us to see how language can finally discover its true function. They are precisely those films that in the past ten years have forged a new concept of the shooting script. It is perhaps not so much the dialogue writers who should be blamed as the directors themselves, who often considered the words spoken by their actors to be unimportant and, instead, put all their ingenuity into finding camera angles or establishing a subtle rhythm in the transition from action to reaction shots. Just because a character repeats a maxim by La Rochefoucauld while repairing his radio or because, while driving a car on a crowded street, he is careful to break up his conversation with interjections and stammering, does not mean that he is speaking the true language of film. The director's art is not to make us forget what characters say but, rather, to help us not to miss a word. Cocteau's best dialogue is the one in *Les Dames du Bois de Boulogne* (*Ladies of the Park*), just as the best of Prévert was in *The Crime of Monsieur Lange* (*Le Crime de Monsieur Lange*), because Bresson and Renoir permitted them to write only what was essential to comprehend the film (and not just the anecdotes). Such a necessity becomes more and more apparent when using a still shot. The weak point of *Citizen Kane* is that speech is still treated too much like sound. On the other hand, in *The Magnificent Ambersons* (which I consider to be far superior), the smallest word is important, because it reveals an aspect of the character that was unknown to us owing to the type of narrative used. The two best examples are undoubtedly the still shot in the kitchen, and the interminable traveling shot in the street. A play between action and reaction shots would certainly have weakened the expressive character of each of these. The immobility of the first is in rhythm, one might say, with the stubbornness of each character's resolution. The aunt's "don't eat so quickly" plays a role completely different from that of the slices of life that cinema spews out with so much complacency. To go back to the classical distinction, the aunt's words are necessary and not placed there for reasons of verisimilitude. As for the traveling shot in the street, the monotony with which it unravels expresses the emptiness of an interminable conversation. The words maintain a rapport, not with the image, but with a purely cinematic element: the dynamism of the shot – even if it is obtained, as in these two cases, by the tension of immobility.

Quite simply, a means must be found to integrate words not into the

Humphrey Bogart, Sonia Darrin, and Louis Jean Heydt in *The Big Sleep* by Howard Hawks.

filmed world but into the film, whether into the shot in which they are spoken or into a preceding or following sequence. In the hangar scene in *The Gates of the Night* (*Les Portes de la nuit*) the weakness of Prévert's text (the dialogue between Yves Montand and Natalie Nattier) is due to his use of an imaginary person situated "beyond" the film, a technique often used in a theatrical narration. On the other hand, the sequence in *The Crime of Monsieur Lange* in which René Lefèvre tells Maurice Baquet what he did during his Sunday afternoon is excellent, both because he refers to a preceding scene in the film and because his story is a lie. There are not enough lies in cinema, except perhaps in comedies. (Nothing prevents us, in any case, from considering the films by René Clair, Lubitsch, and Capra as the best films made between 1930 and 1940, the rare works that do not inevitably make us nostalgic for silent films.) To weaken or control the formidable power of speech, one must not, as was believed, make the significance unimportant but, instead, make it deceptive. One never lies in the theater; that is, whether in tragedy or in comedy, words are never just a simple means of acting on others but are always valid in themselves or, one might say, timeless. There is no room for the ambiguity that is found in the dialogues of Dostoyevski, Balzac, or Faulkner, whereas in the past ten years, we find this ambiguity in the best of films: *The Rules of the Game* (*La Règle du jeu*) by Renoir, *Les Dames du Bois de Boulogne* by Bresson–Cocteau, the work of Preston Sturges, and some American detective films such as *The Maltese Falcon* by Huston–Hammett or *The Big Sleep* by Hawks–Faulkner. In Orson Welles's work, the gap between the signification of speech and that of the visual element, the counterpoint of the text and that of the picture (which is completely different from the sound counterpoint favored in the past by Pudovkin and Eisenstein) functions more by means of commentary. In the past few years, how various directors have used this perhaps too-easy technique demonstrates the need to return to speech's true function and to use it in film.

The difference between film and theater, therefore, does not lie in the importance of speech. We have an enormous advantage over the film-makers of 1930: We are no longer haunted by the ghost of filmed theater, and it is now possible to concentrate all our attention on the essential problem, to write dialogues that are truly made for the film in which they are to be spoken. For the scriptwriter, this assumes a perfect knowledge of the visual language by which the director means to express himself. For the producer (when the two are not the same person, as is desirable) this requires a willingness to consider speech as an integral part of his work.

Up until the past few years, we have not really had a true style of spoken film; we have been content to adapt methods originally created to compensate for the absence of speech. Despite all the material difficulties, the avant-garde – if it is to be worthy of its name – must apply itself to creating such a style. We have already waited too long for proof that the age of talking cinema has begun.

(*Les Temps modernes*, September 1948)

The romance is gone

We no longer love film? A strange desire has come over us to reopen the case that film seemed to have won so definitively. More than ever, we have reason to believe that the art that has already considerably limited the domain of theater and literature will soon become the only possible means of expression. Yet, when we reread one of the many arguments of the last thirty years, arguments that tried to defend film and give it its rightful place, we cannot help but feel a bit irritated. These arguments, to which even the most impassioned detractors were able only to respond with vague and contemptuous banalities, would no longer succeed in convincing us, if we hadn't sworn our loyalty.

"Now that we have won the case ... without bringing in the falsity of the accusations, I would like to plead guilty and to justify the ravages of cinema by the very splendor of those ravages," wrote Denis Marion in *Aspects du cinéma*. This sentence sums up well the state of mind of a generation driven by the legitimate desire to put its trust in a budding art, and convinced that before predicting what it could be or regretting what it was not, it was fitting to recognize its existence and to legitimize it, right down to its poorest examples. Can we now measure the danger of our indulgence? We would like the impolite, capricious child, whose dirty face and bad manners forced us to sympathize with him, to consent to washing his face, even at the risk of losing his greatest charm. A sense of self-consciousness encourages us to abandon his cause until his complete innocence can shine through and open everyone's eyes. And when M. Georges Duhamel declares, as he did just recently, that "the cinema must stir up timeless sentiments, as Sophocles does in *Antigone*," we will no longer dare respond as before; that film's glory is precisely in being "the art of the present"; that it is not in any modern play, but in a gangster film, that one can find the ancient belief in fate in its purest form; that only the rough, inorganic language of the screen has been able to make epic the most ordinary events, a feat to which literature has been vainly aspiring for several centuries; that the arrival of a new form of expression forces us to reexamine the notion of depth in art; and that it is, in fact, from bad literature that good films have been and will continue to be made.

Yet never have such arguments been more likely to find a larger audience: In the past few years, the number of people who have come to see things our way has surpassed all our hopes, and we are the ones who, today, are unable to express these ideas without a feeling of uneasiness, as if the depth of our former attachment were now forcing us to be severe critics. It even seems as if we take great pleasure in stripping film of all the glamour, real or imaginary, that we gladly bestowed upon it. We are almost at the point of adopting as our motto Roger Leenhardt's remark, when he declared his preference for films about which one can say "that's not film." But a demon is already whispering in our ears, telling us to proclaim that the art of film, whose purity we wanted to preserve at all costs, whose rules we insisted must be humbly obeyed, to which we assigned a very limited domain, and which seemed, in its old age, to be independent of all other means of expression, to proclaim that this art of film *does not exist* or at least that it must recognize the strong dependence that links it – no longer to painting or to music – but to the arts from which it has always wanted to differ: literature and theater.

In any case, we have lost our most valued illusions: that miraculously, film was going to bring about a complete and definitive reconciliation of all audiences. To elicit the same reactions from the most refined to the most unpolished sensibilities is undoubtedly a privilege reserved for those arts that have not gone beyond their classical stage. What might have seemed possible at the time of Griffith, Sjöström, and the first American comedies seems today like a utopian vision.

It goes without saying that cultivated and popular audiences will appreciate *Jenny Lamour (Quai des Orfèvres)* for very different reasons. The former will be very careful to show that it does not take seriously the very aspect that is appreciated most by the latter. More and more, the conception and production of a film demand a capacity for hypocrisy on the part of the scriptwriter, the dialogue writer, and the director, a capacity on which they pride themselves with quite disconcerting candor. "For the past ten years, the art of cinema has consisted of being clever with myths," wrote André Malraux in 1940. Turning the argument around, we would like to denounce this regrettable "cleverness," which is no longer justified by any commercial constraint. We are tired of finding, in almost all the best films, a sort of humor by which the director, or even the scriptwriter, means to show that the topic treated is worthwhile because beneath the serial style or melodramatic appearance he can detect a hidden significance. Perhaps our annoyance comes from the fact that we also enjoyed the game they had us play and even have tried to play it ourselves. This explains our attraction to bad films, which at least could show us the primitive state of popular mythology. It serves us right if we are no longer quite sure why we consider *Gilda* to be less valuable than *The Gates of the Night (Les Portes de la nuit)* or *The Grapes of Wrath*.

The confusion was all the greater when film's prestige caused a veritable reversal of literary values. Converted to the new religion, writers, in search of subjects for their novels or films, no longer thought to look beyond cinema's folklore. It is understandable, then, that faced with the best scripts of the past few years, *The Rules of the Game (La Règle du jeu)*, *The Magnificent Ambersons*, and *Les Dames du Bois de Boulogne (Ladies of the Park)*, the critics, blinded by their admiration for the American novel, have had reservations not only about their cinematic worth but also, one might say, about their literary worth. Are we going to advocate a return to traditional values? If we are not afraid to admit that for the past two or three years, the Hemingway or Steinbeck novels we bought to keep our conscience clear remain unopened on our library shelves, it is because we want to end as soon as

Margaret Leighton, Joseph Cotten, and Ingrid Bergman in *Under Capricorn* by Alfred Hitchcock.

possible a period that is no longer our own. Why hide the fact that we no longer receive the same pleasure as our elders did from the display of instincts or violence? Our complexity is not so burdensome as to make us lose interest in the portrayal of anything but the most elementary sentiments. Already, we can no longer understand the prestige this boy wonder of American film had for us, nor that of the generous horseman in westerns, the big dumb guy in gangster films, the naive and smiling Mr. Deeds or Mr. Smith of comedy. If the Marlowe or the Spade of film noir still is attractive, it is only because Humphrey Bogart created such a complex character. It is, moreover, very telling that our preferred directors – Hitchcock, Welles, and Bresson – show a predilection for luxurious sets, for good manners and language. The change in our tastes does not indicate disdain for popular art, which, on the contrary, can benefit from our temporary absence. It is being

Joseph Cotten and Agnes Moorehead in *The Magnificent Ambersons* by Orson Welles.

smothered by our great interest in it. A period when unsuccessful writers compose songs for the radio, stories for illustrated weeklies, or miscellaneous columns for the nightly newspapers may not seem ridiculous to the generations to come, but simply worthless.

Are filmmakers now supposed to make films of nineteenth-century novels or of the great dramatic authors? Adaptations are justified only to the extent that they confirm, not that *Hamlet* or *The Brothers Karamazov were* in fact cinematic works, but that the cinema *can be* Shakespeare or Dostoyevski. That is, it can cease being itself. We are not trying to hide the implications and dangers of recognizing the primacy of literature. Gone are the days when it was absurd to criticize *Broken Blossoms* for being just a bad melodrama, just as it would be absurd to regret that the Greek statues of the fifth century lack psychological pretension. The elementary sentiments expressed were absolutely essential to the splendor of Griffith's art, a pure art of mise-en-scène, not of conversation or narration. The avant-garde of 1925, coming to film through literature, painting, or music, was all the more eager to save cinema's purity. It was perhaps not wrong to restrain cinema's domain to acting, whether the acting of a living character, a landscape, an object, or abstract lines. But professional filmmakers suffered from such an inferiority complex that they wanted to include the conquests displayed by other arts as tangible signs of their superiority. They realized too late the price to be paid for the rapid progress made in the art of telling a story or of organizing the rhythm of a line. Thus, the refinements introduced in editing techniques were less an indication of the desire to develop methods for film than of the desire to bend the new art's style to the general rules of composition used in literature and music. But in deciding to follow foreign criteria, filmmakers lost the chance ever to respond to those who condemned the meagerness or lack of originality of their inventions. The reaction that has been building for some time to the abuse of editing effects sufficiently confirms the failure of an impressionism that was neither able to preserve the expressive character of the shot (which became a simple image) nor reach the degree of abstraction to which it aspired.

Because it has compromised its own purity, film has lost the right to recast all that it borrows from other arts in its own mold. We make no effort to hide our joy at seeing the mortification of the director, who every day must cut a new cog from the machine that he had so lovingly perfected, and of the writer, who, coming to pay his debt of gratitude to cinema, admits to being disconcerted by the apparent simplicity of the machine presented to him.

But it was not enough to have put film under guardianship. Our anger, still unassuaged, raises questions about an element that seemed as essential to the art of film as the word is to language or the note is to the melody. We are a bit surprised when we remember the strange pleasure that glued us to our seats, when, in the darkroom, the familiar surface of the screen came to life. We are a bit ashamed now of the sweet tranquility that overcame us in thinking that the characters, or the world's most varied aspects, as soon as they appeared in the rectangular frame, would be couched in reassuring familiarity. We would like to see some kind of internal transformation of the cinematic shot, which, even in the most objective of documentaries, reduces fragments of reality to its own proportions, distorts them according to its lens, and then presents them as simple recordings. And in our desire to destroy the last of the conventions that made the art of film possible, or so we thought, we wish for perfect illusion, for a physically exact reproduction of things, with their colors and their true relief.

Instead of regretting that these pieces of the world that we have the dangerous power to bring to life will resist all our attempts at uniting

them into a coherent piece, at bending them to the rhythm of our asso-
ciation of ideas, at organizing their structure according to the immuta-
ble laws of proportion and of the golden mean, we now envy the task
of the filmmaker of tomorrow, who will no longer feel obliged to make
sacrifices for what was thought to be necessary for the plasticity of the
image or for the rites of editing, or to seek out a reality that he will
throw in our faces right from the start. He will instead detach us from
the false charm of the visible world, and by directing our attention, as
in the beginning of silent films but in a more subtle manner, toward
the acting, he will build the web of his new language on the luxuriant
framework of words, mime, gestures, and movement. We will therefore
no longer think it impossible to imagine a cinema that will take on a
more austere style, borrowed not from the theater, which is too aware
of the audience's active presence, but from the only art that, like cinema, is at once mise-en-scène and writing, that is, the novel. As a Balzac or a Dostoyevski, whose disdain for the refinements of expression
proves that the novel is not written with words but with beings and
things from the world, the writer-director of tomorrow will know the
joy of finding his style in the texture of the real world.

We are already impatient to see the technical transformations whose
promise so disrupts the tranquility of the faithful troupe, which we
have deserted like cowards.*

(*Les Temps modernes,* June 1949)

Reflections on color

Technology precedes art, but an era dictates its own rhythm of technical
advance and can slow it down when it so desires. There is little doubt we
could have spoken on the screen earlier if we had tired of silence sooner. It
is the same with color, which audiences still cannot bear. But is what we
have seen in the past five years really color? Therein lies the problem,
which it is up to technology to resolve. We reserve all comment. Whether
now or in the distant future, we are excited by the prospect of cinema's
golden years. Allow us a brief excursion.

The color picture is ugly, I agree. You can't shoot a film in violent tones,
the painters say. The more colors are contrasted, the less their "values"
should be. Cartoons are mainly produced in flat colors and are subject to
movement that we introduce almost reluctantly. The screen reveals a
space that is not closed but is spilling over on all sides, like a landscape
from a window or a room from a keyhole. What does it matter if a shot dis-

---

* This article is signed Maurice Scherer (JN).

obeys the rules of painting, because a film doesn't hang on a picture hook. Already, many reels of 16mm film manage to capture a landscape's beauty with such strong illusory power that the image loses its autonomous character, so to speak, and appears more like an exact copy of reality, which alone is subjected to aesthetic appraisal.

What would happen, in fact, if the image became a trompe-l'oeil? This is within the realm of possibility, physiologically and psychologically, because physics and psychology discover new resources every day. To insist on the subjective character of color would be to forget that an optical instrument, the mirror, gives us an absolutely perfect copy of reality and that another, the lens, reproduces in a darkroom an image whose colors differ from the real ones only in their concentration, owing to the smaller surface that they cover. To create a complete mirage, it would suffice for this image to be preserved on film.

Let's hope for this, and the sooner the better. Let's keep black and white as long as we must, while being aware of its shortcomings. Haven't we too often mistaken what we call the *image* for an element of film – that is, a pleasing painting, composed according to the strict laws of plasticity and whose skillful equilibrium we only reluctantly allow ourselves to destroy?

Let's put aside our fears. The camera lens is not a distorting glass or a filter that would jealously eliminate the excess beauty not useful to the filmmaker (as the sculptor must renounce the warmth of a body or the sparkle of eyes). Cinema kneads the dough of reality; its greatest ambition is to accept as much as possible given the richness and precision of the available technology.

Film is the most realistic art: true. But we must understand the appropriate meaning to give this word. Let the filmmaker work with things and leave their reproduction untouched. We no longer believe in the miraculous power of editing but demand, more and more, that the image capture the beauty of the world.

Where is the art, one might say, if nature appears as is? But in film, everything is in a state of becoming. A face matters little until it relaxes or wrinkles following its internal rhythm. Leaves matter little, until they create beauty by rustling. Film works with movement, the only domain in which it must abstract and reconstruct. In film, all the world's beauty will never be excessive.*

(*Opéra*, June 1949)

The classical age of film

We are suffering from a strange complex these days: that of history. Someone was surprised that such a fuss was made over *Les Dames du*

---

* This article is signed Maurice Scherer (JN).

Bois de Boulogne (Ladies of the Park): "What's so new about it?" I would love for someone to dare answer that a work need be accountable only for its own perfection.

In their infancy, all arts require enrichment. Novelty is then the criterion, just as it is in more sophisticated times when feverish construction quickly satisfies the thirst for destruction.

On the brink of its classical age, film is discovering its predecessors, not the relics of the charming, obsolete world of orthochromatic and silent images, but the archetypes of a beauty that it now knows is eternal and whose subtle laws it aspires to decipher. Is it so naive or rash for film, in turn, to wish to build in marble, refusing the label *art of the present* that in its middle age it gladly applied to itself with vain bravado?

Verisimilitude, naturalness, unity of place and action, psychological depth . . . I bet these words are repeated more often than is thought by the critics, who are the most determined to limit cinema's domain to news coverage and detective stories. Who knows? If one of them thought to reread *La pratique du théâtre** by the abbé d'Aubignac, he might find the exact expression for which he yearns. Let us be the keepers of a classicism too young to fear its detractors. But let us be unflinching in our conviction.

There is no need to worry. The classical age of cinema is not behind us, but ahead.

All at once, on the screen, the set expanded and became an actor. Literature, in turn, learned to discover the world: Its clairvoyance, sharpened by thirty centuries of practice, penetrated so deeply into humanity that the day had to come when its sharpened gaze would rest on the absurd and chaotic spectacle of appearances. We can understand this deliberate desire to go against its essential mission, which is to explain and not to show, but by what right can we now forbid cinema to follow the opposite route and discover man? Still far from reaching the summit of the path that the other arts are just now completing, why should it imitate a literature that, born of cinema, can offer cinema only a pale reflection of itself?

I admit that in the beginning, cinema's evolution coincided with that of painting and poetry, which continued to find "rejuvenation" in barbarity. As far as that goes, I find the surrealism of Mack Sennett, Buster Keaton, or Charlie Chaplin to be more authentic than that of *An Andalusian Dog (Le Chien andalou)* or *The Golden Age (L'Age d'or).*

Now the separation is complete. Believe it or not, Diderot is a more

---

* Published in 1657, this treatise served as a doctrinal guide for the classical playwright Racine (CV).

modern scriptwriter than Faulkner is. Besides, there is no need to scour the past for examples. I am sure that our best scriptwriters, fascinated by the glamour of a literature that they believe themselves to be in no position to denigrate, are destroying their secret moralistic or psychological leanings.

Is it so certain that passions, personalities, and states of mind are already dead categories for us and that their portrayal touches only the outer reaches of our intelligence? The only thing for which we can criticize John Ford in *The Grapes of Wrath* or André Malraux in *Espoir* is that their works are cinematic transcriptions of novels that we no longer care to reread.

Art is a reflection of our time; isn't it also the antidote? The cult of brutality is the vice of tranquil times; ours needs a more subtle drug. Not everything has been said about man; a new art impatiently awaits its chance to speak. Let's admit that we are ready to listen; we are tired of a common art to which we gladly lowered ourselves in the interest of being stylish but that our infatuation has killed.

For who in the future will think to rediscover our time, when even its most spontaneous expressions – song, dance, serial stories – are mere imitations?

The world is losing its naiveté. Our time, in which the most natural forms of expression have been degraded, permits us to count on only the more refined resources of our sensitivity and our intelligence. Let's appreciate our luck. Destiny and history are in our favor.

Cinema is cinema. For it to turn against itself is but a clever sham. Let those who still mourn the loss of an imagined purity do what they like with this secret: Deprived of the most ordinary power of signifying, that is, language, the characters in silent films perfected a subtle method of letting us into their hearts. Everything became a sign or a symbol. Flattered by the compliment to his intelligence, the spectator worked on understanding and forgot to see. Now the screen, liberated from this foreign task since the advent of the talkies, should go back to its true role, which is to show and not to tell.

In the talkies, the appearance is the essence, and it draws upon itself the substance of an interior world, a world of which it is the incarnation, not the sign.

Isn't there more in a troubled face than the emotion to which we would like it to refer? How strange it is to proclaim Chaplin the most authentic genius of film! Let's salute Murnau, Stroheim, or Dreyer as our true masters. Beware of all winks to the audience, of the sly quest for complicity, of all calls, even discreet, for pity. We must learn to keep our distance. Proud of being itself again, we bet that

Cesare Gravina in *Greed* by Eric von Stroheim.

cinema will give us more than we could have hypocritically extracted from it.*
(*Combat,* 15 June 1949)

Such vanity is painting

Such vanity is painting, which is admired
because it resembles things whose originals
we do not admire.
                              – Pascal, *Pensées*[†]

* This article is signed Maurice Scherer (JN).
[†] "Quelle vanité que la peinture qui attire l'admiration par la ressemblance des choses dont on n'admire pas les originaux." "Vanity" is used here in the biblical sense (i.e., "How useless is painting…")(CV).

Art does not change nature. In the past, Cézanne, Picasso, or Matisse gave us new eyes to see the world. Such vanity is painting, which has given up telling the world to exist according to its laws. But the truth is that things are as they are, regardless of how we see them. As they align themselves on our walls, the cube, the cylinder, and the sphere are disappearing from our space. Thus art is paying its debt to nature. It makes beauty out of ugliness, but would beauty be truth if it did not exist despite, almost against, us?

Art's task is not to enclose us in a sealed world. Born of the world, it brings us back to it. It attempts less to purify – to extract whatever falls into our canons – than to rehabilitate and lead us continually to reform them. Already this slow work is coming to an end. Emptiness and hopelessness are the subjects of our novels; our painters are content to be monotonous or shocking. One has the feeling that we will soon reach the point of returning to the lost dignity of nobility and order. And yet I fear that different causes will be attributed to the common failure of the art of telling and the art of painting. For the former, forbidding itself to sing, wants simply to show, and the dignity of existence seems to require no further adornment. "I am forming an enterprise that has no example."* For the past hundred years, what written work would not merit this statement? Painting, on the other hand, wanted to make its lyricism – in this case, its vision – into its raw material. No object enters its space that isn't adjusted to the dimensions of painting beforehand. The prechosen theory carries with it an infinite number of applications. In both cases, I see the same desire to sap the prestige of existence. To admit only the unexpected and to reform what is common are, as we see it, quite similar. If the plastic arts characterize our times, it is that our lyricism has been able to find its match in them: The visual world challenges the lyrical one. One might consider this perspective that of the most basic common sense. That's what I'm coming to.

With the discovery of perspective, we realized the respective dimensions that objects registered on our retinas. We then learned that lines did not exist and that everything lay in the interplay of darkness and light, for light itself was color, and that even the simplest color was merely the juxtaposition of several tones. Did our vision change? Show a child a Picasso painting: He will recognize a face that an adult will have trouble seeing. But show him an older painting, and he will like it better. If Raphaël had not existed, we would have the right to call cubism folly or scribbling. *Guernica* does not detract from the *Belle*

* Jean Jacques Rousseau, *Confessions,* Book 1 (CV).

Jardinière, or vice versa, but I don't think it too daring to say that one of these works has been, and always will be, more in conformity with our ordinary vision of objects. "The apple I am eating is not the one I see": Matisse's words define only modern art, not all art. We call *classical* the periods when beauty in art and beauty in nature seemed to be one and the same. We are free to exaggerate their differences, but I doubt that the power of art over nature will be any greater.

An art is born that relieves us from celebrating beauty and making it ours with song. Nothing demonstrates the uselessness of realism better than film does, which at the same time cures the artist of his fatal narcissism. A long familiarity with art has served only to make us more sensitive to the unpolished beauty of things. We are tempted to look at the world with our everyday eyes, to keep the tree, the running water, the face distorted with happiness or anguish, to keep them just as they are, in spite of us.

I would like to disprove a sophism: Without man's intervention, there is no art. Perhaps, but the amateur looks first at the painted object; only as a secondary reflex might he consider the work and its creator. Thus, the primary goal of art is to reproduce not the object, of course, but its beauty. What we call realism is only a more scrupulous search for this beauty. Modern critics have, on the contrary, ingrained in us the idea that we can appreciate only the aspect of things that is a pretext for a work of art. If the artist directs our attention to objects that the masses still judge unworthy, he will have to work harder to win us over. The beauty of a construction site or an empty lot comes from the angle through which we are forced to discover it. Yet the beauty is still that of an empty lot. The work is beautiful not because it demonstrates that one can create beauty with ugliness but because what we considered ugly is actually beautiful. I have now arrived at the paradox that a means of mechanical reproduction like photography is generally excluded from art, not because it can only reproduce, but precisely because it distorts even more than a pencil or a paintbrush does. In a family album's snapshot, what is left of a face but an unexpected grimace that is not the real face? By freezing what is mobile, the film betrays everything, right down to resemblances.

Let us give the movie camera its due. It is not enough to say that cinema is the art of movement. It alone makes mobility, and not the quest for a lost equilibrium, an end in itself. Watch two dancers: Our eyes are satisfied only to the extent that the tension between them vanishes. The art of ballet is in composing the figures, and the movement itself is a simple consequence of the principle of inertia. Think of Harold Lloyd gesticulating from the top of the ladder or of the gangster who awaits the moment when the policeman will be distracted, in order to grab the weapon menacing him. Stability and perpetual movement are just violations of nature. The most realistic art is naively unaware of them.

Nanook of the North is the most beautiful of all films. We needed a tragedy at our own pace, not a tragedy of destiny, but of the dimension of time. I know that filmmakers' efforts over the past fifty years have tried to destroy the limits of the present in which film encloses us from the start. Still, film's primary purpose is to give the present the weight that other arts deny it. In *Nanook,* the pathos of waiting, which in other films is but a vulgar artifice, mysteriously plunges us to the heart of understanding. No artifice is possible here to extend or reduce its duration; all the methods that filmmakers have thought themselves obliged to use – "parallel editing," for example – have quickly turned against them. But *Nanook* spares us these tricks. I will mention only the scene in which we see the Eskimo curled up in the corner of the frame, lying in wait for the flock of seals sleeping on the beach. To what can we attribute the beauty of this scene, if not to the fact that the point of view imposed on us by the camera is neither that of the actors of the drama nor that of the human eye, whose attention would have been drawn to one element to the exclusion of another? Name a novelist who has described waiting without, in some way, demanding our participation. More than the pathos of action, it is the very mystery of time that creates our anxiety in this scene.

The cinema flashes a whole scene before our eyes, from which we are free to extract one of many possible significations. This is opposed to the other arts, which go from the abstract to the concrete and which, in making this quest for the concrete their goal, hide the fact that they aim not to imitate but to signify. Meaning in film is extracted from appearances, not from an imaginary world of which appearances are only the sign. We can see why reality would be useful here, its necessity coming from the contingency of its introduction into the film: It could not have been, but it can no longer help but be, now that it was. For the first time, along with the power of expression, the document attains the dignity of an art. We can already see one of the perilous consequences of this condition: that the cinema will excel in portraying sentiments only as long as they come from the incessant connections with things, and that – these sentiments being things themselves – they will become nothing more than the movement or the mimicry that they impose on us at each instant. What better judge of the authenticity of gesture than its effectiveness? The cinema has chosen not passion but work – man's action – as its theme.

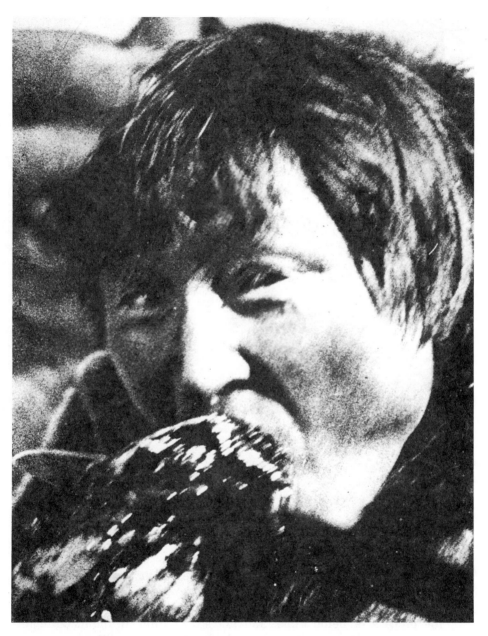

Nanook of the North by Robert Flaherty.

Tabu by F. W. Murnau.

Nanook builds a house, hunts, fishes, feeds his family. It is important to follow him through the vicissitudes of his work, in which we slowly discover the beauty, a beauty that defies description, a lyrical beauty. For, as opposed to epic heroes, it is in the course of his fight, not once victory is achieved, that our man is great. Until now, what art has been able to portray an abstract action at the point of the intentions that give it meaning, or at that of the result that justifies it? I purposely chose a documentary as an example, but at their better moments, don't most films, from the best to the worst, treat something in the process of being done, and not some whim, triumph, or regret? Charlie the tramp, Buster the cook or the mechanic, Zorro, Scarface, Kane, Marlowe, the lady's man, or the jealous woman – so many craftspeople, able or awkward – we judge by their work.

I consider Murnau to be the exact opposite of Flaherty. That they collaborated on the same work, *Tabu,* does not seem like just an unfortunate accident. We know that before filming *Sunrise,* Murnau was careful to construct an entire world that his film merely documents. The desire for special effects comes from a need for greater authenticity. As soon as the actor ceases to be active and must express some interior emotion, he gives himself away. Liberated from the constraint of things, his mask must be molded from a different material. A face doesn't look right if one doesn't feel all of space weigh on each wrinkle. What would a burst of laughter or anxious twitching signify if they did not find their visible echo in the universe?

It is undoubtedly through the metaphor that we rediscover lyricism. One might say that art consists of giving each thing a name other than its own. But delivered from the intermediary of words, we should savor the strange pleasure in making Achilles both a warrior and a torrent, a god and a disaster. Why put two terms together that only the imperfection of language forces us to isolate? *Promontory-shepherd, humid suns, earth blue like an orange,* the efforts of modern poetry tried to shake the primitive inertia of the word; but now that we have the right to say anything about everything, why continue? Long live the cinema, which, attempting only to show, exempts us from the fraud of saying! Cinematic poem, descriptive poetry, the same non-sense. It is no longer important to sing of things but, rather, to make them sing themselves.

During *Nosferatu,* we leave the ghost country to hear a biologist explain to his students the horrifying power of the hydra-headed plants that eat insects. We can excuse the greatest of filmmakers for having indiscreetly disclosed the key to his symbolism through this artifice. To compare an idea with an idea, or even a form with a form, as Eisenstein suggested, discourages the art of movement, and the figure that fascinates us on canvas or in stone exhausts our gaze if it lasts. Movement is the essence of each thing, condemning it to its function, absorbing or shining, sordid or noble, and, as in *Bouche d'ombre,* implying a moral judgment. Two directions, centripetal or centrifugal, share the world, and assign an aptitude to each species. Death is decomposition, evil is ascendancy, life is growth, purity is blooming. The idea springs from the sign and establishes it at the same time, just as an act affirms a tendency. What poetic rhetoric was ever more convincing? Drawn to our lyricism, the previously silent universe has finally decided to answer.

The theme of desire is cinematically one of the richest. It requires that the entire distance, in time or space, separating the man on the lookout for his prey, be displayed before our eyes. The wait is a pleasure in itself, and a neck's tender beauty or, as in Stroheim's *Greed,* the

Emil Jannings in *The Last Laugh* by F. W. Murnau.

glistening of gold, is colored for the impotent desire with a seductive power that is forever new. As spectators we never cease to feel both overwhelmed and disappointed before these impalpable and fugitive images that fix our attention. Yet, doesn't the cinema have any other ambition than to indulge the morose elation of a humanity to which nature has displayed its secrets too soon? There are other relationships that, from the start, the art of the screen has shown itself less apt at portraying. No longer is it the relationship between bodies but, rather, between each desire, one next to the other. Creon or Antigone can no longer use the hemicycle as witness to their sincerity. The lie attracts us, but it is not enough for the event alone to judge deceit. The cheat finds power in the very hypocrisy he wears on his mask. Tartuffe fools only Orgon, and perhaps his power of fascination is so strong because he doesn't trick him entirely. What better homage to Molière than the hideous face of Jannings, sweating falsity from every pore: Onuphrius,* the petty response of a jealous critic.

But, one could argue, why refuse to penetrate man's heart? Doesn't a troubled face betray some interior emotion? Yes, it is a sign, but an arbitrary sign, as it denies the powers of falsity and greatly shrinks the

* Hermit-saint of the fourth century A.D. who is reported to have lived in solitude near Egypt. He is often portrayed in art as a wild man (CV).

limits of the invisible world to which it proudly refers. To go from each of our gestures to its implied intention is the equivalent of reducing all of thought to a few always-identical operations. The novelist will rightfully smile when presented with the neophyte's ambition to give this elementary algebra the name *language.* To go from the exterior to the interior, from behavior to the soul, such is the condition of our art. But how wonderful that, far from tarnishing what it shows us, this necessary detour enhances it, and thus liberated, appearance itself is our guide.

In *The Last Laugh,* Murnau touches on a particularly difficult subject, the pure relationship with oneself, the importance that each person attaches to his failures and triumphs, and the indescribable bashfulness that always prevents our sympathizing with moral suffering, when that suffering visibly alters one's appearance. We should know, then, that the director's intention was not to provoke our pity but, assuming that it was already sufficiently acute, to exhaust it by overwhelming it, just as he would have done with a bad instinct, like cruelty or desire. Thus, art frees us from all our sentiments, even good ones, and justifies its amorality by returning to ethics what it had borrowed. I admit that our pleasure should be condemned if it is derived from pity or sarcasm, but these two very human sentiments have no part in the fascination that the tragicomic destiny of this doorman exerts on us. Name a work, novel, painting, or film that has more deliberately neglected to wring our hearts, while using only the power of the most tangible effects of emotion? I'll add − for those who would blame Jannings's role for its obstinately static character − that the immobility reveals a state of painful tension, not of equilibrium. An overextended acquaintance with the plastic arts has led us to associate joy with restfulness, unhappiness with agitation. What the painter or sculptor obtains only by cunning or violence, "expression," is an integral part of cinema's existence. In order to make it more intense, it is not always appropriate to accelerate the rhythm but, rather, to slow it down to the point of unexpected immobility.

Sunrise carries us a step further to the heart of this intimate world, where the sentiments of love and hate, joy and sadness, desire and renunciation thrive on themselves and die of their own excesses. And yet there are no concessions made to the use of ellipsis or symbol. A kind of preestablished harmony seems to unite their vicissitudes with the rhythm of the changing sky. At the final detour of this interior quest, we find ourselves once again faced with the world. The set participates in the game. Although it rarely gives way to movement, it nonetheless regulates the characters' movements in some way. It substitutes its own laws for the tyrannical limits of the "frame." Let us give way prudently to the appeal of the golden mean and the beautiful

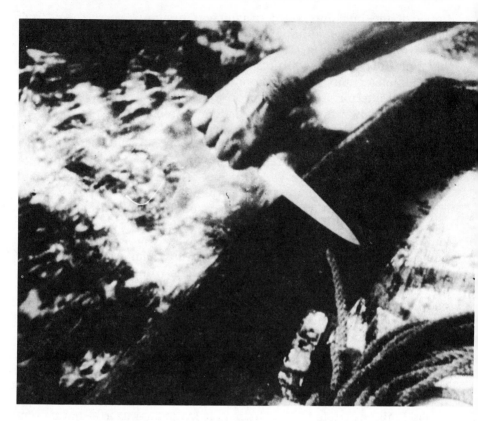

Tabu by F. W. Murnau.

image. What photography will ever equal the smallest phrase? But in turn, which of our poets' most beautiful verses can claim to exhaust the magnificence of the tangible world, which only the cinema has had the privilege of displaying intact before our eyes?

The images in *Tabu* shine with this brilliant beauty, presented without intermediary, and the photographer was careful to cover his tricks with an excess of art. He cheats only to fill gaps that otherwise would have given him away. But he doesn't have to give in to the easy, fantastical play of shadows or to circle objects with a single halo – palm trees, waves, shells, and rosebushes – that the sun's rays have marked with inalterable streaks. Dressed in their own daylight, they illuminate one another through their dissimilarity, and under their manifold bark, they suggest a common pulp. Fascinated by his model, the artist forgets the order that he prided himself on imposing and, in so doing, reveals the harmony of nature, its essential unity. Song becomes hymn and prayer. The transfigured flesh discovers the world "beyond" from which it derives its existence. I am not afraid to call this spontaneous fusion of religious and poetic sentiments *sublime.*

And now that we have reached the realm of finality, we have every right to condemn the insane ambition of our times. We have become so impatient to master the universe that we are unable to grasp more than an abstract and changeable part of it, with which we would like to reassure our anxiety. By breaking off from nature, modern art degrades man, whereas it meant to elevate him. Let's avoid these outcomes, even if we are lured by a distant and problematic salvation. Cinema instinctively rejects every perilous detour and reveals a beauty that we had ceased to believe was eternal and immediately accessible to all. It surrounds the products of our revolt and destruction with happiness and peace. It shows us that we have not lost our sensitivity to the sea and the sky, to the most common display of great human sentiments. It miraculously makes peace between the form and the idea and bathes our eyes, still new, in the even, pure light of classicism.

Art evolved by means of internal spasms, not by history. At most, without changing us, it carries us far away from ourselves and loses itself as it loses us. Let's enjoy our luck; let's carefully hold on to an instrument we know can still portray us *as we see ourselves.* May this very simple certainty reassure us and keep us from pointless exercises. If a filmmaker is reading these lines, he may be surprised that I am praising what his art owes more to chance and its nature than to the fruit of patient investigation. But why repeat that cinema is an art, that is, choice and perpetual invention, and not the blind use of the power of a machine? There are works that prove it. That is why I intended to show not that film has nothing to envy in the other arts, its rivals, but to show what they, in turn, can envy in film.*
(*Cahiers du cinéma* 3, June 1951)

Isou *or* Things as they are (views of the avant-garde)

We must do justice to lettrism for being, since the war, the only literary movement to have the avowed aim of placing itself, to use political terminology, to the left of surrealism. Those who attended the stormy conferences of the Sociétés savantes or of the Salle de géographie three or four years ago, know that for Isidore Isou and his friends it was not so much a question of pushing to an extreme the conse-

* This article is signed Maurice Scherer (JN).

quences of André Breton's experience but of reassigning a place in history to the famous *Surrealist Manifesto,* which our most "advanced" poets still considered the necessary and definitive prologue to all future aesthetics. One might object that there is nothing easier than to go ahead and knock down idols, especially when one makes no effort to replace them with something positive, and the few poems published or recited by the lettrists do not refute this. All the same, the form of Isou's method, if not his object, seems to me to merit consideration. The "treatises" with which he periodically saturates us all result from a reflection on art in which one detects a rather curious defeatism, as compared with the "progressivism" of his theories of the twenties: "Everything has been said: Perhaps in searching I may be able to say 'something else'; in any case, when I'm gone, I don't care what happens." Here is an aesthetic morality to which Breton, I imagine, would have trouble subscribing. If the surrealists, speaking definitively, considered only the aspects of art history that seemed to predict the coming of their era, a quick reading will show us their rival respectful enough of past works to propose only carving himself a modest place, as a final step, on the last page of literary manuals. However modest one may be in expressing it, this idea of a probable death of art is far from foreign to a number of musicians or painters – it is enough to push their backs to the wall to discover that this serves as a substratum for nonfigurative and atonal theories. To be fair, of course, it took twenty years of work for Paul Klee to propose a model of painting that would refuse to represent objects but that would preserve the feeling of their masses and contours. On the other hand, everyone will agree that lettrism is purely an idea of the mind, based on arbitrary induction. Why insist on it?

That said, I do not want to be considered a prisoner of the rhetoric that counts on our perpetual fear of being outdone by artists more revolutionary than ourselves. To clarify my position, I will grant Isou that given the current state of our poetry, I don't consider a reading – or an audition – of his works to be a more unpleasant imposition than that of many contemporary collections. As for the ostentatious publicity that he creates around his name and the bombast of his declarations, they at least alleviate the anarcho-moralizing tone in which our friends revel. Whoever has gotten near the band – I was going to say the gang – of lettrists will admit that it resembles nothing less than a cenacle, and to continue my political metaphor, I will say that if Breton's friends modeled their group's organization after that of an anarchist junta, Isou and his henchman would remind us more of a fascist troop.

I therefore do not know what premonition I had at the showing of *Traité de bave et d'éternité* that the logical end of lettrism was, if not a

Isidore Isou and Blanchette Brunoy in *Traité de bave et d'éternité* by Isidore Isou.

return to traditional forms, at least to the abandonment of this state of mind, which is both antibourgeois and given to denying and which was also that of our literature from between the two wars, from Breton to Artaud, and even Drieu la Rochelle or Montherlant. One senses underlying this film, beneath the provocative variety of tones, the respectful desire to connect with things *as they are*, the concern that once everything has been destroyed or questioned, no substantive material will be left for art. He who has resolved to knock down the other's underpinnings has, understandably, no greater concern than discovering in turn something to cling to. And we find our revolutionary forced by his very own design into acceptably conservative thought. Perhaps the film director was even given away by the strange instrument he imprudently chose to help him elaborate his theories. We know that his goal was to treat the cinema as he had treated poetry, no longer to dissolve the word but, rather, the image. Except for a few passages, however, whose presence is due more to economic reasons than to aesthetic ones (it is cheaper to punch holes in the film than to expose it, even as carelessly as Isou did), he hardly looks to the "abstract cinema" dear to Fischinger, Ruttmann, or McLaren. In short, even if one refuses to take this film seriously, one must admit that Isou doesn't enlist under the colors of this avant-garde – or rear-guard – of Richter, Buñuel, Anger, and so on at the mention of whom crowds gather before films clubs' doors and has – whether or not by chance – a hint of the concerns that are perhaps not completely foreign to our best commercial filmmakers. I am far from thinking that this is good cinema; yet it is not the "literary" cinema as is, for many good reasons, *L'Age d'or*, *Blood of a Poet (Le Sang d'un poète)*, or, closer to us, *Il Christo probito* or *Orpheus (Orphée)*. I mean, Isou shows a definite cinematic sensibility. As opposed to the avant-garde of 1930 that tried to make film the testing ground for its pictorial, musical, or literary theories, the problems Isou means to resolve are specifically cinematic.

The leader of lettrism was too conscientious a spectator of film club showings to delude himself with the illusion, fatal to many others, that until him, film had been in the hands of vulgar craftspeople or shrewd businesspeople. In this domain as well, Isou proclaimed in his commentary, all has been said and well said, and before revealing his destructive theories, he takes care to pay homage to the old masters whom he sets himself the task of equaling, maybe, yet not surpassing. This radical pessimism regarding an art that others persist in considering in its infancy, gives the film a very particular hue, at the very center of the group of avant-garde works.

Even if we are far from sharing his opinion, thinking quite to the contrary that of all the arts, cinema remains perhaps the only one able to do something other than arrange its funeral, we should recognize that it would be futile to count on the help of some technical discovery (I'm speaking of a mise-en-scène technique). There isn't one human gesture, not one single facial expression, that we cannot find photographed many times in the archives of our art. And as Isou correctly states, we should not look to the art of photography for innovation, either.

There is no question that in the past few years one has sensed a certain unrest in the most original directors. They are less confident of the raw power of the image, a power that created the greatness of people like Griffith, Gance, Murnau, and Eisenstein. It may even be from the meagerness of their inventiveness that people like Bresson or Rossellini draw the rigor and novelty of their style.

And doesn't Hitchcock's desire in his latest film (the admirable *Strangers on a Train,* which Hans Lucas* talks about later on) to use only effects that have already been perfected by fifty years of technical research, suggest both an extraordinary mastery and a renunciation of all quantitative improvements in this research?

But what do we see in Isou's film? The director's ability is – as he had to show something – to oppose only trifling images to the emphasis of his text. It was still necessary for them to be selected judiciously, and I admit that they are, for the most part, well chosen: There are none of the facile discordances or concordances that the "discrepant" method of surrealism would have suggested. From these awkward shots we get the feeling of a presence, the presence of actors whom he doesn't want to show us, the presence of a thought behind the director's face, complacently shown, it's true, but having the most expressionless appearance. In short, I believe it is my duty to say that this first chapter in which we see Isou walking on the boulevard St.-Germain affected me a thousand times more than did the best of the noncommercial films I've seen. If it's true that there are places, landscapes, cities, and streets whose appearance mysteriously agrees with the period that made them famous, I would like to believe that because art and literature have moved their staff to this famous St.-Germain-des-Près area, which in the past few years has dictated its style to the world, it's because here, more than anywhere else perhaps, one can breathe the "air" of our time. A long acquaintance has already sealed the agreement between the haphazard layout of its old streets with the clearings hacked out by Haussmann. Past and present blend, gracelessly perhaps, but well enough so that the audacities of one have only half-desecrated the relics of the other. Similarly, after fifty years of enthusiasm, revolt, and systematic demolition, is it possible that our modern art – on the verge of completely destroying the past –

---

* Pseudonym for Jean-Luc Godard (JN).

suddenly feels so modest that the work of the artist who claims to be its most audacious representative had to, like it or not, show symptoms?*

(*Cahiers du cinéma* 10, March 1952)

Of three films and a certain school

One must be absolutely modern.[†]

– Rimbaud

"Yes, you're right: The idea of a neoclassicism is not what I had in mind. If cinema isn't capable of portraying our most current preoccupations, I will think very little of it. But let's make sure we understand each other. You want some examples?"

"Go ahead."

"OK. You lead me to make a connection I hadn't thought of. In all of the productions from after the war, I already see three key films, new in manner and modern in subject: *The River, Stromboli,* and, for the third, *Under Capricorn* ... or better, *Strangers on a Train.* Let's go with *Strangers on a Train.*"

(This took place about one year ago.)

"Renoir, Rossellini, Hitchcock, almost all three are old hands."

"I'll admit that, even for the second one, but so what? If film is an art, which you will agree it is, I believe that true originality must, as in other things, wait a number of years. You know what that sixty-year-old painter said."

"The one who answered, 'The young painters, that's me.' OK. As for the subject matter ... at least if you had said: *Asphalt Jungle, Verdoux, The Bicycle Thief (Ladri di biciclette),* who knows!"

"These films, and many others, portray an era that is, all in all, rather exciting. I spoke a bit pompously of preoccupations, let's say aspirations."

"Art before action, said Rimbaud."

"Yes and no. This idea of a *before* and an *after,* of a unilinear evolution, seems questionable. Beethoven's last quartets are neither more nor less modern that Liszt's first, and Cézanne's *Bathers* is neither more nor less modern than the first Matisses. The films I've mentioned are timeless enough to be less dated than others are, but they express all the better the unrest and hopes of their times. Besides, they inform us about their subjects more than they undermine them, and when they are critical, they denounce things that have not yet taken shape, rather than lingering over the satire of what no longer exists."

* This article is signed Maurice Scherer (JN).
[†] "Il faut être absolument moderne."

Stromboli by Roberto Rossellini.

"A return to good sentiments, to traditional values. A reaction against a certain foolish progressivism, if I've understood you correctly?"

"A return, a reaction, that's a bit much! These films are modern, I said it and I maintain it. They may appear to refer to a certain idea of man that belongs to past centuries rather than to the one in vogue today, but that doesn't bother me in the least. Dialectical progression, our Marxists would say. But watch out: A literary critic may very well complain about the lesser products of formerly existing schools – ersatz Breton, Faulkner, or Kafka – it is a waste of time if he has nothing else to recommend."

"Because for you, film recommends something?"

"In these rare and reassuring examples, yes. It's a pathetic enterprise, and rather detestable snobbery to exalt the wife and no longer the female adventurer, home sweet home rather than the romanticism of bars, if it isn't just a stubborn desire to burn what others adore. If the heroine of *Stromboli* goes beyond freedom and aspires to morality, doesn't that portray a century that is already bearing the burden of emancipation, some say, whose contours have already been sketched? And these tame beings in *Strangers on a Train,* I see them less caught up in daily absurdity, plexiglass puppets in a *Caligari*-esque traveling show, than fighting with the scruples of a conscience that only the automation of modern life has brought to a head. As for *The River.* Perhaps this film attempts nothing other than to reconcile us with a world whose idyllic sweetness takes none of the edge off its cruelty. You are familiar with that poet who sometimes paints ectoplasm and amoeba. Permit me to refuse naively a vision of man that the naive cinema is, well, incapable of making its own. Let's not hope too much that film turns us into insects, just when it discovers itself to be so good at magnifying human gestures."

"Even in modern life?"

"Especially in modern life, since it's quite unwilling to give in to it – and you know how I admire *Nanook* or *Tabu.* What is more unbearable on the screen – grant me this – than the sight of the machine? In our life today, the contact between man and tool has become so abstract (pull a lever, press a button) that it is impossible to interest us in it visually without some outrageous or clever method that produces art. Think of the magnificent scene in which, before the gushing water, the robots in *Metropolis* discover they are alive again. I know that our painting, our music, and our architecture for the past hundred years have been going in the opposite direction. I would admire the filmmaker who dares to say out loud that he doesn't care about all that. I am purposely simplifying this to show you that I couldn't care less about these philosophies of behavior, of failure, or of the absurd about which I was speaking. It's a curious contradiction, a conscience that we reduce to the level of an epiphenomenon, and, at the same time, whose claims to freedom we hail!"

"You would call freedom the supreme value, then?"

"Why not? But I mean that we must be liberated from other constraints. You see, in these very films ... "

This took place a year ago. It happens that in the first months of 1953, further developments provided my thesis with more convincing examples than those to which I referred. *The Golden Coach (La Carrosse d'or), Europa 51,* and *I Confess* are very different works, true – products of temperaments, conceptions, and methods that completely contradict one another. And yet, I wasn't the only one struck by both the similarity of their style and their greater ambitions and also the single

The River by Jean Renoir.

theme that they developed. Don't all three of them orchestrate a spirit-ual challenge to the inertia of the social cement? — I say a challenge, not a revendication, an appeal for some simple pity. The solitude they show us belongs to the exceptional being, or someone that circumstan-ces make into one, the solitude of a genius, not of an outcast or a fail-ure. In place of the hero of classical fiction, they substitute not the famous antihero made popular by Rousseau but someone whose hum-ble condition, candor, and strange destiny are presented, not as an ex-cuse, but for us to judge. All these things one can't say about films like *The African Queen, Limelight,* or *Umberto D.,* films with which my interlocutor last year was manifestly delighted.

I admit that if I decided to praise the three films I just mentioned, I would have no trouble finding the words to correctly express my es-teem for them. I mean that my praise would fall into categories that critics of modern art have carefully determined. One is readily pardoned for referring to them with only the most indirect allusion. I would speak, for example, of the idea of *failure* which, since *Sentimental Education,* has become for the reader or the educated audience the standard for an incontestable pretension of depth. I would point out, in these three works, the presence of a certain notion of the *pure event* which, as we know, has taken the place of the old idea of God or destiny. I would add, just the same, that the moral of these themes is not without a nuance of *black* humor in the first, *discreet* humor in the second two, which is able to compensate for emotion and which is, in any case, just as discreet and *contained.* In this century, such a reversal has taken place in the hierarchy of aesthetic values, that situations or intrigues that our forebears would have presented as the simple outcome of the natural progression of passions, are now denounced as melodramatic. I really don't see in what way the subject of *Europa 51* is more unrealistic than, say, Corneille's *Polyeucte,* in what way our tears are less nobly provoked. The fact that the efficacy of the image adds to that of the words, or replaces it, will certainly not shock a lover of film. The unusual facts – a sly criminal holds a priest in the clutches of moral blackmail, the effects of which Ulysses tested on the young heart of Neoptolene – does not in any way taint the realism of the resulting actions. I believe simply that art's goal is to form a foundation for an extraordinary situation, to proceed toward truth rather than to start with it. Take, for example, one of the most beautiful themes of the nineteenth-century novel, the heroes of Goethe, or Balzac, who identify so well with the fires of passion that it seems they cannot help but suffocate from them. No one dies of love in the movies, or of an excess of scruples, as in *Honorine* or *Elective Affinities.* I cannot help but notice that. But why? Because the art of the screen is not yet able to make tangible the evidence of the soul's influence on the body. I bet that it "will come." Don't we already see the start of this in certain scenes of *Under Capricorn* or *Angels of the Street (Les Anges du péché)?*

But I'll stop these literary references, for fear that they might undermine my intention more than they support it. I simply wanted to indicate that the filmmaker would be wrong in being, in advance, against the entreaty of old, but not outdated, motifs, which not only enlarge one's field of invention but also illuminate a world of relationships already more or less clearly perceived by the painter or the novelist of old (because, to a certain extent, isn't man always the same?), without the latter's having had access to the instrument most apt to express them. It's a strange thing: Considered from the point of view of the symbolism of gesture and of human attitude, literature – say from before Flaubert – was a great deal more than just descriptions of behavior and a free search for metaphors. All things compared, it has lost its early efficacy. To continue my example, have you noticed how the beauty of the images in Goethe or in Balzac has a scientific idea at its foundation that makes our modern artists smile, the sentiment of an affinity between bodies and souls – childish, one may say – but which remains so entrenched in our belief system, which has so strongly marked our language, that I cannot blame film for giving it a kind of new and irrefutable foundation, by simply returning to the obvious?

And yet if I contented myself with saying that these three films are *cinema*, the highest form of the art, whereas the three that I have contrasted with them are only good films by screen writers, I fear that you would agree with me even less. What? Chaplin? – Well, yes! In leaving the limited and safe route of pantomime that he made famous with his comic genius, he might have kept all his intelligence, but he lost the best part of his talent. If I named one of John Huston's works, it's because this director seems to me to be one of the most brilliant representatives of a certain intelligentsia of his profession – richer in intelligence than in true sensitivity – and I admit that his style, although acquired at the best school – the American school – has always seemed, despite some lucky finds, to be lacking in invention. And I would say the same of the Italian De Sica. Excuse me for these points: My goal, in this article, is to enlighten more than to demolish. But this light, which I consider to be the brightest, will shine all the better because of the contrast. And besides, haven't the quasi-unanimous critics crushed *The Golden Coach, Europa 51,* or *I Confess* with their disdain, even their insults? As a supreme insult, they weren't even recognized as exemplifying the failure of an ambition, which in all three was manifestly very great. The choice of their subject was attributed to resignation, to disgust, even to the most material necessity. Yes, there is a cursed cinema, and the serious thing is that this curse is not so much the result of monied forces, censorship, or ignorant audiences, as it is of people whose profession would seem to guarantee, if not always justice, at least prudence and probity of judgment. Undoubtedly some people, very competent people, have already spoken highly of one or another of these films. That's not enough for me. I would like to defend them as a whole so as to reveal better their new and disconcerting sound, which some consider weakness, but which, in my eyes, is of exceptional merit. I know it may be insolent to oppose such generally adopted taste: That is why I am not speaking only for myself. Because Pierre Kast formerly did me the honor of appointing me head of a *school* that shines perhaps more by its impassioned flame than by the number of its members and represents a tendency that, following his survey, André Bazin placed at the very forefront – I'll accept that – of dogmatism in criticism, allow me to interpret the tastes of a fraction – a minority, it's true – but a fraction nonetheless, of the editorial staff of a review whose eclecticism, within a shared love of cinema, is a sufficient guarantee of its competence and seriousness. I don't believe there is one good critic who isn't inspired by an *idea,* whether of art, of man, or of society, and I hold nothing against such and such a political paper for following the narrowest line in its judgments of art. Still, in these issues of *Cahiers,* in which the only object is film, it is not without some precaution, and in a generally analogical mode, that I come to call on convictions that the frequenting of movie theaters has not been alone in forming: I would like my, our, dogmatism – if there is dogmatism – to be inspired first and foremost by the consciousness of an evolution, whose traces are only clearly revealed in film, of all the arts. To associate the cinematic value of a work with the violence of a particular social demand would seem to me, coming from a Pierre Kast, like a "pleasant joke," if the direction of the most fertile evolution hadn't been – even with certain prewar traditionalist directors – precisely toward the left, according to Hugo's old saying "liberty in the social order, liberty in art." I grant that such a precept has been fruitful. It is nonetheless certain that in the Byzantium in which we live, it has lost its reason to exist.

That is why I want to conclude by returning to the aspect of these three films to which I first paid particular attention: the social aspect. Ever since the cinema attained the dignity of an art, I see only one great theme that it proposed to develop: the opposition of two orders – one natural, the other human; one material, the other spiritual; one mechanical, the other free; one of the appetite, the other of heroism or grace – a classical opposition, but one that our art is privileged to be able to translate so well that the intermediary of the sign is replaced by immediate evidence. A universe of relationships therefore appeared that the other arts may have illuminated or designated but could not show: the relationship between man and nature and between man and objects – directly perceptible relationships that are quite beautiful – but also, since the age of the talkies, the less visible relationship between the individual and society. It is a difficult theme, as pure convention replaces experience or instinct. One of *The Golden Coach's* greatest assets is that it goes beyond satire – for which the director is still labeled – and is marked by a sort of sublime buffoonery which to my knowledge has no precedent in art, even in Shakespeare. It provides man with a sort of second nature, thereby magnifying the comedy by its perfect imitation of one of the most profound aspects of life, which is, of course, comedy. Thus, the challenge that Magnani launches at the court of Peru acquires all the more relief. It is not so much a question of denouncing the order as such – an easy and futile undertaking – as of revealing its necessary contradictions. If art is fundamentally moral, it is not because it reveals the path to abstract

Ingrid Bergman in *Europa 51* by Roberto Rossellini.

equality or liberty but because it glorifies the exception that is made possible only by the rule, and in a sense – as shocking as this idea may be – because it exalts the inequality of each person before destiny, or even salvation. But here I am on the topic of the modern *Europa*, whose fundamental blemish Rosselini was able to sketch with a few bold strokes: a tolerance more tyrannical than intolerance, because it does not even allow us to choose our own incentives, a justice

Karl Malden, Dolly Haas, and Montgomery Clift in *I Confess* by Alfred Hitchcock.

more unjust than injustice is, because it returns to each one only what doesn't belong to him. In the frigidity, the pettiness of modern manners, don't we find an echo of the mind's confusion, too quickly concerned with freeing itself from the forms prompted until now by the familiar contact with nature, refined by the long workings of time? I have always admired Alfred Hitchcock's acute sensitivity to cinematic things, joined – a remarkable fact for a director who was never a writer – with the permanance of a very pure line, and the unity of an extremely ambitious goal. We readily praise him for having been able to maintain the tension in his *suspense*. This suspense is always coupled with an *ulterior* interest, a wait, not so much for an event as for its repercussions in thought, whose flexible and fleeting contours remain unaltered by the almost metallic precision of the image. And now we've revealed the richness, not only psychological but also moral, of this famous theme of *suspicion*, of a certain *blackmailing* of courage, purity, and innocence that we find in each of his films. No, it is not the weakness of heroes or heroines, so disdained by our aesthetes, that, thanks to Hitchcock, was so ruthlessly exposed, but, I would say, the heightened scruples of a conscience that was suddenly rejuvenated at the point of strangulation. Think of how, in this director's works, such an idea was enriched little by little, deepened, cleansed of some implausible elements that never really bothered me anyway. The only criticism I would allow myself to make concerning Hitchcock – that he directed our attention more toward a situation than to a character, toward a state rather than a personality – is dwarfed when compared with the grandiose fresco – such is the word to describe it – which I can compare only with the most accomplished works of the screen. Unlike so many others, who use the plasticity of the image to create art at all costs, Hitchcock uses it to express the fragility of the ecclesiastical state in a society less impressed by the charm of the pomp and the robe than by the strict impassiveness of a face, in a society in which the slightest trace of joy or human suffering tends to elicit surprise, worry, irritation. What more beautiful scene than the fall of the priest, suddenly aware of the sense of the cross that he undoubtedly did not want to carry, the rush of the crowd on the solitary man, the ice that he cracks with his elbow, just as Scarface used his fist to shatter the window of the cell where his rival awaited a death sentence. An easy effect, one may say, but I believe that the use of the most direct means, the means to which our nerves are the most sensitive, is reserved for the greatest filmmakers, whereas the recourse to allusion or ellipsis so dear to others, is only too often a mark of dryness and indigence. If there is a system, dogmatism, formalism in Hitchcock, it is because his much criticized form is not just ornamental but is also so closely linked to the content that any form of expression other than film would be entirely unthinkable.

I wish that film criticism would finally free itself of the ideas dictated by its elders and that it would begin to consider with fresh eyes and minds those works that, in my opinion, will count much more in the history of our time than the pale relics of an art of days gone by.*
(*Cahiers du cinéma* 26, August–September 1953)

Of taste and colors

Color is slowly but surely conquering film. And the sophisms are collapsing one by one. "Color's fine, but only for certain subjects," they proclaimed ten, even five years ago. Today who would maintain that color is less at home in a modern setting than in an ancient one, in a civilized setting than in an exotic one, in a serious setting than in a comic one, in realism than in the fantastic? Go see *Rear Window, The Barefoot Contessa, A Star Is Born,* to name only recent films. The *thriller* draws as many effects from the hotel room's red carpet as does the *western* from the vague green of the prairie; and the moralist will be better able to scrutinize faces, washed of their wan masks, even if he cannot detect every fleeting blush or passing pallor.

If certain films, among the best and the most ambitious, continue to

---

* This article is signed Maurice Scherer (JN).

be shot in black and white, it is not because color doesn't suit them but because they are not suitable for color, that their very ambition forces them to limit their estimates. To claim that they would have gained nothing from color doesn't make much sense, because we don't know what effects the director would have achieved. We see, on the other hand, what other films would have lost had they been in black and white.

This is why I divide the best color films to date into two categories. On the one hand, those that we remember for their harmony, their general tonality, in which the director, the set designer, the costume designer, and the photographer wanted to create a work, if not of painters, at least of men sensitive to pictorial matters. *Gate of Hell (Jigoku-mon), Romeo and Juliet,* and *Lola Montès* had hardly any trouble being recognized for their merits. Color is an additional refinement, a luxury, which, for these luxurious subjects, is almost a necessity: It touches, it underlines, it substantiates the dramatic texture, yet it is never its only source. In the second category, on the other hand, color is occasionally, but then unquestionably, in charge. These films haunt us not so much because of their overall climate as because of the power of certain details, of certain colored objects: Harriet's blue dress in *The River* or the green one belonging to the "lonely heart" in *Rear Window.* It is not enough for a blue or a green to bolster the film's expression; they bring with them new ideas, their presence at a specific moment evokes an emotion sui generis.

I vote for this second concept, because it is, if I may say so, *positive.* We've accepted color. Good. Let's do more, let's welcome it. It is still too often the case that we recognize it only negatively. Let's consider what it brings, not what it doesn't destroy when mastered. Let's simply count the film effects *that color alone makes possible.* I know that they can be counted on one's fingers, but they exist.

Nine out of ten people who have seen *To Catch a Thief* will talk about the famous "cigarette in the egg" shot. Would Hitchcock have conceived this very effective gag in black and white?* No, of course not, and yet if you think about it, what does color have to do with it? It's not the yellow as such, but the egg yolk itself that produces this effect on us, funny for some, powerful enough to nauseate others.

But, and this is the crux of the matter, without its color, this egg is only partially an egg. It *exists* fully only in color. It is only in color that cinematic expression attains absolute realism. We find this egg, almost as conspicuously placed, in a very recent still life that is

---

* The black-and-white equivalent is the jar of cream in which the English tourist in *Rebecca* puts out her cigarette.

greatly esteemed by our young painters. But in all honesty, is it the same egg? This first one existed only *through* color; Buffet's egg lives only *for* it. Modern painting's great idea is to have given color a life of its own, or at least to have made it the absolute ruler of the canvas, the supreme value. For van Gogh, Cézanne, or Matisse, the sky is *blue* before it is sky. The green of a fruit spills onto a table, or to a face, if harmony so demands. The painter has intentionally overthrown the barriers separating the three natural kingdoms: animal, vegetable, and mineral. Only the greatest have been able to resuscitate them by an artifice that is no longer academic, to express the "substance" without the use of "relief," like depth without the use of ordinary perspective.

What was a paradox in Manet's time is merely commonplace today. The modern schools, and perhaps one hundred years of black-and-white photography, have taught us to distinguish "value" from "nuance." We know, as Gauguin, I think, said, that oranges are brighter, more "orange," when the weather is gray. We have learned to see like painters.

Is this way of seeing suitable for the screen? "You liked *To Catch a Thief,*" someone said to me! "All those picture postcard shots! And the costume ball," my interlocutor, a man of good taste and an esteemed painter to boot, added. "What unbearable disorder! I could see that loud colors were in!" Such objections leave you dumbfounded! How can you not consider your adversary to be right, to admit that, in fact, you had hardly thought about it, in short, that you were too easily taken in?

Does cinema lead us beyond the norms of good and bad taste? Might it be in every way an art such as the art of Epinal, whose vulgarity must be accepted or rejected as a whole? I don't believe that, either. If we do not notice certain discordances on the screen, it is not that our senses have been dulled but that we view them with a different eye than we would a painting. In the film in question, I did not notice the picture postcard images any more than I notice them when I walk from Cannes to Menton (the landscapes make me think more of Matisse, Dufy, or Bonnard). Don't misunderstand me. The screen is not *reality,* but it is even less a *painting;* it must be approached from a different angle. The concert goer is disappointed by records, but the record lover is also disappointed by concerts. Whoever hears a recording on FM might think that his radio is poorly tuned. This true sound seems loud and impure to him. Little by little, he purifies it, forgets the noise, and retains only the harmony.

So it is with color in film. Our eye is used to toning down naturally violent shades. It must learn to purify the screen, just as it purifies reality. If, by an excess of taste or attention, we make this purification unnecessary, we may tarnish the object's natural brilliancy which the camera recreates very well on its own; we would betray reality without even managing to create art.

Beware of filters, of chemical toning, and of all other tricks. There is a kind of intensity belonging to the raw image that we must respect. Photography's ability to show objects spontaneously is something very precious, and we should play on it. One emulsion may be more sensitive to the yellow of a flower than to that of a rug, and vice versa. It may establish a difference between the two colors that the naked eye could not appreciate, but that the eye will find later. Film, just like museums, teaches us to see. There is no shame in taking lessons, even under such an unassuming master.

Let's believe Jean Renoir when he tells us: "I'm convinced that our profession is that of a photographer. If we arrive at a set saying, 'I want to be Rubens or Matisse,' I'm sure that we will wind up making huge mistakes."

So what if there is a bit of ingenuousness in this declaration! Renoir is free to love painting, even to owe the reliability of his taste to its familiarity. I would like to believe that the two conceptions, that of the painter and that of the filmmaker, are not irreconcilable.

To the mob of tasteful people, to which we can only be flattered to belong, color seems unsuitable for the screen. But not too long ago, it was all film that they almost unanimously condemned. They condemn it still, wanting, with undue pretension, to impose on it their tastes and their colors.

(*Arts* 59, March 1956)

The taste for beauty

The love of the beautiful is as widespread as good taste is rare. Passions are identical, but they aren't all for the same objects. The man in the street or the philistine professes a love that it would be wrong to underestimate. It is often that indifference sets in along with culture.

My colleagues at the daily or weekly papers, collaborators or not, friends or not of *Cahiers,* will therefore not be shocked, I hope, if I am surprised to see them, especially lately, say little about the very notion of *beauty* in their film criticism.

I realize that the word is dull and cannot be used in place of an argument. But it is not the absence of the word that I deplore, but of a certain perspective through which it would seem natural to judge films, if we truly consider them works of art.

Now, what newswriter at the most obscure provincial paper is not deeply convinced that film is an art, a major art? Who, today, would dare to confuse the analysis of a film with the study of its script? Who would try, as before, to support his judgment with only political or moral considerations? Such progress has been made in this direction over the past few years, that in France today, we would be hard pressed to determine the bent of a publication by reading only the film column.

In any case, I would be out of line in voicing doubts as to the competency or objectivity of my colleagues. This is not my intention. At the same time, they would quickly agree with me that it is not always easy to escape being affected by the questions of the day. I might add, as they probably will themselves, that in giving in to these questions, they are no less correct than we are at *Cahiers* to maintain the ambitious goal of judging films for what they are.

It is normal for an art critic to act somewhat as a prophet, for his role is to advise an investment. The same thing is true of literary critics: Their readers appreciate not crowding their bookshelves with works they will not reread. But the film critic does not have to worry about looking to the future, because usually this future does not exist and because the film is an ephemeral piece that he will never again have occasion to quote, nor his readers to see.

The cinema that we work on at *Cahiers* is perhaps, as someone wrote, a cinema "in itself" and even, I agree, a mind-set. But our concern with the eternal should be more readily excused when one considers that our monthly appearance prohibits us from sticking closely to the present. This disadvantage must be turned to our benefit. It's our only raison d'être.

We address a limited public with a museumlike perspective. On what grounds can this be condemned? A film is not made for the repertory any more than the *Mona Lisa* was painted for the Louvre. If film museums worthy of the name do not yet exist anywhere in the world, it is up to us to lay the foundation. That is the best part of our struggle, which we plan to follow up in the years to come, in a more active, specific, and direct way.

This does not imply that we are better prophets than anyone else, if not in general, at least in specific cases. In deciding to go back to the beauties of four recent films, beauties that went unnoticed, I do not mean to say that posterity will necessarily find me right. Rather, I want to show that from a certain point of view, less dependent on circumstances, these works present *beauties* – yes, that is the word – which easily erase the faults that others have been happy to point out.

Beauty – or beauties – is a concept that on this occasion I judge to be preferable to that of mise-en-scène, which I ordinarily advocate but which, just the same, I do not wish to ignore. The first notion incorporates the second, which, however, also has a purely technical meaning. Now in a pinch, from a purely technical perspective, one can obviously

defend the works of – let's say so as to hurt no one – Clement or Clouzot, Wyler or Zinnemann. But as soon as you say the word *beauty,*
their works deflate like balloons.

I do not think that our critics in France have lessons to learn from
anyone concerning the specific merits of cinema, which they always
discern with insight. I would not criticize them for failing to indicate
how film differs from the other arts but, rather, for failing to show how
it can be considered an equal. Unknowingly, they often make it out to
be a poor relative. An initial theoretical indulgence turns out to be the
cause of their individual complaints. They do not think that the *beauty*
they are proposing is of the same quality, of the same height, as the
beauty that can be admired elsewhere. They refuse to believe that this
beauty may hide beneath the same barren façade as in a painting or a
poem and that a long and patient familiarization may be necessary to
reveal it. They do not admit its capacity for secrecy or mystery, which
is, nevertheless, one of its most certain powers.

Take *Why Change Your Wife?* By today's standards, this film may
seem to lack the provocative or endearing virtues by which the works
that preceded it in the same theater, or which are showing at the same
time in the area, were able to win over the critics. A dryness that cannot be construed as hiding a sense of modesty, a refusal to use the
notations that are the bread-and-butter of psychological description, a
systematic preference for downbeat action, none of that interests us.
But without even waiting for a second or third viewing to rekindle our
interest, which I am sure it would do, you should simply compare this
film with the greatest the history of cinema has to offer. You will see
how much that – far from losing – it gains in comparison. One of art's
paradoxes is that those who can do the most cannot do the least. And
the old Aristotelian that I am, I do not hesitate to write that one of the
most beautiful works of cinematic art is not necessarily the best
choice among the listings of one of the poorest weeks of the season.

Don't get me wrong. I do not mean to say that *Why Change Your
Wife?* is not for our times. To the contrary. Set in history, this film will
appear a thousand times more modern than do so many of its compet-
itors, which are judged at the moment to be more "advanced." But here
again, in this respect, we would have no argument if we approached
the film from only a technical viewpoint. Our perception of novelty is
in this case inseparable from the feeling of beauty. And this beauty,
although it is not exempt – as is its prerogative – from pictorial or literary references, merits consideration above all for the kind of beauty
that the great works of the screen have taught us to appreciate.

We talk of specificity, and that's all very well. But normally it is
only a question of the specificity of means and not of *ends.* It is true,
for example, that *L'Avventura* or *La Notte* are great films, and it would

be quite stupid, in only considering their means, to accuse them of being literary. The most correct and original use has been made of powers that belong only to cinema. Just the same, one has the right to think that the kind of beauty that these films reveal could have been, or would have been, captured equally well by the painter or the novelist. I accept the idea that cinema has invented nothing – even less than its detractors think – if we limit ourselves to the means of expression or themes it uses. It is not a language but an original art. It does not say things differently but says different things. It has a unique beauty that is neither more nor less comparable to that of a painting or a sheet of music than a Bach fugue is comparable to a painting by Velasquez. If film must equal the other arts, it is by seeking the same degree of beauty. This is the only goal they can share.

I love only great subjects. This film is one of them, with all due respect to those who see in it only a Bernstein type of drama, which it is, perhaps, on paper. But today I will avoid the quicksand of the debate over form and content. Besides, the film's fundamentals were defended here last month, and I need not return to that. I would simply like to express my astonishment that my colleagues are ordinarily so satisfied with a very mediocre, commonplace concept of profundity on the screen. True, it has been a while since we have been taken in by propaganda films. But have we made so much progress? What we call *profound* is a description, often a very correct description, of characters or of morals, but it is limited to the dismal borders of an academic realism. We simply cannot believe that cinema can tackle real tragedy. Each time a film attempts to do so and succeeds – without, for all that, plagiarizing the Greeks or Shakespeare – we find it, ipso facto, baptized as melodrama. If our art has not, as the others have not, lost the gift of exploiting strong and simple situations, why not rejoice, instead of wanting to take away its good fortune?

Criticism, in a unanimous agreement, has skirted the subject of *Les Godelureaux,* which, here again, is also a great subject. Never has there been so great a misunderstanding regarding a film. There are reasons for this, but not excuses. Following a certain hullabaloo by the press and the myth of the New Wave, we insisted on finding an exemplary or romantic side in Chabrol's work, which it does not, in any way, possess. As A. S. Labarthe said in regard to *Les Bonnes Femmes,* what counts here is not the "message" but the "gaze." Now, through the gaze of the camera, the simpleminded women and the dandies are privileged beings owing to their excesses: The former's sin is being excessively natural, which is their principal characteristic, and the others' sin is being excessively artificial, which has become their second nature. Simply by persevering in their characters, these people fascinate us and finally touch us, just as anything does that

Jean-Claude Brialy, Bernadette Lafont, and Charles Belmont in *Les Godelu-reaux* by Claude Chabrol.

is simple and naive, without recourse to the tender winks and other Fellini-like pathos. This theme is so dear to the screen – there is not one great film that has not used it – that I am surprised that no one, or almost no one, has congratulated Chabrol for attacking it head-on and for having followed his logic, without faltering, right to the end.

But where is the *beauty?* I am afraid that we have a rather affected, academic idea of beauty. Isn't caricature an accepted genre? There is some beauty in this film, as in the preceding one, and of excellent quality. I mean that it does not come from manneristic writing but from a vision that comprehends things. Do I dare say that Chabrol's art is the most "metaphysical" of all our young filmmakers? Why not, if it is true that he draws his beauties less from the embellishment of themes than from the discovery of *ideas?* In Ambroisine's character, for example, there is an idea of the woman, of femininity, that I don't find expressed with the same plastic, biological, or moral force in the heroines of contemporary films, even though the latter win in regard to their delicacy of detail and all that we are accustomed to calling psychology. Whether dowdy or nude, bantering or sugar sweet, a nymph or an old hag, a cow or a butterfly, Ambroisine, through all her metamorphoses, is the bearer of eternal femininity to such a degree only because she chooses the severe graces of the *archetype* over the convenient seductions of her sisters in film.

Les Godelureaux has another sort of beauty that should at least have affected audiences, as it is more like the tastes of today. By the presentation of the characters and the treatment of the narrative, this film is the furthest of them all from the norms of classical dramaturgy and the closest in spirit to the contemporary novel's research. For I do not believe it is so "modern" to impose on situations or on conventional groups the iron collar of Byzantine rhetoric, which places cinema in literature's wake, as literature alone oversaw its formation. Here, on the contrary, the perpetual desire for transition comes not from an arbitrary assumption but from the actual fluidity of perspective, which is, as I said, one of metamorphosis. A slow ascension leads us from the asphalt of St. Germain-des-Près up to the iridescent skies of the final reels, skies that, though in no way mystical, place us all in the perspective of Sirius and change the slightly fashionable puppets of the beginning into disquieting science fiction heroes. Chabrol does not hide the fact that there is symbolism – and even an esoteric symbolism – but on the contrary, I see nothing in this desire to signify something between the lines that would be opposed to the generous canons of art, and therefore, to the habits of our century.

La Pyramide humaine is in no way a cursed film, but the praise granted it was astonishingly moderate and centered more on the interest of the *experiment* performed than on the merits of the *work of art* itself. The anthropologist Jean Rouch is perhaps not a born artist, even though the fantasy – one could say the poetry – of his research is more closely related to art than to science. He undoubtedly has truth in mind to start with, and beauty, it seems, is given to him only in accordance with the axiom "truth is beauty." Yes, this is true, if we consider only the undertaking, the production, the method. But from the point of view of this "cinema in itself" that they love to saddle us with and whose burden we so happily accept, I wonder whether the reciprocal "beauty is truth" doesn't reveal a more accurate perspective. Painting, poetry, music, and so forth try to translate truth by the intermediary of beauty that is their domain, which they cannot leave without ceasing to exist. Film, on the other hand, uses techniques that are instruments of reproduction or, one might say, of knowledge. In a sense, it possesses the truth right from the beginning and aims to make beauty its supreme end. A beauty, then, and this is the essential

La Pyramide humaine by Jean Rouch.

point, that is not its own but that of nature. A beauty that it has the mission of discovering, and not of inventing, of capturing like a prey, of almost abstracting from things. The difficulty is not, as we think, in creating a world of its own with mirrors – the tools at its disposal – but in managing simply to *copy* this natural beauty. But although it is true that the cinema manufactures nothing, it doesn't deliver things to us in a neat package either: It arouses this beauty, gives birth to it according to a *Socratic art* that constitutes the very basis of its method. If it gave us nothing but things that were known in advance, in principle if not in detail, all it would capture would be the *pictur-esque.* And, believe me, our critics, if you read them, are quite comfort-able with the picturesque.

But on this point, I see that I must use an example, at the risk of denigrating a work that is not the least worthy of films. *Shadows,* which I like, and about which others have made a big deal in compar-ing it with *Pyramide,* is, in my eyes, the quintessential picturesque film. It is, as we know, the story of a man who seduces a woman whom he believes to be white, and who, after they make love and after seeing her more ethnic-looking brother, realizes that she has black blood. I know that the racial problem is on today's agenda, but permit me to say that from the "eternal" perspective in which we place our-selves, this current event is not so important. The situation as it is portrayed would not have been greatly changed if, for example, instead of a black woman, it had been about a married woman. It is therefore *just any* situation. The heroes of the film are young people, and youth is also a fashionable theme. But they could just as well have been in their forties. The story would have lost only a few, entirely external, details. Their age is therefore also *just any* age. The fact that it was more or less about "dandies" again adds to the modernity and the pic-turesque quality, but a portrait of the human species cannot be painted with just these details, as it is in Chabrol's film. Even Amer-ica, from where such movies come, does not emerge as the center of the world, as it has been made to seem in so many Hollywood films. We are, then, really in a *just any* social milieu.

On the other hand, the race, age, and milieu of the heroes appear constantly as a *privileged* theme in Rouch's work. And this is so not only because of the opportunities that they offer the filmmaker. I said that I considered the ends, not the means. The privileges here are shown to be the result of the plurality of races as such, youth as such, Africa as such. Race, in particular, no longer appears, as before, as a single issue or as a particular case stemming from a blemish or a freak of nature, but as the expression of abundance and freedom in nature. If there is tragedy in this psychodrama, in which the mouths of the high school students transform the lead of psychoanalysis into the gold of confession, respond in terms of morals when one talks to them about science, it is because this tragedy rests, as does all true tragedy, not so much on the idea that the world might be good but that in fact we cannot really conceive of it other than it is. It is no longer a question, as before, of a contingent theme, to be chosen from many possibilities, but of a great and necessary subject, the likes of which the cinema *had to* tackle someday, and it has hardly found a more beautiful one in the course of its history.

Preminger's work is pure beauty. But it is precisely because of this beauty that he is criticized, this taste for the beauty of nature or for beautiful lines, for which, they say, especially in *Exodus,* he sacrificed verisimilitude, realism, psychology, and other major virtues. His earlier films were excused because of their violence or the bitterness of their subject matter. In *Exodus* he is denied even this indulgence, which is generally accorded works more naively attached to their theses, works confined to the limits of a popular genre, as if there were no salvation for the director of a historical film other than the perspective of the *Song of Roland* or that of Fabrice at Waterloo.*

Here again we are faced with an important subject, not so much because it shows big powers in action, but because it mobilizes all of cinema's resources, which are not a luxury but its daily bread. This birth of a nation is able to give substance to the idea of a people, by adding the idea of a race, which is more concrete, and therefore better suited for use on the screen. It is true that the director, with little concern for this advantage, did not let any ethical consideration come before his choice of actors. Having a "star" in such a spectacular production was compulsory. Yes, certain things are conventional, but what does it matter when they no longer are a hindrance but are useful to the material and become one of the tools by which the filmmaker creates his beauty. What counts is not the similarity of a group or its appearance, but the permanence of its blood under its many masks, even if the concern with diversifying these masks can be partly attributed to a certain – quite legitimate – coquetry, as is shown in the very humorous scene in which Ari, dressed as an English officer, fools the governor's adjunct, who claims to know a Jew when he sees one.

One may be content to see in Preminger – and it is a sufficient cause for admiration – one of the purest representatives of classical cinema, Goethian, one might say. We see this in the kind of unhurried serenity one detects in the actors' eyes, the disdain for vague yearnings or for the bizarre, the cult of the ordinary, the search for essential things and for the act in all its fullness, a love of order and organization, and a taste for exceptional yet vulnerable beings who are closer to the "king's sons" dear to Gobineau than to the romantic model. We

---

* In Stendhal's *La Chartreuse de Parme:* Fabrice watched from the outskirts (CV).

Eva Marie Saint and Paul Newman in *Exodus* by Otto Preminger.

can notice to what extent the royal simplicity of the style escapes analysis, because each problem is resolved according to a constantly alert sensibility and not according to a loudly proclaimed system.

But we also can see all that is *modern* in Preminger's art. Cinema's evolution is not linear. To praise Rouch does not prohibit admiring Preminger, who is at the other end of the spectrum. And in the end, the two find a common respect for nature. The great technical means that the director of *Exodus* has at his disposal, which have their little shortcomings, have the enormous advantage of allowing us to forget the human intervention in art by trying to bring us closer to this natural beauty, which in both cases is the goal. The maker of a documentary film, for better or worse, tires himself out pursuing reality, gives himself away by being one step behind, and, as objective as his intentions may be, introduces subjectivity in his composition. But here the camera, which is always present at the right moment, which is always *where it should be,* finds itself at the heart of things and, by means of this precision, shows these things in their natural state, whatever arti-fice may have preceded their placement.

Look at the photographs that illustrate the "Interview" featured in this issue.* (They do not give, either by their centering or by their im-ages, an exact idea of the films, but for our example, they represent the spirit well enough.) You will be struck, at first, by the simplicity of perspective, the asceticism of the set, even sometimes the convention-ality of the actors' stances. But on closer inspection you will discover a thousand small innovations beneath this apparent dryness, especially regarding the *hand* movements, which are always distinctive, always eloquent, always sensitive, always intelligent, always beautiful, always true. These *small* beauties constitute *great* art: We accept this in painting, why not in cinema?

I am not pretentious enough to think that my words cannot easily be refuted. That is why I mean to *prove* nothing. On calling on my col-leagues' natural taste for beauty, which I have every reason to believe is robust, I want to avoid a sterile battle of words, of which our com-mon love of film would risk being the first victim. Allow me, then, to hope that I will be considered correct, just a little, in theory, even if it is true that we all do not agree on the details.

(*Cahiers du cinéma* 121, July 1961)

Letter to a critic [concerning my *Contes moraux* (*Moral Tales*)]

My films, you say, are literary: The things I say could be said in a novel. Yes, but what do I *say*? My characters' discourse is not neces-sarily my film's discourse.

There is certainly literary material in my tales, a preestablished nov-elistic plot that could be developed in writing and that is, in fact, sometimes developed in the form of a commentary. But neither the text of these commentaries, nor that of my dialogues, is my film: Rather, they are things that I film, just like the landscapes, faces, behavior, and gestures. And if you say that speech is an impure element, I no longer agree with you. Like images, it is a part of the life I film.

What I say, I do not say with words. I do not say it with images either, with all due respect to the partisans of pure cinema, who would speak with images as a deaf-mute does with his hands. After all, I do not say, I show. I show people who move and speak. That is all I know how to do, but that is my true subject. The rest, I agree, is lit-erature.

It is true that I can write the stories I film. The proof is that I did

* *Entretien avec Otto Preminger,* by Jacques Doniol-Valcroze and Eric Rohmer (JN).

write them, long ago, before I discovered cinema. But I was not satisfied with them because I was unable to write them well enough. That's why I filmed them. I was searching for a style, but I didn't look to people like Stendhal, Constant, Mérimée, Morand, Chardonne, or others of whom you claim I am a disciple. I read these people very little or not at all, whereas I never stop rereading Balzac, Dostoyevski, Meredith, or Proust: rich, prolix, involved writers. They present me with a world living its own life. I love them and read them often, just as I go to movies often; they too reveal life to me. And when I film, I try to extract as much from life as possible, in order to fill out the line of my argument. I no longer think about this argument, which is just a framework, but about the material with which I flesh it out, such as the landscapes where I situate my story and the actors I choose to act in it. The choice of these natural elements, and the way I can hold them in my net without altering their momentum, absorbs most of my attention.

Where do I find my subjects? I find them in my imagination. I said that I see cinema as a means, if not to reproduce, at least to represent, to recreate life. Logically, then, I should find my subjects in my own experience. But that's not the case: They are purely invented subjects. I have no special competence in the subjects I treat; I use neither memories nor books. There are no keys to my characters, I use no guinea pigs. As opposed to the novelist in my film (*Claire's Knee/Le Genou de Claire*) I do not discover; I combine some primary elements in small amounts, as a chemist does.

But I will use a musician as an example, instead, as I conceived of my moral tales as six symphonic variations. Like a musician, I vary the initial motif, I slow it down or speed it up, stretch it or shrink it, add to it or purify it. Starting with the idea of showing a man attracted to a woman at the very moment when he is about to marry another, I was able to build my situations, my intrigues, my denouements, right down to my characters. The principal character, for example, is a puritan in one tale (*My Night at Maud's/Ma Nuit chez Maud*), a libertine in others (*La Collectionneuse, Claire's Knee*), sometimes cold, sometimes exuberant, sometimes cross, sometimes feisty, sometimes younger than his partners, sometimes older, sometimes more naive, sometimes more cunning. I do not do portraits from nature: Within my self-imposed limits, I present different possibilities for human types, for both women and men.

My work is thus limited to a vast gathering and sorting operation that I do without a guide, it is true, but that I could very well have given to a computer, as do some of today's musicians.

When I began to film my moral tales, I very naively thought that I could show things – sentiments, intentions, ideas – in a new light, things that until then, had received attention only in literature. In the first three I made ample use of commentaries. Was that cheating? Yes, if it contained the main part of my subject matter, relegating the images to the role of illustrations. No, if from the confrontation of this conversation with the characters' conversation and behavior a kind of truth was discovered, a truth entirely different from that of the text or the behavior – and that would be the film's truth.

For example, the filmed action and the words said off camera were never in the same *tense.* One was in the present or the simple past, and the other almost always in the imperfect. The commentary generalized the individual case shown on the screen, linking it more tightly to preceding or coming events, and also, I admit, destroying some of its uniqueness, its charm of something in the present and only in the present. At the same time, it took away quite a bit of my characters' mystery and the sympathy that the spectators were ready to feel for them. But it would have been an easy mystery, a suspicious sympathy, beyond which, for better or worse, I convinced myself to lead my audience.

In *My Night at Maud's,* on the other hand, the protagonist explained too much about himself in the presence of his different partners for us to endure more lengthy confidences on the side. He confirmed himself as narrator only through the title of the film, by two short sentences intended only to keep us from going astray.

As for *Claire's Knee,* it was written, in its novelized version, in the manner of St. Jerome, describing the progress of the protagonist's thoughts. How can one show this purely internal emotion on the screen? The commentary was necessary, but superimposing it on the image seemed to me even more useless and artificial because at the beginning of this thought process was a single event whose uniqueness made it valuable. Here, it was no longer possible to play on the gap between the *tense* (in the grammatical sense of the word) of the action and that of the thought. Showing an action and giving the exact thoughts of the person involved, at the very moment when he performs the act – is that "cinema" or not? I do not know. In any case, it goes against the commonly held belief that most things witnessed happen in less time "than it takes to tell them."

Therefore, instead of superimposing, I chose to juxtapose. In two of the film's key passages, the one in which Jérôme contemplates Gille's hand posed on Claire's knee and the one in which, in the cabin, he in turn places his hand on her knee, I first present the facts in a direct, objective manner, while leaving my character's thoughts unknown. Then, during a conversation, I have my character tell his thoughts directly to the critical and amused novelist: "What do your thoughts matter," she says, "the important thing is that you form a pictorial grouping." But film, at the risk of falling on its face, would like to go a bit beyond this simple painting, which it is.

Laurence Monaghan and Jean-Claude Brialy in *Claire's Knee* (*Le Genou de Claire*) by Eric Rohmer.

Speech goes over very well on television, and people talk a great deal in my stories. But what do they talk about? Of things that must be shown with all the luxury and precision of images: of thinness, for example, of fragility, of the smoothness of a knee which must be made perceptible in order to understand the attraction it exerts on the narrator? Now, the best television screen in the world is not very good at showing these characteristics. In short, the television screen erases not only the effects of light belonging to a specific hour, a specific season, but also the feelings of warmth, cold, dryness or humidity, a stifling environment or an airy one, which the image, whether naked or reinforced with sound, has the power to evoke.

In a western, the change to the picture tube can underline, consolidate the picture, and can make the principal lines, too often masked by a conventional appearance, stand out. But the originality in my work, if there is any, is to be found in its *rendition*. And besides, is television more intimate, as they say, than cinema? I am not so sure.

Even alone, in front of your set, you feel less isolated from the world than in the anonymous crowd of a movie theater. It is more difficult to be swept away by the illusion of penetrating into the fictitious universe presented. You are not in the screen but in front of it, as if it were a stage.

That being said, I admit that the audience's reaction, even if favorable, disturbs the unfolding of my films, which I dream of adjusting to individual sensibilities, more so than to the collective conscience of a movie theater.

(*La Nouvelle Revue française* 219, March 1971)

Film and the three levels of discourse:
indirect, direct, and hyperdirect

In the past, the worst comment one could make about a film was "It seems like a play." Today it would be "It seems like a film."

Modern cinema has more to fear from its own clichés than from an external influence like that of the theater. And is cinema's influence so bad? Everyone said so at the time of Pagnol and Guitry, whose reputations are almost assured today. Everyone agreed that film was beneficial in the 1940s, when it had Orson Welles and, to a lesser extent, Jean Cocteau, as its source. It disappeared in the 1960s, stifled by cinéma-vérité. Now it's back again. All flattery aside, what films in the 1970s, in France or elsewhere, put cinema in the forefront more than do those of Marguerite Duras?

Yet I believe in the distinction between genres and their specificity. The fact that the cinema can safely explore the theater's domain does not prove that "theater and cinema are one and the same," as André Bazin remarked, but that the latter is mature enough to face the former as an equal. Differences remain in the classical conception and, more subtly, in the modern conception of each one. These are differences that have been discussed a thousand times. It may be futile to search for others, but let us try just the same.

We shall use the text as a point of departure: not the form – more or less relaxed or lofty, colloquial or literary – that may be used here or there but its content and, more specifically, the amount of information revealed.

The answer is clear: The theater's text is richer, because during a presentation, it alone provides information. The other elements of the performance, the so-called mise-en-scène, convey only a tiny amount of information in comparison. A play read or heard on the radio often loses much of its charm and impact but little of its clarity, whereas the sound track of a film is generally not sufficient to follow the story.

Yann Andréa and Buller Ogier in *Agatha et les lectures illimitées* by Marguerite Duras.

The sequence of images serves to connect the text and to complete the information provided.

We are familiar with the Aristotelian distinction between "verisimilitude" and "the necessary." Corneille speaks of this in his *Discours* and applies it to the action, but not without extrapolating. Extrapolating in turn, we shall allow ourselves to apply it to the text and shall say: Everything in the text that is indispensable to the clarity of the intrigue is *necessary*. All that the characters say among themselves in a given situation that is not concerned with informing the audience is *verisimilitude*. For example, in Racine's *Andromaque,* the fragment of the first verse, "...since I find such a faithful friend again," is absolutely necessary (it informs us that Orestes and Pylades are friends and were separated) but not very true to life, as the interlocutor does not need this information: It is meant only for the reader. The "yes" that begins the verse makes the rest of the sentence seem like the continuation of a conversation that has already begun and is there to provide, among other things, the verisimilitude that is lacking.

Thus, we see that in theater, the necessary takes precedence over verisimilitude and that its presence, even diffused, limits the sphere of the true-to-life. A film's dialogue, on the contrary, must use the necessary only as a last resort. Information is presented in an inoffensive manner, cloaked by pure verisimilitude. It reaches the attentive spectator, whose vigilance increases as he learns more, by a ricochet effect. Film dialogues from before 1960 seem encumbered with necessary lines that modern film has left as commentary, monologues, or graphic signs, with an ease that is beginning to seem dated as well.

Nothing goes out of style more quickly than the necessary – except verisimilitude, whose excess in the 1970s is beginning to show. In order to give free rein to the true-to-life, we have done away with written texts and have the actors say "just anything." It was believed that from this absolute contingency, a new necessity would be born, without any reference to the "rules" of the theater that were always lurking in the background. It did happen, sometimes felicitously, with Rouch, Godard, or Rivette. The *true* killed the true-to-life: The stopgap realism of the scriptwriters became unbearable. And here we are, once again, faced with the demands of necessity.

The novel does not have these problems. The marriage of verisimilitude and necessity has never been impeded. Therein lies its strength, its specialty. It has such an arsenal of informational methods at its disposal that it can afford to reject any part of them, according to its particular period. As for verisimilitude, it can dispense with it, owing to the license that writing gives it to remodel reality slightly, without this obsession with absolute truth, the repetition, the stammering, and the moments of silence, which the cinema had to endure, did endure, and which it would now like to leave behind.

Putting aside the *narrative* and its thousand syntactical resources, the relationship among the characters' spoken words is shown on the different *levels* or *planes* (in the concrete sense of the word, as in "perspective plane") of what we traditionally call *discourse.*

One is *direct discourse,* introduced specifically in the novel by a typographical sign: quotation marks and an inserted clause indicating the speaker. This presentation has the advantage of linking the discourse to the narrative.* But it has the disadvantage of not always being clear, when, to avoid the monotony of "he said," "said Mr. X," or the ridiculous sound of its synonyms, "he started," "she groaned," and so on – the writer eliminates the insertion. What reader, lost among

---

* And gives it the dimension that we call *epic.* Like the *épopée* from which it is descended, the novel is an oral art form. Not so long ago adults read aloud to one another.

these interjections, has not had to climb the list one by one, counting them in order to determine which character said what? But no novelist likes to use theater's simple method – that of preceding each passage with the speaker's name in capital letters.

Except, as we know, the countess of Ségur. Addressing herself to children, she means to help their reading. This effort, however, which was originally typographical, creates a new plane of discourse, situated at the forefront: it pulls the character toward us, isolating him from the narrative background, conferring an autonomy on his words that are uninterrupted by necessity, and giving him as long as he likes to express himself in his own manner, with all his idiosyncrasies of speech, including (as with Georgey, Foelichein, Cozrgbrlewski) his accent:

JEANNOT: Where's it, m'sieur?
PANTOIS (laughing): Well spoken, my friend. Such pure French! Where's it? There, on the counter.*

And farther on:

... He sits down at a small table and calls out: Waiter!
A waiter hurries over.
No, I wasn't calling you, my friend; I want to be served by Simon.
The waiter goes away a bit surprised and tells Simon that a gentleman has asked for him.
SIMON: Monsieur asked for me? What can I get for monsieur?
THE STRANGER: Yes, Simon, I asked for you. Bring me two cutlets with spinach and a fresh egg.

In the second example, at the beginning, verisimilitude unites with the necessities of a narrative whose length is fairly limited. It stops entirely for a moment – we will return to that – and as soon as Simon speaks, expands suddenly. The preceding was only an introduction. We are at the heart of the scene. Everything, even what seems useless, has its place. The stranger's order, "two cutlets with spinach," sheds light on neither the story nor the character. It is a pure tribute to verisimilitude[†] and makes the character jump off the canvas in an almost hyperrealistic fashion.

Another interesting point in this passage is the use, though fleeting, of a third type of discourse that appears at the point mentioned in the text when the waiter "tells Simon that a gentleman has asked for him."

---

* Jean grunts, and Jean laughs.
† What could be more annoying for a director, while shooting a scene in a café, than to have to have his characters served specific drinks in the interest of "realism," with the subsequent connotations in which he has no interest and for which he will be accused of clandestine advertising? Realism is becoming a necessity in film, the first and foremost, and therefore an enslavement from which one naturally wants to be freed.

It is the indirect discourse, rare in the countess's work as it is too abstract for her young audience. It weaves speech into the narrative and its *rhythm* and permits it to remain in the background when it is not interesting in itself, but only as a bearer of information. The text, from one end to the other, may contain only "necessary" elements without shocking the true-to-life quality.

Of these three planes of discourse, the theater and the cinema have only the second one, the "hyperdirect," and it's a pity.

We can skip over theater, in which an eternal unvarying present seems to reign.* But these nuances are essential to film, and it is awkward to put a dialogue whose tense refers us to the present into a scene that might take place in the past (sometimes even a habitual past). Silent films were more at ease. The "abridged" passages in talking films still imitate their example – and are dated.

Still, a careful examination of every film will turn up the discrete, but definite, existence of our three types of discourse. To see them, one must simply believe in them. The problem is that we do not, as can be seen by the curious way in which scripts are still written. I am not talking about the now-abandoned method of retaining two columns (image and sound) but about presenting a dialogue, whatever or wherever it may be, in the manner of the theater, which does not match the impressions that the audience will get from the film.

It is entirely natural for the scriptwriter, to get a better grip on the realism of his film, to be tempted to use a novelistic device, like quotation marks or an indirect style. I gave in to this temptation when writing my moral tales. I did not do it out of laziness; I put off working on the scenes that "bored me" – if I was bored while developing a scene, it was because it was not in its place as a scene and it was necessary to give it the role and appearance of a connecting scene. Sometimes I even scribbled down certain sequences of exposition or transition using a direct style, and I noticed that the tone and length they would

---

* We should nonetheless mention *lyrical* discourse, which manifests itself quite differently from the *chorus* of Greek tragedy – in which it indicates an interval of time between the events of the drama, and possesses a certain informational function as well as a basic verisimilitude – and the aria of the opera, which is stagnation, a stretching out of the instant at heightened moments of action, and whose informational power and verisimilitude can be considered nonexistent. The "necessary" in these two cases results from an order different from that of communication: *incantation.*

We know too that lyricism also has its place in film, although it is restrained and often contested in the name of "purity." Moreover, more than in theater, it is linked to movement and dance.

Certain playwrights have tried to vary their discourse by using different rhythms. For example, the verses in Corneille's *Le Cid* or *Polyeucte* offer both a suspension and a lyrical elongation of time. In *Käthchen von Heilbronn,* Kleist alternates prose and verse, but contrary to what one might expect, he uses verse for the most action-packed scenes in which the dialogue is the choppiest and uses the most colloquial prose for the almost-lyrical tirades.

have "realistically" in life went beyond the limits of their function in the narrative. In order to be able to eliminate the unnecessary part, I had to use the indirect style and merely put them into the direct style on the day of the shooting. Thus, in the prologue of *Chloe in the Afternoon* (*L'Amour l'après-midi*) we find "on paper":

When one of the secretaries, Fabienne, arrives, I am sitting in front of the typewriter typing an urgent letter. She apologizes for being late, and I tell her that I am early. She offers to replace me. I tell her that I haven't yet composed the letter and that I will give it to her to retype if there are any mistakes. Instead, she should look for such and such a document in the archives.

It sounds like this on the sound track:

I: Good morning, Fabienne.
FABIENNE: Am I late?
I: No, I'm early.
FABIENNE: Do you want me to type that for you?
I: No thanks, I'll do it myself. If there are any mistakes, you can retype it.
FABIENNE: OK, in that case I'll finish Dossier number twenty.

I realize that the transposition is far from faithful. The second text is more concrete ("Do you want me to type that for you?"), less rich in information ("I tell her that I haven't yet composed the letter" disappears), and richer in unnecessary true-to-life details ("Dossier number twenty" is the equivalent of Mr. Abel's "two cutlets with spinach").

But using the indirect style allowed me to give the film a tone that, when viewing it, corresponds more closely to the first text than to the second. This is to be expected: The first was made to be read, and the second was to be heard as part of a film whose context is missing here.

There is an enormous amount of indirect style in Kleist's short stories. All the people I spoke to in Germany about my project to film *The Marquise of O*, book in hand, with no other script than the text itself, in an effort to maintain its integrity,* threw up their hands and said, "But what will you do with the indirect style?" To which I responded that I would merely take out the subjunctives in the German. My interlocutors then condescendingly explained to me that there is much more than a difference of mood between the two styles and that neither the words used nor the expressions and thoughts were the same. I objected that the same was true in French and that it had not prevented me from writing certain parts of my tales in the indirect style that I later transcribed, as was my plan here. "Yes," they said, "but if

---

* In fact, the script that I wrote for diplomatic reasons (to show to the producers and technicians) had the corresponding page of the novel glued opposite each sheet: I used only the latter.

Bruno Ganz and Edith Clever in *The Marquise of O* (*Die Marquise von O*) by Eric Rohmer.

Kleist used indirect discourse, he had his reasons." "That is why I don't want to change anything. This story is interesting and easy to film precisely because it has a lot of indirect discourse. It even is a preliminary script. If it had been in the direct style, it would have seemed theatrical. And the most difficult dialogues to speak are certainly the direct ones, because of this theatricality."

The shooting confirmed my predictions beyond all hopes. The indirect passages, less somber, less marked by interjections and metaphors of the period, resemble real film dialogues. Sometimes, it is true, a line may be so long as to seem overly literary, for example, the one in which the count's false death is announced:

The messenger who brought this news to M—— had himself seen him, with a mortal bullet-wound in the chest, being carried to P——, where, according to a reliable report, he had died just as his bearers were about to set him down.*

Dividing up the sentence would have meant playing with the natural speech of two centuries ago which was unknown to me and which I did not know how to manipulate. Instead, the text continues, at times off camera, throughout the entire scene, thereby giving it value as a transitional scene. And is it so unrealistic for a soldier or a messenger to express himself concisely in such grave circumstances?

On the other hand, when they came to a part with short, lively sentences, the actors, who had been magnificent up until then, suddenly stumbled. It is the point at which the mother and the daughter, back from the country, await the arrival of the father, who is coming to make amends:

An hour later she returned with her face very flushed. "Why, what a doubting Thomas!" she said, though she seemed secretly delighted. "What a doubting Thomas! I did need a whole hour by the clock to convince him! But now he's sitting there weeping." "Who?" asked the marquise. "He himself," answered her mother. "Who else but the person with the most reason for it!" "Surely not my father?" exclaimed the marquise. "Weeping like a child," replied her mother. "If I hadn't had to wipe the tears from my own eyes, I would have burst out laughing as soon as I got out the door." "And all this on my account?" asked her daughter, rising to her feet, "and you expect me to stay here and ... ?" "You shall not budge!" said her mother.

As the rehearsals progressed, we floundered more and more in an atmosphere resembling that of the "théâtre du boulevard." I knew that hinting at an action off camera and the father's expected appearance at the back door were not enough to create this very trivial atmo-

---

* This and the following passages are adopted from Heinrich von Kleist and Jean Paul, *The Marquise of O——*, trans. David Luke, in *German Romantic Novellas*, ed. Frank G. Ryder and Robert M. Browning (New York: Continuum, 1985), pp. 1–28.

sphere. All of a sudden, I understood. "It's the direct discourse! That why it's so difficult to say!" Not the direct discourse of grand, pathetic tirades, marked by an appropriate eloquence, but rather an effort at verisimilitude as it was understood in the theater of the 1800s, and which seems naive to us today. But I had resolved to keep *all* of the text. This "natural" part had to be conveyed, as had the artificial parts of other sequences. It was more difficult, but we managed, I think, by refusing to fall into its traps. We used a diction that was more sensitive to the musical quality of the words than to their meaning and that reestablished the lofty style of this falsely colloquial scene.

I plan to do my next film, Chrétien de Troyes's *Le Roman de Perceval,* in the same way, "book in hand." There is no indirect discourse in it, but a great deal of direct discourse, linked by a narrative whose atmosphere can never be replaced by an image or cinematic montage. I'll use it as is and will have it spoken not only by the narrators but also by the characters – who will speak of themselves in the third person, including occasionally the "he says" that the cinema, like the theater, does not need. But indeed, who knows?

PERCEVAL: Faites-moi chevalier, dit-il,
   Sire roi, car aller m'en veux.

(*Cahiers Renaud-Barrault* 96, October 1977)

CHAPTER II
For an impure cinema

André Bazin's "summa"

I anticipated writing this article with great joy, far from suspecting the circumstances in which it would appear. The publication of the first volume of *What Is Cinema?* was not only going to allow me to pay a tremendous debt to my teacher and friend but also to draw attention to an event in the history of cinema no less important than the production of certain films or the development of a particular technical method. I even hoped that it would explain or excuse the minimal attention we usually give our book section at *Cahiers*, despite Bazin's own pleas. Each time a new work came out – and recently there have been many – I noted with continual bitterness that however honest or intelligent it was, that although it brought a new block to the building of cinema's theory, it was practically useless, as the framework was missing. The aisles and side chapels of an aesthetics under construction sat proudly in bookstore windows, while the blueprints for the nave were confined to the newspaper! Works were published that, if not unreadable at the time, would be so in two or three years, while the person who had turned the contemplation of cinema into as engrossing an activity as reading a novel, had published only two books, and collaborated works at that! A beginner would offer the sum total of his reflections, whereas the thoughts of the greatest contemporary critic had to be plucked out among the rubbish of weekly papers, reviews, or pamphlets.

This book was supposed to be the introduction to André Bazin's future work, which was no longer going to be that of a journalist, even an exemplary one, but that of an author. Alas, we are now compelled to consider this as the completed work, to contemplate the "summa" instead of a merely promising beginning! We were getting ready to celebrate a departure, a birth; now we must honor a death. But is it appropriate to speak of death when it refers to a work and not to a person? I know that what we have in our hands is only a tiny fragment

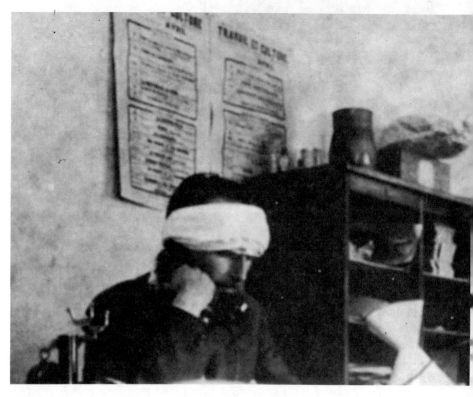

André Bazin.

of the work we had hoped for. And yet, beyond our sadness and our regrets, we at least have the consolation of knowing that the manuscripts that Bazin left us will appear more important in retrospect, more polished than we had judged them during his lifetime. As I read this first volume, and the proofs of the second,* I am certain of one thing: They are not collections of notes or outlines. Although it may not be crowned by a roof, this edifice has a solid foundation. Not only is the structure there, but also the walls are in place, some of them have been there for a long time.

This is an important point. Allow me to linger over it before going

* Bazin himself had assembled and arranged the material for four collections that were to appear under the title *Qu'est-ce que le cinéma?* I. Ontologie and Language, II. Le Cinéma et les autres arts, III. Cinéma et société, IV. Le Néoréalisme (Editions du Cerf, Collection 7e Art). Let's hope that the series will add more new volumes, as almost all of André Bazin's articles deserve to be reedited. [Bazin's work is available in English, in two volumes, translated by Hugh Gray under the title *What Is Cinema?* (Berkeley: University of California Press, 1967, 1971).]

on to consider the work itself. Despite its appearance, we are not dealing with a collection of articles. A selection was made, of course, but it seems as if the articles chosen, most often in their unrevised state, were written with this selection in mind. Nothing in them reminds us of the restrictions of the journalist's profession, which we nevertheless know that Bazin practiced with fervor and a sense of urgency. These pieces, all of which were inspired by specific events, were part of the development of a methodical outline that is now becoming apparent. And there is no doubt that they are part of an *outline* established beforehand and not of an argument assembled after the fact. The order of the logic found here does not necessarily correspond to the chronological order, and yet it is interesting to note that the first piece in the collection, "Ontologie de l'image photographique" ("Ontology of the Photographic Image"), is one of the oldest. Bazin does not give us a series of similar discussions of the same subject, but definitive answers to different problems. It was, at least in each section, important for him to resolve one problem before moving on the next.

I would first like to bring to light the scientific aspect of his work, but not to ignore the artistic aspect, to which I will return. One can speak of both the example of the natural sciences, which he frequently invoked, and that of mathematical methods. Each article, but also the whole work, has the rigor of a real mathematical proof. It is true that all of Bazin's work is centered on one idea, the affirmation of cinematic "objectivity," but it does so in the same way that geometry centers on the properties of the straight line.

It is not a question of a rigid principle, of a "Dada" repeated *ad nauseum* in many different forms, but of a general hypothesis that the author's several verifications lead us to consider as true. His constant references to this hypothesis, whether explicit or implicit, are far from monotonous. Instead, they give the work its diversity. It is constructed just as Euclid's work is. What I admire most in Bazin is that the purpose of each new article is not to complete or clarify a thought that was partially expressed elsewhere or even to offer more convincing examples. Rather, it adds, it creates a new thought whose existence we had not suspected. It gives life to critical "entities," just as the mathematician gives life to numbers or theorems. So many categories were opened to our inspection, thanks to him, beginning with that of ontology (the concept, not the term) which was absolutely disregarded by theoreticians before 1940!

If Bazin does not repeat himself, he does not contradict himself either. Without doubt, he has sometimes changed his mind about a particular film. In this case, he did not choose to do it sneakily, but with gusto, with an honesty that I dare not praise too much for fear of doing injustice to his other merits. In fact, if Bazin likes to make amends, this asset should be credited to the integrity of his system more than to his character. It is because for him, as for the scholar, there are objective truths and errors, whereas there are none for the doctrinaire or the impressionist. If he can say "I was wrong," it means that it is a rare event. He did not fundamentally change any of his written works, and yet we would have as hard a time finding even a tiny contradiction in his work as we would finding one in Euclid. Because he established himself in truth – or in the most fruitful hypothesis, as modern science would say – from the start, the exploration of different branches of his original tree of thought never induced him to rebuild this tree.

True, the deductive method has its dangers. I know the objections one might have: If Bazin never risked seeing his theories weakened, it is because he had more or less created a cinema for the sole purpose of verifying them. It is true that with respect to certain films, he proposed constructions that were too tempting to us to stick to the film's reality. So tempting that we couldn't help but forgive him, impressed as we were by the intrinsic perfection of his critical edifice. But at the moment, I am speaking of the scholar, not of the artist, although it is true that we had to await the artist's arrival for cinematic criticism to reach the same "literary" perfection as that of the other arts. To celebrate Bazin in this way is to honor him in a manner unworthy of him. Yes, his method is perilous, but rereading his texts has convinced me, if I were not already completely convinced, that the ever-present perils were always avoided at key moments. It is possible not to agree with Bazin when he judges certain films. No one can honestly disregard his own tastes: Bazin, who was the opposite of a dry theoretician, never hid his own taste any more than he left us in the dark concerning his philosophical or political convictions. What is rare in his work is that the principles guiding his judgments are never altered to agree with principles from another aesthetic world. His judgments are always drawn from his own thoughts on cinema. And this creates the strength and permanence of his conclusions. Thus, for example, he is always careful to distinguish actual realism from doctrine. If he defends, let's say, Wyler against Ford, it is not to explain Roger Leenhardt's slogan but to strengthen his knowledge of cinematic language. Bazin's study "Le janséniste de la mise en scène" has lost none of its value or even its timeliness: It is the work of a historian; it is not a manifesto. Compared with Bazin's basic serenity, all the rest seems polemic: naturally our own articles and works, those of his emulators and contemporaries, and also the great prewar theories (including those of Balasz) which were too busy trying to propose a new Aristotelian poetic to return to the basic facts.

But doesn't the inductive method present even greater risks? To infer a law from an example is, in art or history, to make a rash decision about the future. It is to define cinema only by what it was, to refuse sound or color, for example, on the pretext that film was silent or black and white for a certain time. Before Bazin, the theory of cinema had used only a model drawn from the experimental sciences, and because it was unable to achieve the same precision, it remained empirical. It noted the existence of certain facts — especially the uses of language, close-ups, and editing — without being able to give the reasons for them. Bazin introduced a new *metaphysical* dimension (we can use the word, as he did so himself, though at the same time he was careful not to play the philosopher) or if one prefers, a *phenomenological* approach. Sartre's* influence was, as he said, a decisive factor in his career. We can admire the disciple's subsequent independence from his teacher.

One of the proofs of the perfection of Bazin's construction is his success in formulating the basic framework. All is contained, if not said, in one sentence. It contains a definition of cinema, just as the definition of the straight line contains the seeds of those of the plane and space. One probably cannot be any more "comprehensive," but the concept will hereafter seem to extend infinitely: "Cinema," we read, "appears as the completion in time of photographic objectivity." By means of this small, this modest, sentence, Bazin makes a Copernican revolution in cinema theory. Before him, the emphasis was placed on the subjectivity of the "Seventh Art." It was generally reasoned as "Is cinema an art? When speaking of art, we speak of interpretation; we should therefore collect proofs of infidelity, highlight traces of the artist's intervention." This is a useful, a necessary, step, but one that long hid the fundamental *essence* of an art whose originality we failed to recognize in trying to discern its analogies with other arts. What is important to Bazin is not how cinema resembles painting, but how it differs from it. Like photography, it is the child of technology: "For the first time, nothing but another object comes between the original object and its presentation. For the first time, an image of the outside world is automatically formed, without the creative intervention of man. All arts are founded on man's presence; only in photography do we enjoy his absence."

We know that the extraordinary fecundity of this point of departure has been confirmed in the past thirteen years. Everything takes on new color in this light, and unknown fields of investigation will surface.

* Malraux's as well. In his case, Bazin borrows his ideas more than his method, but only to the extent that the justifiably famous article in *Verve* clarifies all preceding critical ideas. The study "Ontology de l'image photographique" is less the counterpart than the antithesis. A new age of dialectical film theory is beginning.

The chapters that follow do not paraphrase the first, nor are they variations on a common theme, or even particular applications of a general law. Like an explorer, Bazin investigates the interior of cinema as an entity. He has a line to guide him through the labyrinth, but he does not know in advance the riches awaiting him, which we discover with the same astonishment as he does. I have borrowed a few lines from the next chapters that convey both the unity and the extreme diversity of his remarks:

The guiding myth of the invention of cinema is therefore the fulfillment of the one that confusedly dominated all mechanical reproductive techniques of the nineteenth century, from the photograph to the phonograph. It is the myth of concrete realism, of a recreation of the world as it is, as an image on which neither the hypothesis of free artistic intervention nor the irreversibility of time would depend. If cinema in its infancy did not have all the attributes of the adult cinema of tomorrow, it was not by choice, but only because its fairy godmothers were technically incapable of peeking into the cradle.

. . .

The fantastic in cinema is made possible only by the realism of the photographic image, which imposes on us the presence of the improbable and inserts it into the visible world.

. . .

Thanks to cinema, the world is skillfully saving money on its war budget, as wars are used for two purposes, history and cinema, like producers who shoot a second film using the costly sets of the first. In these circumstances, the world knows best. War, with its harvest of corpses, its innumerable migrations, its concentration camps, and its atomic bombs, leaves the art of imagination which attempted to reconstitute it in the dust.

. . .

Such is the miracle of scientific film, its inexhaustible paradox: At the extreme end of self-serving, utilitarian research, among the absolute interdiction of aesthetic intentions as such, cinematic beauty develops as well, like a natural grace. . . . Only the camera can enter this universe where supreme beauty identifies with both nature and chance, that is, with all that a certain aesthetic tradition considers to be the opposite of art.

. . .

Just as cinema transforms it, hard and fossilized by the bony whiteness of orthochromatic color, a world already past returns, more real than our own and yet fantastic. Proust recognized the reward for the remembrance of things past in the ineffable joy of being enveloped in their memory. Here, on the contrary, the aesthetic joy comes from a division, for these "memories" are not our own. They exemplify the paradox of an objective past existing outside our conscience.

. . .

The representation of real death is also an obscenity, not moral, as with love, but metaphysical. We die only once. Photography does not have the

Paulette Goddard and Charlie Chaplin in *The Great Dictator*.

power of film in this domain: It can only show a person in agony or a corpse, not the elusive passage from one to the other.

· · ·

We can see from these few quotations how Bazin was led to reveal a world of new relationships between the work of art and nature. Cinema abolishes the traditional distance between reality and its representation. The model is integrated into the work; in some ways it is the work. We judge the work at the same time as we judge the model, and vice versa. Jean Jacques Cousteau's *The Silent World (Le Monde du silence)* leads us to admire the wonders of the deep, but it owes its beauty not only to these depths but also its value as a work of art.

The model may even be assigned a lower reality coefficient than is the film that reproduces it. These borderline cases, "Le mythe de Staline" ("The Myth of Stalin") [*Qu'est-ce que le cinèma*, vol. 1, p. 12],

"Pastiche et postiche ou le néant pour un moustache" ("Hitler and Chaplin") [*Bazin,* vol. 1, p. 13] were given particular attention. Bazin is unique on this issue. This critic, serious among the serious, displayed verve and fantasy when necessary, which in no way altered the depth of his observations. Besides, these are not the only moments in which we can admire Bazin's humor. To tell the truth, it is everywhere, not so much in his remarks or sudden changes of subject ("*Kon Tiki* is the most beautiful film, but it doesn't exist" [*Bazin,* vol. 1, p. 51]), as in the actual understanding of problems. It is less a question of style than of thought. Cinema's true nature is contradictory. One can enter its temple only by the door of paradox, therefore through that of humor. This type of humor is like a supplementary show of respect.

"On the other hand," we read at the end of the first chapter, "Cinema is a language." Although Bazin may have drawn his ontological reflections on cinema from scratch, he is not the art's first grammarian. The term *language* appeared in 1918 in the writings of Victor Perrot or Canudo. It was above all the problems of expression to which Delluc, Eisenstein, Pudovkin, Arnheim, and Malraux paid attention, and it might have seemed that there was little left to say. But the study of syntax was carried out to the detriment of the study of the contributions to reality that the art of film fosters. Armed with his discoveries in the latter domain, Bazin gave the research on language a new orientation. Thus, in "Montage interdit" [vol. 1, p. 16], the study of *Ballon rouge (The Red Balloon),* and the animal films, he does not examine the method from the perspective of the relationship of images among themselves, but of their relationship with reality: What is allowed in a fictional film is not allowed in a documentary. The syntactical rules vary according to their application. They lose their fixed character.

And then language evolves. It is useless to harp on this point. Bazin owes most of his renown to the fact that he became the champion of a new aesthetic, that of "depth of field." As I said, this is, to a large extent, a distortion of reality. André Bazin cannot be reduced to an advocate of a cause, even the most just one. For him, the evolution of language is a fact, by the same token as is, for example, the majesty of documentaries. With complete impartiality, Bazin intends to take into account one as well as the other. That is why, once again, his study on Wyler, which I reread with a certain degree of apprehension, remains valid. We cannot explain the evolution of film since 1940 simply by the depth of field or the love of the still shot. But let's go back to the source, that is, to the text. Let's not put words in Bazin's mouth. Notice that all the amendments that others believed to have contributed to his theory were already formulated in his work, that the famous depth is considered as only one of the signs of a certain progression toward objectivity that was not denied by his later works or by new technology,

beginning with CinemaScope. The next to the last chapter, "L'évolu-
tion du langage cinématographique" ("The Evolution of Cinemato-
graphic Language"), a collection of three articles, is likely to satisfy
the most demanding, as this sixteen-page essay is both dense and detailed. We enjoy praising Bazin's analytical talents. I believe it will be
a while before another person can give us a synthetic view as clear, as
seductive, and as difficult to attack as this one is. These few lines,
borrowed from the conclusion, demonstrate:

> In the past ten years, it is no doubt mostly with the Stroheim–Murnau ten-
> dency, which was almost completely eclipsed from 1930 to 1940, that the cin-
> ema has more or less consciously renewed its ties. But it does not just prolong
> this tendency, it extracts the secret of a realist regeneration of the narrative.
> This narrative is once again becoming capable of integrating the true duration
> of things, the duration of an event, for which classical editing substituted an
> intellectual and abstract time. But it is far from eliminating the triumphs of
> editing and gives it, instead, a relativity and a sense. It is only in relation to
> the image's heightened realism that additional abstraction becomes possible.
> The stylistic repertory of a director like Hitchcock, for example, graduates from
> the powers of hard documentary to superimposition and large close-ups. But
> Hitchcock's close-ups are not like those of Cecil B. deMille in *The Cheat.* They
> constitute one stylistic figure among many others.

These thoughts came to me while reading a very small portion of
Bazin's work. It is appropriate to begin here, as this is the way he
wanted it, but in reading the proofs of the second collection – currently in production – which is dedicated to the relationship between
cinema and the other arts, I am convinced that it is in no way inferior
to the first, neither in the value of each chapter nor in the coherence of
the whole. My first intention was to present all of Bazin's work, but, as
familiar as it is to me, I quickly gave up this enterprise, given the limited amount of time.* Not that his work is so eclectic that one cannot
find a guiding thread; rather, the links among different sections are so
strong, so essential, that one runs the risk of proposing weaker, more
tenuous links in trying to highlight the main ones. Excuse me if my
summation is slightly subjective, if I am proposing a particular interpretation to the detriment of other, equally legitimate ones. What I especially wanted to show was that Bazin's mind, whose analytical
capacity is denied by no one, also possessed, as I just demonstrated, a
no less admirable ability to synthesize. My colleague Jerzy Plazewski
lamented that Bazin was unable to give us his "summa." We regretted
this as well, which made it even worse. But here, at least, is some consolation for our pain: We have this sum total thanks to the simple addition of different parts of his work, each as homogeneous and as

---

* I even had to leave one section out, an important section on the sociology of cinema.

irrefutable as a mathematical theorum. I do not believe that the famous works of Eisenstein, Balasz, or Arnheim can compete with this work in terms of rigor or coherence.

As with the problems of language, the relationship between the cinema and the other arts had often been discussed before Bazin, but the true nature of this relationship had been misunderstood because the question was reversed. A particular conception of art was used as a starting point, and there was an attempt to fit cinema into this conception, even while trying to single out certain qualities specific to cinema, but secondary qualities nonetheless. Bazin, on the other hand, made a clean sweep of all preconceived notions and proposed a radical change in perspective. The proof of this new point of view's promise is that it sheds light not only on the art of cinema but also indirectly on the other arts. With his usual modesty, Bazin does not try to trespass on a domain that is not his own, but while following the meandering path of his work, and as if unbeknownst to the author, we suddenly catch invaluable glimpses of the nature or the evolution of the novel, the theater, or the painting. No, it is not a matter of showing off his cultural background, of applying the specious method of reasoning by analogy. It is because there is no question that if, on the one hand, knowledge of the other arts has been able to provide interesting insights into the cinema, the reverse is no less true, and an exploration as deep as Bazin's, though limited to a narrow specialty, cannot help but bring with it discoveries about the nature and future of art as a whole. A few random quotations will take the place of further commentary:

> Mounet-Sully's success and efficacy were undoubtedly due to his talent and also to the audiences' complicity. It was the phenomenon of the "sacred monster" that today has landed in cinema's court. Saying that the conservatory's auditions no longer produce tragic actors does not mean that no more Sarah Bernhardts have been born but that there is no longer a match between the period and their talents. Thus Voltaire went out of his way to plagiarize seventeenth-century tragedy, thinking only Racine was dead, when it was, in fact, tragedy as a whole.

. . .

> A painting's frame forms a zone of spatial disorientation. It opposes inwardly oriented contemplative space, opening only onto the interior of the painting, to that of nature and our active experience that borders its outer limits.

. . .

> The Mystery of Picasso (Le Mystère Picasso) does reveal not what we already knew – the length of time needed for creation – but that painting's temporality can be an integral part of the work itself.... Moreover, painting's temporality has always been present in a latent state, notably in sketchbooks,

and the "studies" and "steps" of etchings, for example. But it has revealed a more demanding potentiality in modern painting. In painting *The Roumanian Blouse* several times, what does Matisse do but spread his creative invention in space, that is, in a suggested amount of time, as in a card game?

One of Bazin's contributions, and not his least original one, is his denunciation throughout his book of the "specific" characters by which, before him, we claimed to define cinema. He makes a case for the art he loves, but without creating false virtues for it and by refusing to allow himself to be seduced by superficial differences in order to discern better the true ones. He does not try to avoid the most dangerous problems, to which we, the critics, generally provide a partial solution, valid only for the case at hand, not having found the complete answer. I had given up ever finding this answer when I suddenly discovered it in an aside in the first chapter, dedicated to the *défense du cinéma impur* ("defense of impure cinema"). We know that Bazin always attached a great deal of importance to the problems of adaptation. This is a primordial question: It is a matter of pleading innocent even when the cinema shows all the signs of guilt. It is important that film still be film, and when it finds its inspiration elsewhere, this borrowing is not an irrefutable proof of sterility or dependence. We can consider that his answer is the thesis of the second volume, just as objectivity is that of the first. Quite honestly, they are related. Each is founded on the recognition of the close relationship between cinema and reality. In sum, contingency is also a necessary quality of film.

Let's not allow ourselves to be fooled by an analogy with other arts, especially those whose evolution toward individualism has made them almost independent of their audiences.... Cinema cannot exist without a minimal public. Even if the filmmaker challenges current tastes, his audacity is valid only to the extent that one can admit that the spectator is wrong about what he should like, and will like, someday. The only possible comparison would be with architecture, because a house makes sense only if it is inhabitable. Cinema is also a functional art. To use another reference system, one would have to say that cinema's existence precedes its essence. Critics must begin with this existence, even in the most farfetched extrapolations.

It is a great pleasure to see these sentences and the ones quoted earlier flow from my own pen. Such phrases are myriad and shine, not as vain ornaments, but through the density of their matter. They furnish additional proof of a rare gift of synthesis on which I do not believe it is superfluous to insist once again. They bear witness to Bazin's equally apparent talent as a writer. It is true that no one can speak of cinema without finding inspiration in Bazin's works, but I think it would be not so pretentious as risky to undertake any mildly serious study without quoting a few of his sentences.

We arrive now at his style. It is a reflection of his thought and is marked by the same qualities. But this praise still seems too thin to me. True, Bazin is not a purist: As a journalist, as a theoretician of a brand-new art, he bears no prejudice against the neologisms of vocabulary and syntax. Above all, he wants to persuade, to leave out no step in his proof or turning point in his logic: The *fors, moreovers, therefores,* and *that is whys* appear at crucial moments and are indispensable. And yet there is no dryness, no heaviness, no pedantry. Considering how ambitious his remarks are, the technical terms dealing with philosophy are fairly few. If a slightly scholarly term slips in, a few lines later we find the familiar, but not vulgar, expression, which serves as a humorous substitute. The beginnings are slow and subtle. Bazin, who, as far as I can judge from having often seen him at work, wrote quickly, almost never crossing out, liked to let his pen get away from him. And then, abruptly, comes the brainstorm, the admirable turn of phrase that, far from satisfying him, inspires a second, a third, and finally a cascade of dense, colorful, explosive, and yet unpretentious maxims.

Here again, I must choose: Among the many ornaments, if ornaments they are, the *comparisons* invite the greatest admiration, if not envy. Are they really stylistic effects? Not if it is true that they cannot be considered purely ornamental, for assuredly, a metaphor was never less gratuitous. They serve to reinforce the proof and are never ashamed of their didactic origins. In the beginning they emerge cautiously. In the chapter on Wyler, Bazin excuses himself for looking to minerology for his arguments. Elsewhere, they seem less scientific, even if their contents are almost always borrowed from the author's preferred science, natural history: zoology, botany, geology. But didn't the old didactic poets do the same, starting with the author of *De rerum natura?* Armed with this example as well as that of Balzac's *Human Comedy,* we can unabashedly answer yes to our question. In addition to reinforcing pure convictions, these examples add to the enjoyment of our reading. I find them more poetic and persuasive than the often-praised metaphors of Albert Thibaudet. Their beauty must come (a rarity in modern literature, in which a naturally affected style is necessary, as a good metaphor rests on an idea of finality in which our century does not believe) from the correspondences they suggest between the natural world and the world of cinematic art. They indirectly translate the kind of primordiality that Bazin accorded the universe of ends over causes. This is demonstrated by the surprising introductory paragraph that he wrote for the interview with Orson Welles and that ended in Balzacian-style fantasy. Which, among the thousand gems, should be quoted? Only this one (regarding Bresson's "stylized" noises) owing to the lack of space, for its rare density and the perfect suitability of the metaphor to its object of study.

They are there for their indifference and their perfectly "foreign" situation, like a grain of sand that jams a machine's mechanism. If the arbitrariness of their choice seems like an abstraction, then it is a wholly concrete one; it scratches the image to betray its transparency, like a speck of diamond dust.

I have just reread Bazin. My reading, while filling me with an exaltation that I was only partially able to communicate, also filled me with an equally poignant feeling of discouragement. We, at *Cahiers,* who had almost daily colloquia with him, believed ourselves exempt from returning to his writings. If not for this, we might not have dared to restate what he had already definitively stated or to contradict him at times, forgetting that he had already answered our objections. Besides, we all have taken the lower road of polemics and frivolities, leaving him to tackle and answer the main question, What is cinema? Now we are left with the difficult job of continuing his task; we will not falter, no matter how sure we are of our inability to go as far as he did. If cinema did not evolve, we might be more apt to give up the task. Only the surprises of the future permit us to hope to be, if not the successors, at least the not-too-undeserving disciples of André Bazin.

(*Cahiers du cinéma* 91, spécial issue, André Bazin, January 1959)

Lesson of a failure: *Moby Dick* by John Huston

From its beginning, *Cahiers* has followed the principle of critiquing "beauties." The critique of a film is ordinarily assigned to the one among us who finds the most arguments in its favor. There is no question of our abandoning this method which, believe us, is the most equitable.

Some of our readers, however, have written to us saying that a disdainful silence is sometimes too generous and that certain "losers," especially those favored by the public, merit a more severe punishment than a two-line execution on the monthly list of films, or several black dots from the Conseil des dix.* That is why we have readopted the system of notes dedicated to works that seem of minor importance to us and that find only detractors or lukewarm advocates among our editorial staff. As for the rest, they have nothing to teach us, except as a part of French or foreign cinematic production that concerns only the industry, as Malraux would say.

In short, there is undoubtedly more to learn from a detailed accusa-

* *Cahiers's* ten-member council.

tion of certain ambitious, honest works than from a lukewarm defense. Our review's goal is not so much to encourage or discourage seeing such and such a film (this job belongs to the weekly or daily papers) as to add to the thoughts you might have had, or will have, concerning the film. It happens that these thoughts lead us further when they are *against* a film than when they are for it. In this case, the length of an ordinary critique may seem insufficient, and such articles, like the one that André Bazin wrote on *Ballon Rouge (The Red Balloon)* and *Une Fée pas comme les autres* or even like this one, find a place in the "general" section of the *Cahiers*.

Huston, alas?

The failure in question is that of *Moby Dick*. I know that John Huston's last film had its supporters, but their articles suggest that it did not arouse as much enthusiasm as did *Red Badge of Courage* or *African Queen*. We cannot deny his preference for novels. The battle, they say, was not equal. Equal between whom and whom? Between one of the great novelists of the last century and the filmmaker considered by many the best in Hollywood? That indicates a rather poor idea of cinema in general and of American cinema in particular. This idea is implied in the comment of our New York correspondent, H. G. Weinberg, who used [André] Gide's words concerning Hugo: "The greatest American filmmaker? – Huston, alas!"

Let us not get caught in this dilemma. It is too easy to say that either Huston did the best job possible and this is glaring proof that cinema is still in its infancy and that perhaps the domain of poetry shall forever be off-limits or that our director did not have what it takes for such an enterprise; he is simply a man of taste, and taste never took the place of genius. If I had to choose, I would choose the second explanation without hesitation, but I prefer to suggest a third option, which I hope will have the advantage of better highlighting the obscure relationship between a film and a literary work.

A useless adaptation

I would first and foremost condemn John Huston for his choice. An adaptation of *Moby-Dick* was not so much impossible as useless. A stroke of genius is a stroke of luck. It doesn't happen twice, and especially in art, "you can't cross the same river twice." Whether the filmmaker kept the novel's form or changed it, he added nothing to the sublimity of a work that is perfect in every respect, and we have placed our discussion at too high a level to consider the arguments that some of my colleagues propose in such a case (that a film can popularize a literary classic and attract new readers). I intentionally said *perfect:* It is not a matter of a myth like that of Orestes, Faust, or Don Juan, which in the hands of ten different artists can produce ten works of art of equal importance. In this case the filmmaker has no disadvantage compared with the painter, the dramatist, or the novelist. But Melville has nothing of the naive or primitive man, leaving to posterity a still poorly organized work. He is, on the contrary, typically modern, placing his erudition at the service of his experience, conferring – owing to his talent and culture – the dignity of a work of art on a ship's logbook. To bring *Moby-Dick* to the screen is to treat a subject that has already been treated, to undertake not an adaptation but a *remake.* What makes such an enterprise so futile is not that Melville's sentiments are unable to be expressed in images but, rather, that of all the world's novels, it is the one that best displays the type of beauty that the screen is most able to highlight: In short, that this novel is already a true film.

The novel and cinema

Huston, therefore, did not aim too high but, more specifically, too well. Of *all* the American directors, he is – we gladly grant his admirers this – among those who choose the "best" scripts. Such scripts depict the kind of relationships that film expresses effortlessly, those that give their characters, words, and actors' gestures the ambiguity with which the screen sharpens the faintest silhouettes. Huston, then, gave us the "thickest" scripts, but because their thickness was already entirely on paper, the mise-en-scène could not introduce a new dimension and instead threw this famous literary depth into an ordinary perspective, squashing it, flattening it.

I will not go so far as to say that one can make good films only with bad literature but, rather, with works in which literature did not assume the very task that the filmmaker performs: transforming the myth or the news item into a work of art. And of all the literary genres, the novel is the one that uses for this purpose the means closest to film's. The contemporary novel (I include those of the last century) learned the art of making things almost as visible to us as if they were shown on a screen. Many of the things we have said about cinema and its specificity would almost apply to the novel. Might there be only a difference of degree and not of nature between these two genres? That is what we would be logically led to admit if we assume, as do the admirers of Huston and other "literary" directors, that cinema is leaning toward a kind of novelistic perfection, like a curve toward its apex. Thus it could never go beyond this. But who is to say that there is nothing "beyond"?

Beyond literature

This world *beyond* is precisely what we try to define in these *Cahiers,* for better or worse. We do so by praising those filmmakers whom we may have been accused of celebrating too systematically, but who, consciously or unconsciously, have tried to extend the limits of the literary aesthetic by which films are hastily judged. This world *beyond* can undoubtedly not be reduced to a formula; we may perhaps never find a term to designate it. What is certain, however, is that it derives from the mise-en-scène and that it appears only when the latter has room to function. When a composer sets a poem to music, he substitutes the song of the verse with another song, different enough so that his project seems futile only if it is truly damaging. In the same way, a play leaves a space between lines that the director fills in his own way. It is revealing that screen adaptations of modern plays have recently been more successful than have adaptations of novels. Does this mean that film is moving closer to the theater? On the contrary, it is because sound, color, and the large screen have made things easier that the adaptation of a novel is riskier today. At the time of silent films there was an important margin left to invention. Now that we can, and therefore must, be faithful, the spectator's demands have increased, at the same time as the filmmaker's freedom has begun to shrink. He is therefore compelled to look in a completely different direction in order to maintain his integrity.

The fantastic and realism

One might say that I am moving rather quickly. The present example does not support such a theory. Two major obstacles make the adaptation of *Moby-Dick* nearly impossible. The first is the fantastic nature of the tale, and the second is the vivid richness of the style. The novel finds its poetry in these two aspects, which cannot be imitated in film.

My answer is, first, that cinema need not bother with a certain fantastic quality. In this it resembles the novel, which is the genre most enslaved by the laws of verisimilitude. In any case, *Moby-Dick* respects these laws, except for the evocation of a monster of incredible proportions. By this enlargement, Melville's work gains in epic grandeur, but not in its novelistic quality. But cinema is suited better than any other art to enable daily actions, ordinary things, to attain epic dignity. The example of *Nanook of the North* or other such documentaries proves this. It was not so much the dimensions of the whale that were important, but its true-to-life quality. Huston would have been better off (it would not have been easy, but this type of film would have greatly benefited from the material difficulty of the shooting) filming real sperm whale fishermen that still are found in the Portuguese Azores,[*] and not this papier-mâché whale worthy at most of a science fiction tale. This betrayal of natural history – based on nature itself – condemned this film to failure from the start. Melville's work is a meditation on an experience, Huston's is a meditation on a book. In no case can the latter substitute for the former.

Yes, film is very capable of portraying a sentiment in every way identical to that inspired by the novel, of showing the type of anxiety unique to stalking a prey, of evoking nature's veiled hostility to human endeavor. It can do it: The proof is that it has done it in the documentaries that I have just mentioned or in the admirable tuna-fishing sequence in *Stromboli.*

In search of a metaphor

It is useless to continue. I suppose I am preaching only to converts. The second point remains, a matter of another kind of fantastic. How can one express Melville's magical style on the screen? Is the cinema merely an art of reporting, of dry reviewing? Are the heights of poetry inaccessible to it? What is the equivalent of metaphor in film? Maybe we are wrong in conceiving of this equivalence as an exact copy, a reflection. Many filmmakers have pursued it, like Achilles pursuing his tortoise. They did not notice that their art could reach in a single step what the poet attains only by a series of successive approximations. The metaphor comes from language's inability to make a reality concrete. By comparing the incomparable, by systematically using the incorrect term, poets have never ceased to lie throughout the years, but the lie was more respectful of the secret essence of things than were the pale, flat, abstract descriptions of ordinary speech.

Whether by luck or misfortune, the filmmaker is not familiar with this art of felicitous lying. If the failure of attempts by Eisenstein, or more recently those by Abel Gance, show that the filmmaker cannot, without some clumsiness, go from one form, one thing, one sensation, one idea, to another, he is nonetheless entitled to include all the wealth of the cosmos in the briefest appearance, the most insignificant object, the most limited space. The means he uses are innumerable and vary according to the temperament of each director. There are, here again, a thousand ways of lying, but the lie does not center on the same points and appears to us only on second thought. We can see it in Orson Welles, in the adoption of a certain optical dogmatism; in Hitchcock or Lang, in the rigor of a certain visual or spatial rhythm; in Rossellini, in the constant interference of two types of phenomena,

---

[*] As Mario Ruspoli's documentary shows us.

physical or moral; and in Renoir, in a certain touch that is difficult to define in words. We have been criticized, and one could say the same of all film critics, for using too "flowery" a style. This is because a film is full of metaphors, and it is difficult to talk about it without using the metaphors implied. Cinema offers us a vision of reality and contains the seed of comparison. A poem bears a potential reality and leads us to it by way of comparison.

Error or lack of imagination?

Of all the means available to him for finding the equivalent of Melville's style, Huston chose the most ordinary and the most dangerous. Of Orson Welles's lesson, he retained only the use of skillful framing, and the student crawls lamentably where the master alone maintains himself by stunt riding. The affectation of the camera angles only highlights the images' emptiness, only makes the numerous special effects more irritating. Because the director is incapable of trusting the power of what he is showing, he summons the resources of a dialogue and a diction that are vulgar imitations of the Shakespearean tradition and that convince us only when Welles himself briefly fills the screen with his great stature.

We find the same mistake in the use of color, as unpoetic as it is unreal. Unlike the painter, the filmmaker does not use color as a material but as fragments of reality itself: He knows neither red nor blue, but only a red boat and a blue sky. Color in cinema is useful only to make the objects' reality more precise, more tangible. It appeals to the touch as much as to the eyes, one more proof that poetry can spring only from the most scrupulously respected truth.

An imported philosophy

Literature has gone a long way since its inception: It has reached the point that certain themes are automatically assigned more significance than others are. Pessimism, absurdity, "failure" are important ideas to modern writers. But although optimism may be outmoded in books, on the screen it is couched in the densest meaning. The portrayal of a success in *Le Vent souffle où il veut** is no less rich from this point of view than that of an aborted effort. I do not want to infer a rule from one example. The fact remains, however, that film's Olympus is peopled by more benevolent gods than the ones adored by this century's great novelists. Nonetheless, we do not have the right to mock them.

---

* The subtitle of Robert Bresson's film *A Man Escaped* (*Un Condamné à mort s'est échappé*) (JN).

Thus, his mind clouded by a certain literary myth, the most "intelligent"* filmmaker believes that he has completed the essential part of
his task once his script has been written: He needs only to find
mouthpieces in his characters for his ideas. Of course, he has experience and knows that the actors must move, and so they move, but only
because they have to. In certain scenes of *Beat the Devil,* Jennifer
Jones says her lines while doing stretching exercises: It is a clever
idea, but nothing more. Ninety-nine percent of John Huston's shots are
based on this model, minus Jennifer Jones's legs.

One last word: I will take an opportunity on this occasion to make
amends with John Huston in the name of *Cahiers.* It is against our
wishes that *Beat the Devil* was deprived of an article, which, written
by Pierre Kast, we had every reason to expect would have been favorable. This caricature of a certain film is, in my eyes, our filmmaker's
masterpiece. He is more at ease in the satirical apologue than in the
epic tale. Not that he rebels against poetry (see the end of *Asphalt
Jungle*), but lyricism is no more his forte than silliness is. To reduce
cinema to John Huston is to reduce literature to Voltaire, the author of
Candide, but also of the *Henriade.*

(*Cahiers du cinéma* 67, January 1957)

Explanation of a vote: *South Pacific* by Joshua Logan

If we judge by our usual criteria, this film is not worth much, even
less than *Sayonara,* after which Logan's popularity plunged. Would
the director of *Picnic* and *Bus Stop* be merely the least scrupulous of
frauds? A patented imitator, delivering, on request, a designer product
or a mass-produced one?

Logan's first two films are worth about the same as certain Broadway productions. His fourth gives us a faithful copy of what must be
the world's worst genre. The American musical has no reason to be
jealous of our Châtelet. Vulgarity wears similar costumes on both
sides of the ocean. Such an art, if we can we can use the word *art,* is
not even blessed with the privilege of universality granted to most
Made-in-the-U.S.A. products. It is doubtful that *South Pacific* would be
appreciated by French audiences, who are moved by Mariano, not by
the ineffable Brazzi, in whom no native of Paris's Belleville would con-
descend to recognize a compatriot.

Comedy musicals such as the ones done by Minnelli, Kelly, or Donen come out on top by comparison, although they may not need such
a comparison to shine. First, they are grounded in good cinematic

---

* "Here is true intelligence (how Huston must laugh and find that bookish, like the little nitpicking of a Hitchcock!)" Bernard Chardère, *Positif,* nos. 14–15, p. 40.

earth, borrowing only their points of departure from music halls, and flying with their own wings after that. Next, they are works created by refined men, for an audience that is, after all, select. They constitute the aristocratic form of a genre of which we have here one of the most common specimens.

That sums it up, it seems. There is no point in continuing this savage criticism. I will therefore not pursue it any further. The sin of vulgarity is an unpardonable one. And yet, as I wrote in the preceding paragraph, I was plagued by doubt. If instead of *common*, I wrote *popular*, the entire argument would crumble, for *popular*, like *rustic* or *naive*, is one of the recognized, established categories of art.

But one could argue that popular is not the correct term, at least in its more noble sense. I will respond, first, that the notion of an aristocratic people seems, at least to me, contradictory. One could then object that I am playing with words, using pages and pages – many more than this review can contain – of examples drawn from the ancients and the moderns, from classicism and romanticism, from cinema and elsewhere, finishing, of course, with Chaplin, who was so good at reconciling the crowd and the more refined. But all in all, the crowd is the crowd, and if we admit a small part of what comes from it, on what grounds can we refuse the rest? That it is in bad taste? That means introducing the idea of a delicacy of the palate, and therefore the existence of a limited circle of connoisseurs, beginning with an aristocracy of art.

What makes my position difficult is that this aristocratic conception is mine, and ours, at *Cahiers.* Unlike some film buffs, we do not always value the bizarre or the melodramatic, and we do not label filmmakers who display taste and ambition as aesthetes. And yet no matter how warmly we defend this ambitious, uncompromising cinema made of gold and marble, we believe it would be dangerous for film, now on the edge of its intellectual – or if one prefers, its reflexive period – to shut itself up in a tower, haughty with disdain for the still-soft clay on which its foundations are built. Cinema is not too young to die, either from a strong lack of curiosity or from overly thin blood.

To tell the truth, I do not mean to defend *South Pacific,* only to encourage people to see it. At the Conseil des dix – an expression that must be taken to mean not only *council* but also *counsel* – I could not convince myself to mark it with a black dot. A star would not have sufficed, for it is not a film to see "if there's nothing else," as is a contestable work. It is incontestably bad but incontestably interesting.

I know what Bazin would have thought of *South Pacific.* Allow me to restate one of his arguments, the one with which he defended CinemaScope. "Cinema," he said, "is a functional art. Its existence precedes its essence." This *existence* was previously accorded to each film, even the worst of films, as a natural attribute. Even in the worst one, there were always those ten minutes so dear to Man Ray, which were worth the bother, which proclaimed the birth of an original art, an art irreducible to any other. Today we cannot deny that it is more and more difficult to watch a bad film: They are superficial, substitutes, fakes, the products of never-ending dismal recipes. If all masterpieces look as if they belong to the same family, all the world's losers carry their inherited blemishes more boldly than do the rejects in Zola's *Rougon-Macquart*. This is a common phenomenon in the arts. Perhaps it came a bit later to film than to the others. When department-store dishes copy Picasso's ceramics, when low-income housing projects copy Le Corbusier, when songwriters of little ditties copy Prévert's or Jean-Paul Sartre's words, one can say that popular art is dead. Art as a whole is quite sick, for throughout the ages it has not stopped borrowing its best material from folklore: tragedy its myths, painting its subjects, music its themes, novels their stories, and so forth. And this is perhaps proof that cinema in its entirety is really Art with a capital A – and therefore less "naive" than some say, because fundamentally it has invented nothing. To take just one example, all the themes in cinema's most fertile and incontestably original branch, silent American comedy – all its gags, one could say – are perfectly sketched, shaped, and staged in the famous *Famille Fenouillard**** that appeared the year before the Lumière brothers' first screening and in which most of the episodes – quite an impressive omen – took place in America!

No, it is not true that almost everything deserves comment. What I am saying about *South Pacific* could never apply to, say, *Sérénade au Texas* and other pseudocomedy musicals or operettas filmed by Pottier, Boyer, and company. Whatever we may think of Logan's film, that it is the epitome of infamy, whatever, it still *exists*. Beautiful or ugly, stupid or subtle, vulgar or distinguished, this film resembles no other.

That is not hard to do, one might say, if you pay no heed to taste or to rules and you are ready to do anything. But that is not so certain: All ink spots look alike, as do all children's drawings: If one haphazardly hits piano keys, the same noise is created. *South Pacific* is not just anything. There are two reasons for this. The first is, as I have tried to say, that it belongs to the last living branch of an art that we are obliged to call popular, or even naive, though it may be factory made, may have used enormous capital, and may result from the self-serving calculations of people as different from douanier Rousseau or the gallant Méliès as are the producer Buddy Adler, the authors Rodgers and Hammerstein, and the director Joshua Logan. It is imagery, it is conventional, it is postcardlike, all that, but it is just as difficult to

---

* Based on a well-known French comic book. In 1961, a film of the same name was made by Yves Robert (CV).

create something original in the postcard genre as in cubism or in abstract painting. We may note parenthetically that from a sociological point of view, the film contains a thousand interesting themes concerning the average American's position on political, sentimental, and technical problems. My concern is only with the aesthetics, which furnish sufficient food for thought. *South Pacific* is therefore definitely cinema, because it contributes a new look, much as did *The Cheat* after World War I, which nevertheless has not entered the Seventh Art's Parnassus.

What does this novelty consist of? Because I cannot say that it can't be defined – which is what I believe at heart – for fear of being accused of sophism and laziness, I must now mention the second reason, which does not weaken the first. Whether popular or not, a film never springs out of Jupiter's thigh fully armed, and Joshua Logan sharpened these arms with such care that we are forced to use the word *art*. This film, as we know, was shot using the Todd–AO process, which alone is worth the trouble of seeing, even if it is true that the Hermitage's auditorium and screen are not adequate to the film. But it is not so much the process in itself that deserves attention (the beginning short serves only to make it seem like a type of Cinerama playing simply on the purely physical impression created by forward movement, an effect that becomes as tiresome as the train of [Lumière's] *La Ciotat*) as the remarkably intelligent way in which Logan uses it. What attracted me, but what might have shocked some people, is that the filmmaker makes his new raw material undergo the same treatment as did that in *Picnic* or *Bus Stop.* He plays with Todd–AO in the way he played with CinemaScope in the two others, seemingly against the grain, but in the right direction if we assume that the physical potential of a means of expression and its aesthetic are not necessarily equal and that the close-up, for example, that would have seemed uninteresting in the demonstration reel has an undeniable appeal in the film. Here, as in *Bus Stop,* the close-up that earlier bored us now astonishes us, as it must have shocked audiences of the first Griffith films. The different uses of the wide screen have certainly made film progress toward photographic realism. This, as Bazin showed us, is an essential realism that nonetheless, in an extreme case, kills art, hence the concerns with Cinerama. Many filmmakers have made the mistake of combating this realism by traditional means (by staging the image) or of believing, on the other hand, that it signaled the death of the classical shooting script, whereas it was not this script that it condemned (that is, the possibility of placing the camera farther away from or nearer to the subject), but the frame itself.

Destroying the frame does not necessarily mean constantly moving the camera and reframing the image, like a reporter holding a camera in his hand. In this case, the curve of the screen makes panoramas risky, and Logan works with the still shot in principle, if not always in practice. To destroy the frame is also, and especially, to fill it with a set endowed with such a power of fascination and architectural solidity that one forgets the limits imposed by the borders of the screen. I know that though it is natural, this set is in bad taste, and it is undoubtedly quite irritating to see otherwise appealing marine landscapes transformed into gaudy or sweet picture postcards through the combined craftiness of Logan and cinematographer Leon Shamroy. And yet, even under the glare of blinding colored floodlights, which resemble the floods used by James Wong Howe in the night scene of *Picnic,* in the way that the Gare d'Orsay resembles the Invalides; yet, even at these moments, in that awful sort of colonial garden of the first sequence, we are not sorry that nature, or what is left of it, has not been replaced by painted canvases as in Gene Kelly's ballets. Logan will always know how to use what painters call the "raw material," as degraded as it may be. His film has a sensual charm that is strangely lacking in works *ad usum multitudinis,* in which symbolism and planning reign, to the detriment of sensation.

I am purposely defending this film's least defensible aspects. As for the directing of actors, the case would be easier, even for Rossano Brazzi, who no longer inspires laughter in this film, having achieved a kind of archetypal beauty. One need only compare his character in *South Pacific* with the one in *A Certain Smile.* Watch the acting carefully. You will never find it poor or monotonous, although it is governed by the most unrefined psychology. Particularly rigorous work was done on Mitzi Gaynor and France Nuyen. Both have some charming moments. But they are not my concern . . .

My sole concern was to maintain an active curiosity in us, cinema lovers, which our exclusive viewing of masterpieces is liable to kill. Luckily there are still times when it is *worth being bothered!*
(*Cahiers du cinéma* 92, February 1959)

Faith and mountains: *Les Etoiles de midi* by Marcel Ichac

Is it our place to pass judgment on a work whose beauty – and quite a beauty it is – seems to be more sporting than cinematic in nature, which seems to fill us with admiration more for the model than for the art with which it is reproduced? My answer is yes, and for two reasons. The first is that cinema, as André Bazin demonstrated, invites us to revise formerly antithetical notions of art and nature. As for the light that a film like this can shed on the paradoxical merits of the documentary genre, one should read volume I of *What Is Cinema?* For what could I say that has not already been said in this work? Concerning the new "adventure film," one could also reread what Jean-Luc Godard wrote last year on Haroun Tazieff's *Volcano* (*Les Rendez-vous du diable*).[*]

Now for the second reason. We shall no longer consider the ontology – or the definition – of cinema but, rather, its language or its history. It is unfair to treat Marcel Ichac's film separately, under the pretext that we like it better. It does intimidate us, and we feel a certain reluctance to talk about transitions and lenses when actors and technicians have risked their bones for many a week to provide our evening's pleasure. And yet, speaking for *Cahiers,* I believe that praise is more flattering when it is attributed to the talent of the filmmaker rather than to the genius of the genre or the sport. No special allowances need be made for this film, which is ambitious from an artistic point of view, for it means precisely to present itself as a film, even an exemplary film. A short prelude gives an idea of what should not be done, before showing us what it is proper to show over the next hour and a quarter. And we are convinced: Yes, it is pointless to weigh down, with false, novelistic embellishments, material already sufficiently rich in poetry and pathos.

I purposely said *false.* One could also say inadequate. If I claim that *Les Etoiles de midi* (*The Midday Stars*) is worthy of being compared with the fictional films showing these days in Paris, it is not because I believe that documentaries are superior. Quite the contrary: I think, as did Bazin, that fiction has always been, and will be, cinema's preferred route and that the most beautiful documentaries, such as Flaherty's, are able to allow some – if not anecdotes – at least drama. If this film can stand up to comparison with others, it is not because it shows that they are pointless, but because it equals them or beats them on their own turf. It is because this film, which doesn't bother with intrigue, gives us the same type of pleasure as a well-told story does. It is because the fight against nature, fatigue, and doubt that is portrayed is no less dramatic than are the vicissitudes of a story of passionate love, the itinerary of a repentant criminal, or a prisoner's preparations to escape.

Just as we praise *A Man Escaped* (*Un Condamné à mort s'est échappé*) and *Pickpocket,* or even *Paisan* (*Païsa*) and *Viaggio in Italia* (*Strangers*) for having mixed fiction and documentary, we should be glad to see a specialist, though he remains largely a craftsman, allow fiction to enter his genre through the front door and no longer through the service entrance.

Though traveling in the opposite direction, Ichac encounters Bresson and Rossellini on his path. I admit that he imitates them, but this

* *Cahiers du cinéma* 93, March 1959 (JN).

Les Etoiles de midi by Marcel Ichac.

is not to his discredit. On the contrary, what better teachers are there? So what if the episode with the German reminds us of Rossellini and if many details of the climb, and even a certain tone in the commentary and dialogue, make us think of Bresson? What does that prove, if not that we are dealing with a filmmaker who is up-to-date in a genre that is usually a bit archaic? We cannot say that Marcel Ichac "makes good films without knowing it," as Godard could write about Tazieff (and yet, what filmmakers, even the greatest, even Eisenstein, have not sometimes happily played a Monsieur Jourdain?).* In short, this work's greatest asset is that finally in the history of the documentary since Flaherty a film is absolutely and consciously modern, free of the verbal or plastic mediocrities apt to ruin the most beautiful material in the world.

This film is modern because it was able to throw out many of the

* Character in Molière's *Le Bourgeois Gentilhomme* (CV).

clichés associated with the genre since its beginning and to open our eyes to the facts. Because fictional film is slowly getting closer in style to documentaries, why shouldn't documentaries end their lofty isolation and profit from the windfall? Acting is becoming less theatrical; many nonprofessionals are used; and these people, wherever they come from, carry themselves a thousand times more naturally in front of the camera than they were able to do before. Lionel Terray's, René Demainson's, or Michel Baucher's diction will not seem "quite right," I imagine, to fans of Pierre Fresnay or Kirk Douglas, although it is, of course, less shocking than the diction of François Leterrier or Martin Lassalle. But we Bressonians would say that *Etoiles de midi* is one of the best-acted films showing today, not only for the movements, which cannot be criticized, but also for the speech. As for the text of the dialogue itself, I cannot think of another dialogue writer on either continent who could have written a better one, even for the chalet scenes which are a bit didactic (but isn't didacticism the weakness of athletes at rest?). It is not the first time that a documentary accords such importance to dialogue, but until now we had never really been convinced that the old principle whereby one must recreate truth by means of artifice was false, even though filmmakers increasingly prefer to create truth with truth.

I know that what I am saying is not new. Who is not convinced of cinema's realist calling? It even is appropriate to define this realism as absolute, but not in the relative way that different schools who claim the title define it. What distances us now from certain postwar Italian works is not their alleged realism but their extreme theatricality. It is not enough to want to be a realist to become one. Art does not reproduce reality, it *discovers* it, a bit like the scholar discovers his material. In both cases, these searches take us on roads far off the beaten path. That is why realism is not the enemy of style but, rather, is its best companion. Just as we are taught by the history of cinema – which these days evokes the fascinating memoirs by Henri Fescourt[*] whose title I took the liberty of borrowing – it is the love of the real that little by little led film people to create their own style, far from theatrical pomposity, and to carry this style to the degree of economy – entirely relative, we will say in ten or twenty years – where it is today. The best way to characterize the evolution of the past ten years is by the progressive abandonment of a notion that was quite suitable and successful in its time: that of the photogenic, in the sense that Louis Delluc, the inventor of the term, gave it. The advent of color, the wide screen, the zoom lens, and high-speed emulsions all prove that the filmmaker has not finished destroying nature and that the silt of yesterday will become the diamond of tomorrow. The number of themes

* Henri Fescourt, *La Foi et les montagnes.* Publications Photo-Cinéma Paul Montel.

that have lain barren until today is greater than we like to believe. Take, for example, sports, a "moving" thing if there ever was one, and one to which our eyes are sensitive. Boxing is photogenic, but athletic competitions are not at all, at least not yet. A one-hundred-meter race, a jump, so exciting in the stadium, lose all their power on the screen – and what should we say about an eight-hundred-meter race or a throw glimpsed on a news bulletin! Leni Riefensthal's film revealed a type of beauty in physical exercise that is certainly genuine but that is not quite what the specialist likes to revel in.

I believe that cinema's mission is no longer to enshrine realism but finally to discover it as it appears to the naked eye. It is incorrect to think that certain themes have been overdone: They have simply been misused. Some say that it is no longer appropriate for our art, refined by the years, to find pleasure in the spectacle of pure movement and physical force or even of great natural rhythms: Its path is in the conquest of the interior. Of course, but can't we find a more refined *idea* in these old external appearances than the one we believed to be connected to them? What is important to me, and what attracted me in *Les Etoiles de midi*, is not, as Rossellini said, "the image, but the idea." This film, in which space and movement are kings and that instinctively recaptures certain secrets lost since the silent period (the audience, as breathless as it is, is surprised to laugh at some of Harold Lloyd's or Buster Keaton's blunders), introduces the modern notions of continuity and duration. In this battle between man and gravity, the obstacle that seems the most difficult to overcome is not space but *time,* that is, the long and tedious repetition of each movement, the bearer of a more subtle vertigo than that caused by heights. Little by little, through the intervention of time, we perceive the futility, the vanity, and at the same time the true glory of the undertaking, the rare pleasure it brings. Thanks to time, we enter these men's souls, and the suspense, which is physical in the beginning, becomes psychological and moral in the end. In devoting itself to painting a rare passion, this film allows us to touch the common foundation of all passions. Far from being an interruption in our frequent visits to the movie theater, it reinforces our attachment by discovering new powers in it, making us more demanding but also more confident.
(*Cahiers du cinéma* 106, April 1960)

The photogenics of sports: The Olympics in Rome[*]

I know, *this* is not a film. Yet, *this* was listed on the program of a Parisian movie theater and thus perhaps deserved to be listed in our

---

[*] The following article was written about the live televised broadcasting of the Olympic Games at the Bosquet-Gaumont cinema (JN).

Counseil des dix. Without hesitating, I would have given *it* three stars, if...

If we could honorably advise seeing what no longer exists. But good films were so rare over these vacation months that the best picture show – because it is projected on a movie screen – of the season, has the right, it seems to me, to some commentary.

Now, from what viewpoint should I approach this? I am not lacking in angles, but they hardly correspond to *Cahiers*'s traditional perspective. Because we are not electronic specialists, I leave it to others, elsewhere, to analyze the technical achievement by which the small screen was able to centuple its dimensions. Nor will I not go into the possibilities that this experiment opens for the cinema industry and the chance it may give two rival but related activities to end a misunderstanding that has lasted too long. Art is not directly touched by this, even though it does depend, in one way or another, on the vicissitudes of business.

I will not venture to write a critical study of this "program." Our review does not contain a television column – though this was considered earlier on – and as sound as the notion may be, I have qualms about adding an innovation with no future. I thus think it wise, for the moment, to approach the problems of TV only from a generalist perspective, as we have done on several occasions.[*]

In fact, I will address myself less to the form of this newscast than to its *content:* sports in general and athleticism in particular, dedicated to elegance of gesture and pure movement, and thereby it would seem, to the highest photogenics. Now, things of this type that I have seen on the screen have never offered me – in quality or in quantity – one-one-hundredth of the emotion I ordinarily feel in the bleachers of a stadium or even in reading the sports newspaper. I have already touched on this concerning Marcel Ichac's beautiful film *Les Etoiles de midi.* Allow me to take this new and precious opportunity to pursue my thoughts and to remove a few of the obstacles they have always come up against.

Despite its great beauties, *Les Dieux du stade* (*Gods of the Stadium*) remained very distant from its subject matter. As for the film shot by a group of French filmmakers at the Melbourne games, its demonstration of both artistic and technical incapacity was even more irritating because its directors had obtained exclusive rights to the shooting. But here I was pleased beyond all expectations. Far from envying the spectators whom I saw crunched together at the Olympic stadium, not

---

* See, in particular, *Pour contribuer à une érotologie de la télévision,* by André Bazin (42); *Propos sur la télévision,* by André Bazin and Marcel Moussy; *L'Ecrivain de télévision,* by Paddy Chayefsky (90).

knowing where to look, handicapped by their binoculars, I rejoiced in the fact that the TV offered such a convenient telescope, blessed with the double power of ubiquity and discrimination. Its many cameras, its panoramic views, its traveling shots created a privileged spectator's box, anxious to satisfy my gaze's every wish, aside for a few false maneuvers. This was the wonderful proof that athletic exploits could be shown within the space of a screen, but not in a film of normal length. For condensing this spectacle even just a little by the cunning methods of editing would have ruined it. I was introduced to a world in which Space and Time reign supreme and do not tolerate even the slightest disobedience. It would no longer be enough for the entire duration – or the entire trajectory – of a race, for some of the most outstanding feats of a competition to be shown us *in extenso.* It was essential that they not be artificially extracted from the mass of real time in which they took place. The "suspense" was not a function of the feat itself but of the empty moments – sometimes long, never boring – that preceded and followed it. The very austerity of the spectacle did not allow it to be separated from the thousands of secondary events, which were nonetheless essential to its comprehension: preparations, false starts, aborted attempts, nervousness visible on the faces or bodies of jumpers or throwers, the athlete's behavior after his success, the crowd's reactions, and so on. The simultaneous progress of races and competitions – difficult for the spectator in the stadium – intensified our interest and increased the cohesion of the whole.

For example, the twenty minutes during which we saw two of the greatest world records fall, the four hundred and the fifteen hundred meters, was a great moment in sports. A filmed digest of the Games would have to eliminate the time interval that in reality separated the two events. Besides, nothing happened during this interval, except – and this is what made the audience's hearts pound – the wait for the results and the "times" of the first race and then for the racers of the second event to enter the track.

We have now cut into the problem, but in the manner of a Gordian knot. No more cinema, no more problems. Screen? No, but a magic window, open more than one thousand kilometers away onto a present that after leaving the room, I could have seen transformed into a future by reading a recent edition of the nightly newspaper. I looked for the illusion of reality: It was reality itself, presented in its absolute truth.

But in thinking it over carefully, this truth was perhaps not so faithful: The poorly defined image did not allow me to read signs of fatigue or apprehension on the athletes' faces, and the absence of sound prohibited me from noticing their breathlessness. What is more, the use of wide-angle lenses and panorama shots falsified the notion of space, flattening distances, accelerating movements. Worse were the changes in shots, even the most successful ones, that created an illusion of "ellipsis" against which I had to fight with all the force of my reason ("because it's *live,* there cannot be any cuts").

To these imperfections, which were partially due to the newness of the technique, another was added that pertained to the nature of our perception. We know that directors of silent films forced their actors to slow their movements in order to make them "seem more real." Filmed as it is, reality offers an inconsistent, choppy quality, associated with reels projected at a higher speed than that of the camera shooting. Although it is no longer always done, I think that the modern actor instinctively continues to slow his *tempo.* The athlete, of course, is not concerned with slowing down his movement for the audience, but the filmmaker is greatly tempted to do it for him by using "slow motion." Can we really call our perception of a one-hundred-meter run's finish *true* when we are absolutely incapable of distinguishing who is first and who is second? It is a strange thing that in this universe of movement, truth can be measured only by the standard of immobility: the photo finish projected onto the screen a few minutes after the race.

But all in all, in a movie theater at least, I would opt for Hercules over Parmenides, however admirable and necessary are certain snapshots taken from the stadium. Let's leave sculpture to the Greeks and photography to the photographers. In speaking of the photogenics of sports, I assign the word a different meaning in the case of a film than in that of an album. For – and this is the main point – what I saw, seventh or eighth art, what does it matter, immersed me in the same delight as have the most beautiful works I have admired on the screen.

This spectacle, which lasted ten times four hours, had the same internal cohesion from start to finish, the same steadiness, as do the best-meditated films. It was also much easier to watch, as the woman announcer's introduction – which took the place of the usual ad for ice-cream bars – and a brief filmed retrospective served as a backdrop. In such circumstances (more so than in the case of ceremonies, parades, coronations, and heads of state's visits, in which order attacks liberty), television attains a nobility that is usually denied it. What ordinarily keeps me away from it, I admit, is not so much the questionable weakness of its means, as its profound *vulgarity.* This vulgarity, in France or elsewhere, is contingent, it is true, on its idea of its audience, but I also fear this is due partly to the fact that it is never destined, as is film, to be judged by posterity. The concern with detail, with the picturesque – in which it excels – limits its goals: Realism leads to indiscretion. But here we find only a few out-of-place "shots," aimed toward the audience. The athletes' reactions (the males, in any case), even the least controlled, contributed to the general serenity of the climate.

I hope that the friends of television forgive me this attack, which could just as well have been launched against radio or journalism. Or even against cinema, in its ordinary production. It would be too much for the arts born in this century to be promised immediate sublimity. It is more accurate to think that the best can rise up only in an often-brutal reaction against the worst of their lot. If cinema is good, as advertisements, scandal sheets, or many well-wishing aesthetes claim, no one in the world, you can be sure, thinks worse of it than I do.

Therefore, I will not say that this program was as beautiful as a film, but as beautiful as a film I love, beautiful as are, let's say, Howard Hawks's films, if this example can help clarify my idea. I am not speaking of a resemblance in their language – as far from one another as possible – but in their tone, in the quality of the pleasure afforded. In both cases, the physical exploit is no longer clad in the decorative beauty so dear to photographic aesthetics, but in another splendor, more arid, more abstract, more austere, more scientific, one might say more sensitive to the intellect, more foreign to all sorts of complacency. And this argument has its counterargument. Hawks – or at least what he represents – has nothing to fear from a confrontation with what I will call the raw artistic material of our civilization. He does not need run after the modern, because he possesses modernity from the start. I bet that his example will long continue to be at least as successful as that of the Picassos, the Joyces, and the Brechts, with whom we became familiar not after, but *before,* him.

This is why, from *Cahiers*'s perspective, which continues to be "Hawksian" despite the current proliferation of schools and tendencies, it is not at all futile, it even is necessary, to consider all that can be projected onto a screen, even when, in our case – a borderline case – we are no longer talking about film. One of the new aspects of our review, at the beginning, was that it mentioned films that were not talked about; it considered the so-called commercial films as the works of art that they were. It is important to continue this exploration, without forgetting the parallel or allied activities – functional activities, as Bazin would have said – of a means of expression that, backed by its good conscience and the imprudent zeal of its admirers, runs no greater risk today than that of allowing itself to be enclosed in the same ivory tower as are the other contemporary arts.

(*Cahiers du cinéma* 112, October 1960)

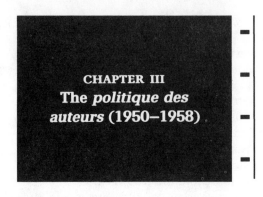

Roberto Rossellini: *Stromboli*

Stromboli is the story of a sinner who receives God's grace. But Rossellini does not show the odyssey of a conversion, with its hesitation, remorse, hopes, and slow and continual victories over oneself. God's majesty shines here with such a hard and terrible brilliancy that no human conscience could bear even the dullest reflection of it. This grand Catholic film solemnly unravels its exterior pomp and shows nothing of interior life, except what we are left to imagine of the hideous motives of a soul sensitive to the call of the world. The heroine of *Stromboli* is brought to a savage island by a man whom she married for ulterior motives and who forces her to share his austere fisherman's life. Like a trapped animal, the heroine spares us none of her lamentable struggles. We contemplate her with disgust, never sympathy. This weak creature seemed just the type to touch us. Yet, the most disinterested movements, the feelings of disgust and the delicacies of the fragile, protected woman, are nothing here but the mark of a sordid appetite for a comfortable life and only persuade us all the more of her fundamental abjection. God's boundless mercy is shown by the absurdity of his pardon for her, just as the mystery of reprobation is shown by the incommensurability of the punishment with the crime. He pardons at the moment when man, turning himself into an administrator of justice, makes insensitivity a rule.

I will therefore comment on the biblical verse that Rossellini gives as an epigraph to his work: "I am sought by them that asked not for me; I am found by them that sought me not" (Isaiah 65, quoted by St. Paul). Everyone is free to find other aspects to this film. As for me, I see only a few works that in our time have as magnificently, as directly, exalted the Christian idea of grace, works that, without rhetoric, simply by the evidence of what we are shown, proclaim more loudly man's misery without God. Perhaps of all the arts, film is the only one

Ingrid Bergman in *Stromboli*.

today that knows how to walk without faltering on these high summits and with all the magnificence required, the only one that still leaves room for the aesthetic category of the *sublime,* elsewhere discarded because of an excusable sense of modesty. Since Victor Hugo's voice was silenced, what writer would dare not banish the words *magnificent, terrifying,* or *grandiose* from his pen? The poetic beauty of *Stromboli* borrows none of the pomp of the verb or the metaphor and thus does not fear an abuse of their power. The idea and the symbol are so indistinguishable that we no longer question the artifice of the person who united them for us. God's grandeur springs not from the mouths that speak of him but from the actual presence of the volcano, the lava, the waves, and the Italian shore, which the beautiful foreigner in her beach outfit desecrates with her awkward, Nordic-girl grace. Perhaps the filmmaker's conscientiousness led Rossellini beyond his intentions as an author. We feel he has some pity for the creature whose fall he portrays, and we often fear that he will succumb to the base pity that earlier caused some Italian films to be successful. To attribute his discomfort to a exaggerated concern with formal research would be to fail to recognize the deeper sense of modern art. American literature today, whose influence on postwar Italian filmmakers we know, is one of the most brilliant illustrations of the Nietzschean myth of the "death of God." Each being, each event, is clad only in the charm of its pure existence. What *is* must be, in a world in which all hierarchy of religious or moral values is deliberately cast off. We can imagine the temptation of a philosophy that seems exactly suited to the filmmaker's purpose. Giving in to this temptation would mean failing to recognize that the portrayal of the small, true fact – "realism" – is the requirement of an art whose very existence is paradoxical, but poetry, song, its end. And what other subject would be more immediately poetic? We condemn Rossellini only for having given too much to the literary objects that he admires and for having sacrificed a bit of the tradition of Gance and of Eisenstein to the false gods of Caldwell.

Some people are born filmmakers. The author of *Stromboli, Païsan* (*Païsa*), and *La Macchina ammazzacattivi* knows all the importance that his art bestows upon the objects, places, and natural elements of a set. By mastering the power he gives them, he makes them his primary instruments of expression. The set will automatically form the actors' movements: the room with thick walls, the narrow courtyard, the steep or sheer slopes. They tell us of an obsession with a closed world, a world that confines into an always narrower matrix the large graceful body of the imprudent woman who wanted to remake it to her liking. And just as he makes things act, Rossellini considers his characters to be "things" as well. Rossellini's art is one of the least apt to express interior life. The whimpering, the gasping, and the rattling with which Ingrid Bergman fills the walls and shores signify nothing more than the leaps of a small rabbit strangled by the carnivorous stone marten or of a tuna pierced by the fisherman's pike. They *are* her and, stripped of all mystery, reveal only her interior emptiness. In this respect, it is significant to compare *Stromboli* with *Under Capricorn,* a work of protestant inspiration, in which we see, once again, the same actor climb the long road separating despair and self-disgust from the peace of rediscovering a conscience. If cinema were merely the art of probing the soul's interior, I would be ready to give all of *Stromboli* for the Hitchcock shot in which Ingrid Bergman's face, sunk against the edge of her bed, heavy-lipped, eyelids half-closed, reflects, in the space of an instant, such a wealth of diverse sentiments (fear and self-mastery, candor and calculation, rage and resignation) that the most concise writer could not express it in several pages. But Rossellini's design is different, and it would be unfair of us to condemn him for denying us what others put so much science into revealing. In his work, each thing is in the present, is an appearance, a palpable form, and admits nothing beyond the divine hand that presided over its creation. What this film loses in moral depth, it finds in religious grandeur. A kind of tragic horror fixes our gaze and imposes a view of the world that is neither that of man, in that it excludes compassion, nor that of God, in that it still inspires terror. At a time when almost all the arts base their hierarchy of values on ideas of revolt and blasphemy, I am glad to see that among them, the youngest and the lowliest in appearance, in the process of one of its more questionable procedures, "realism," suddenly begins, as if in spite of itself, to rediscover the meaning of the virtue of *respect,* which was formerly the symbol of art.

It would be futile to search this film for the echo of an adventure that is still in the news. A director never treated his actress with less love or consideration. If, in the course of the projection, our distracted gaze leaves the character to linger on the woman who brings her to life, it is not the destiny of the woman that draws our attention but that of the actress who, docile under a tenderless master, patiently learns to splinter the royal allure of a great tragic actress on the piles of pumice and the pebbles of the banks.[*]

(*Gazette du cinéma* 5, November 1950)

[*]This article is signed Maurice Scherer (JN).

Howard Hawks: *The Big Sky*

I'm not crazy about westerns. The genre has its requirements, its conventions, like any other, but they are less liberal. The plains, the herds, the guitars, the chase scenes, and the eternal good guys and their rugged bravado, their traces of Scottish or Irish humor, are apt to tire anyone from this Old World who carries a more resounding, more distant past among his baggage. Yet the great masters, the Fords, the Wylers, were able to affirm their mastery in this domain without compromising themselves. I must even apologize to Fritz Lang in the name of *Cahiers: Rancho Notorious* was not honored here with an article. It is true that we learn nothing about its director from the film, except that the idea of his pseudodecadence is wrong. But maybe we, as critics, are more sensitive to the call of the new than to the strict law of equity, which should be our rule.

I am therefore jumping at the chance to denounce a strange prejudice, according to which every filmmaker has a short life: Counting one's days is even an exercise in which most of my colleagues find the greatest of pleasure. What master of the screen has not been called decadent? From Gance to Renoir, from Clair to Ford, from Lang to Hitchcock... As for me, I give more credit to the man than to the work and, only very slowly, when necessary, alas!, give in and see the light. In short, I'm all for the *aged*, not that I am impressed by their age, but it seems difficult to admit that one can plunge so low from such heights – if one really attained such heights. Some say that chance rules the art; this is yet another sophism. I do not believe it great enough to have prevented any cinematic genius – and perhaps this alone is proof of his genius – from having done what he wanted to do, exactly as he wanted to do it.

As for the *genius* of Hawks, one must read the excellent article that Jacques Rivette contributed a few months ago. I see nothing that can be added to this study, which is as thorough as possible.* I also consider Hawks to be the greatest filmmaker born in America, except for Griffith. For my tastes, he is far superior to Ford, who is generally more esteemed. The latter bores me (what can I do?), whereas the former sweeps me off my feet. Quite a pointless criterion, one might say. Is it really? I remember Alain's naming Stevenson's *Treasure Island* as one of his favorite things to read: It is true, as he said, he did not care to be considered a good, voracious reader. But whoever has read *The Master of Ballantrae* will agree that if the author of the story who charmed him at twelve years old had the making of a wise storyteller, he was also a great connoisseur of men, a great novelist altogether.

---

* *Cahiers du cinéma* 23, May 1953, *Génie de Howard Hawks* (*The Genius of...*) (JN).

"Art's goal is to make you see," said Conrad, in his preface to *The Nigger of the Narcissus* — a sentence as specious as the style of this author, whom I wish I liked more. For is it so much a question of suggesting with words as of probing with them? If the novelist's sole concern were to approach the outside of an object with words and to remain outside the object, I would unquestionably prefer the least film to the best of novels, if only because, saving me from the boredom of description, it brings me into the whirlwind of action which the most beautiful prose slows down or freezes. One of cinema's assets is to have made us more critical of words that sound nice but have little expression, more sensitive to a vigorous style than to a bombastic one, to the verb rather than to the adjective, to intention and movement more than to sensation and state, and to the moral rather than to some nebulous cosmogony.

In any case, such is the esteem in which I hold Stevenson. Cinema is responsible for my taste for the adventure classics, to which his works belong. Nowhere else have I seen the secret roots of desire better brought to life, better sketched: the instant when a decision is made and the action begins, less drowned in pomp. The development is so well arranged only because it is left to itself. Even an accidental event would turn the hero away. Would the wait and the more than tragic anguish be this heavy if the least of the hero's decisions did not threaten his freedom even more than his life? Read the astonishing *Ebb Tide* (what a script for Hawks!);* see how, pursued by constant peril, the characters become strong or weak, how the darkness brightens and the bright begins to darken, but as if of their own accord and not by the storyteller's tricks. Because I believe that man is free and always ready to be renewed, I do not it like when, in order to preserve an unknown part in man, a hero disappears before my eyes by means of some stylistic artifice, an ellipsis, or a sudden blank; disappears at the very moment when I expect him, watch for him, judge him.

Such is Howard Hawks. Except for a few violent flashes, sometimes unbearable, all is preparation in his work. No swelling, no rhetoric in the exposition of the facts, too dry even to be resolutely brutal. The wait is satisfied, not because the developments overwhelm it but, just the reverse, because they realize it fully. Once the act is accomplished, the impossible becomes possible, necessary. A difficult act becomes the easiest act in the world. Just as Hitchcock plays with fear, which heightens the danger and inflates reality with imaginary phantoms, so in Howard Hawks's perspective, which is that of courage, what remains of an action but a dry indication of its material, geometric pos-

---

* It *had been* filmed in 1937 by James Hogan and remade (as *Adventure Island*) in 1947 by Peter Stewart (CV).

Elisabeth "Coyote" Threat and Dewey Martin in *The Big Sky*.

sibility? In this world of physical ability in which the heroes of Yankee folklore live, no false move is allowed: Whoever tries to portray this world has no room for slipups, haziness, or metaphors. I know of no other director who is more indifferent to plasticity, whose shooting script is more ordinary, but in exchange, who is more sensitive to the exact outline of a movement, to its exact duration.

And just as for the athlete, an efficient style is a beautiful style, poetry here is a bonus. But at the same time, this poetry is primary, it cannot be separated from the utilitarian part it heightens. Hawks is undoubtedly more personal, more astonishing, more regally elegant when working with comedic exaggeration, with gritty excessiveness, than with the halftones of the heroic comedy into which he is blocked by Dudley Nichols's skillful script, a script that is more traditional, more in accordance with Ford's mind than with the virile and flamboyant *Red River*. But what luxurious detail lies beneath the uniformity of purpose, what refusal to exploit the easy horror of an amputation, of a burnt face, of a fight between a man and a woman, what mathematical beauty in these battles, these reversals in which the equilibrium collapses, the system of forces inverts itself but does not cancel itself out!

I see Hawks as having a special place reserved for him. Others, some great, Renoir, Stroheim, or Vigo, shone with different virtues: the disdain for recognized forms, or a stiff intransigence; others still, by a desire to be abstract, systematic, a desire with which the director of *Scarface* is not concerned, either. Should we hold it against him? I'll admit that his place is not the very first, for it is only fair to give this prize to risk and ambition. But can we blame a filmmaker for being merely a filmmaker, for not seeking to transgress his art's boundaries, for remaining, on the contrary, always within them, and for bringing the popular genre of the western, or the adventure story, or the musical comedy, to a classical perfection? There are two ways to love film that I do not at all appreciate. Some, strangely enough, make a practice of protecting everything in the art that is not the art, even of admiring the projection of pretentious dramas, shoddy operas, and autodidactic poems, which elsewhere their good taste would disapprove of. The others – are they any less harmful? – are quick to praise anything, saying they are sensitive to the mere naiveté, even if this entails inventing it where it does not exist. I understand that when masterpieces are lacking, it is easier to adjust to the commonplace than to the pretentious and that all in all, a Java would be less hostile to the ear than a contemporary sonata. But cinema is already too old and too respectable to be treated in such a haphazard way. Were things ever any different? Who would dare speak of Griffith's simplicity today, or of Chaplin's? I do not believe in involuntary poetry, in this domain even less than elsewhere. I think, all things considered, that the best westerns are those signed by a great name. I say this because I love film, because I believe it is not the fruit of chance, but of art and of men's genius, because I think that one cannot really love any film if one does not really love the ones by Howard Hawks.[*]

(*Cahiers du cinéma* 29, December 1953)

Skimming Picasso: Henri-Georges Clouzot's *The Mystery of Picasso* (*Le mystère Picasso*)

Is Clouzot's *Picasso* a good or a bad film? It all depends on what one expects from it. I enjoyed seeing it very much, enjoyment that would have been perfect if it had not been for the music by Georges Auric, which seemed rather mangled and overwhelming. I did not want to find out any secrets, but to see a painter, whom I admire, at work. I

[*] This article was signed Maurice Scherer and was entitled *Les Maîtres de l'aventure* (JN).

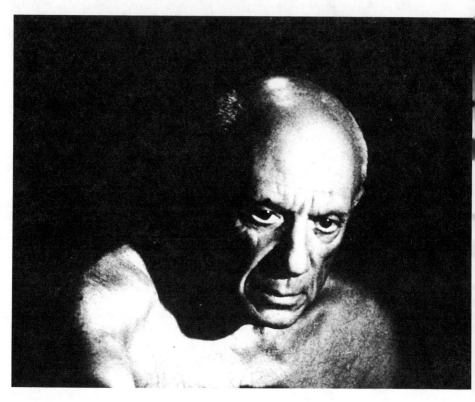

Pablo Picasso in *The Mystery of Picasso.*

went, I saw it, and I was not disappointed. Picasso, in the background, takes a charcoal pencil and signs. He adds a new work to his already-full catalogue: a work that is just as appealing as the others.

Who is the director of the film, in fact? I singled out four types of answers. Picasso for the man on the street, Clouzot for those who are in the know, who see through the trick. Picasso, in the third degree, if one notices how he winks behind the director's back. And finally, venturing out to the fourth degree, André Bazin brings Clouzot to the forefront, ignores the question of who's pulling the strings, and discovers a new kind of art film that combines Resnais with McLaren. His argument is solid, especially when he praises the filmmaker for filming everything in black and white except for the painting, thereby giving it its rightfully privileged position.

I will not go as far as he did, however, but will stop at the next lowest level. Picasso is a strange fish, who is no less loath to bite than to swim off into the unfathomable night. As opposed to a Braque, a Dali, or a Matisse, he has always remained silent about himself but does not mind showing his colors. Probing the mystery of creation is rather an ambitious task, but what we are shown is already very solid food for thought. We see our painter enough to take him seriously, even when he mystifies us. Clouzot sticks to the drama, the good classical melodrama, and portrays a man galloping against the clock, like an outlaw followed by the sheriff. Picasso has his own suspense, of a better nature. As an emulator of Hammett or Gardner, he places his pawns according to a plan that he alone knows; with a flick of the finger he demolishes a work that seemed to lead directly to the goal. The flowers that change into fish, then into roosters, then into the mask of a fawn: It's good fun, from which none of the other passages are exempt. "Taurus, table or face, all that flows from my brush," he seems to say, "is worthy of admiration. I alone, by my demanding playfulness, am able to decide what should be left as is and signed, or brushed off and destroyed."

Here he is showing off for the crowds. Showing off, OK, but not like most people: It is a luxury allowed a genius whose true difficulties are not those that make others pale. His able strokes, which are a difficult conquest for so many painters, come to him naturally, like a gift from above. They are a comfortable, but also a perilous, point of departure. He does not stop until he has corrected what seemed to be perfection itself, smears, destroys, dirties the pure gems of his first sketch, with no concern for our distress. "Enough! Stop!" one feels like screaming. And, in fact, he stops, but never on the tonic chord. The pause fades; the painting gives way to another before we have time to recover. "OK! I'm leaving it like this!"* he says in his neutral voice, at once unpretentious and commanding. Yes, of course. He is the only judge. It is for him to lead, for us to follow and to admire. We want to, we must take him at his word.

I am not being ironic. In Picasso, more than in any other, we find the embodiment of the regal pride common to the painter of our times. The individual work is far from constituting an end in itself, as it did for the classical painter. It is only a pocket of momentary fixity. "Each of his paintings," said Malraux, in the preface to Faulkner's *Sanctuary*, "is but a milestone in the progress of a high-strung genius." This film invites us to carry his thesis to an extreme. Each step in Picasso's painting is to the definitive "Picasso" that will result, in turn, what this one painting is to Picasso as a whole: An atom in a microcosm to which only the macrocosm, that is, all the works together, gives the

---

* This sentence is genuinely Picasso's. Clouzot, on the other hand, added the following "I don't worry about the audience" and other fragments that we can rightfully judge as third-rate.

key. What counts for our painter, who is a god in his universe, but a god only after the creation, is that a certain line be faithful, but the points of inflection are not known in advance. Thought and hand go together; one cannot be known without the other. Whatever he does, success lies at the end of the road, and yet the anguish is there, anguish that he may not be good enough, that he cannot surpass himself. Artists through the ages have known this drama. In fact, for them it was not a drama: The outcasts dawdled in a mannerism, and the elected went forward, slowly adding precision to their style. The progress of our modern Proteus is more tenuous, despite his nonchalant appearance: In addition to the kind of fine tuning that always comes with experience and age, he imposes the stubborn desire always to move on to new ground.

I remember an extraordinary instant in a short film on Matisse. The painter, with his back to the camera, had placed a young boy in front of him and was drawing his face with a sure hand. All of a sudden the stroke, which had been exact and supreme, was lost. "No, it's not possible!" True, it isn't: Matisse takes his eraser and erases... Clouzot's film did not show us any of these moments, but I believe that this is because of his model. There is nothing more disturbing than Matisse's method, even though it aims for a certain asceticism (I am thinking of the contours of the frescos at Vence, [France]). Picasso's movement takes us more from a given, primary purity to a conquered, restored purity, but so abruptly that the most attentive viewer has trouble following it. Filming with a rear projector, and at intermittent times, Clouzot adds still more to this impression of discontinuity, but, at least in my opinion, he neither clouds nor reveals a mystery that the presence of the painter's hand, in the rare instances when we are able to see it, leaves no less intact. The gap between the cause (the movement) and the effect (the stroke) is too obvious. From in front or from behind, in our minds or in Picasso's, perhaps it all is the same.

In sum, the most serious thing in the film – as is normal – is the painting. One cannot fool with it, provided that the painter is playing the game, and the proof is there, he played it. He did not dawdle during the filming, he worked for himself as much as for us. He did not stop at laying out some samples. He is not a salesman. The use of colored inks posed a technical problem and, for him, a current problem. After the expressionist and neocubist period started by *Guernica,* we have seen, since Vallauris, a period dedicated to softer colors and to "graphism," as was the case after the other war. And he had never pushed this graphism so far. As long as he draws, he works in familiar territory, finding inspiration in the series of *Grotesques* that he gave us one or two years ago. But once the bottles are open, the difficulties begin: He must transform the sketch into a painting with this intractable material, and, as was once the case with pasted paper and ink in 1955, suggest a new style.

Is he returning to oil? His ambition is growing as large as the canvas. Picasso has never seen CinemaScope, but he envisages a theme worthy of its regal proportions, the proportions of a fresco. And the result will be the *Beach*. He wants to create a complete work, to crown the series of studies with a more meditated sum total. He begins to work, and it is not surprising if things do not go well. Not following his usual method, he may have wanted to give a digest of his previous work. In any case, the ghosts of the past reappear with a more and more troublesome insistence. He flounders, to Clouzot's great joy, who discovers an unhoped-for ending. He abandons it, paints a few canvases, all just as impressive but more modest in nature, which are inserted into the editing at the beginning of this final part. Then, because the film has to end, he returns to the *Beach,* brings it to a state of a rare perfection, and close to the design of his earlier ink drawings. We must at least be satisfied. The film is over, but to this day Picasso, so I hear, works on the famous *Beach.* Who can say that he is not serious?

Let's not ask more of this film than it can give. Picasso only passes through it, but his presence is continuous. Paradoxically, this film gave me what art films generally deny: the freedom to admire what I want. The tyranny of time, even arbitrarily concentrated, is sweet compared with the tyranny of a commentary. Picasso is the modern painter who has seen the most books dedicated to his reproductions. He is an author to skim; the picture rails at exhibits are too solemn for him. Here then, is a new album, if not an entirely new period, as I said in the beginning. And because he is not addressing himself only to those who are already knowledgeable, we should not condemn Clouzot, the editor, for having included an introduction that is a bit too obtrusive for our tastes.*

(*Arts* 572, June 1956)

A twentieth-century tale: Orson Welles's
Mr. Arkadin/Confidential Report

The revolution brought about by Welles seems greater every day. Without him, as we said in the dedication to our Christmas issue, "the new American cinema would not be what it is." From Wyler to Robert Aldrich, through Kazan or Preminger, following a meandering but never entirely broken line, his influence has never ceased to obsess Hollywood. True, like Eisenstein, he is not the type that can be imitated,

---

*This article was entitled *En feuilletant Picasso* (JN).

and with the help of time and ingratitude, the many errors committed in his name have caused us to turn to other gods. Little by little, we allowed ourselves to consider him the majestic and already-faraway portico to modern cinema, without dreaming that he could one day return to our ranks and dazzle us with unequaled brilliancy.

Othello reminded us in time that our god was not dead, but as much as we admired this film, we did not rediscover the fiery vitality that, ten years ago, had inflamed our young eyes. We resigned ourselves to believing that the meteor had absorbed the shadows of history, leaving behind a mere precious tail, whose glowing dust alone was left for us to gather, perhaps with somewhat less haste than our elders did.

Then came *Arkadin*. We cannot say that the critics were harsh. Yet, I would have hoped for less measured praise. What, the best Orson Welles film? Why not? It is just as great as *Citizen Kane* or the *Ambersons*, and before time imposes a more objective judgment, it is normal for my current choice to be for the most recent. Far from a *remake* of the preceding films, it continues a tendency that I had sensed at a recent showing of *Lady from Shanghai*. Although the director admits that the latter was taken from the first novel he picked up, until today it had been my favorite. It is appropriate to compare *Arkadin* with this film and not with *Citizen Kane*, as is usually done. Neither claims to be realistic, or at least if there is realism, it is only at a secondary level. These are *tales*, in the strict sense of the word, fables, yet not abstract allegories. It is surprising that a period so quick to get carried away with the many revivals of Kafka's *The Trial* or *The Castle* would so confuse genres in this case. Unlike *thrillers*, whose moral system and structures they borrow, they are not embellished myths of popular or scholarly origin but brand-new myths, *pure myths*. The fantastic springs from a primary source, but Welles does not treat it with the grain of condescension detectable in Raymond Chandler or in Aldrich's *Kiss Me Deadly*. If the story's significance surpasses the director's explicit meaning, it is because it also surpasses analysis, as do all tales, of all ages, in all countries.

According to Pierre Kast and his followers, *Lady from Shanghai* is a demythification (or demystification) of a certain Hollywood idea of the woman, the denunciation of an entire moral and social system. Granted, but saying that *Orestes* is the expression of a Greek consciousness crisis linked to an economic infrastructure does not explain why this myth remained fertile until Giraudoux and Sartre, by way of Racine. For *Monsieur Verdoux* (which was Welles's idea, I know), OK, I agree it is merely a pamphlet in allegorical form, a tale like *Zadig*, to which we are free to prefer *A Thousand and One Nights*. In this case, Orson Welles preserves the naiveté and polyvalence of the fable. In place of an optimistic, if not a completely inane, myth, he

Akim Tamiroff and Robert Arden in *Mr. Arkadin*.

substitutes another, more bitter one, whose truth far surpasses the circumstances. "Innocent or guilty, it doesn't mean a thing," murmurs Michael the sailor. I just mentioned *Orestes:* The ancient idea of fate is replaced by a more obscure, more dubious one, somewhere between Kafkaesque absurdity and "politics," that is, human plotting. We find this idea of universal deception in *Mr. Arkadin* but associated with another, just as profound, idea: that of the invulnerability of the secret, of a *killing truth,* which reminds us of Pandora's box.

Arkadin asks the explorer Van Stratten to lead a strange search: to reconstruct a past that he pretends to have forgotten since a certain day in 1927. Van Stratten accomplishes his mission and little by little discovers the secret reason for it: to eliminate troublesome witnesses whose traces were lost. Everyone can interpret these rather extraordinary facts as he likes. What matters is the tone of this search, which is that of rape, of *violation.* Watch the improvised detective shaking the old Jacob Zouk, pulling pieces of truth from him as he pulls off his blanket. "The main thing is to age well," said Michael: Arkadin and Van Stratten refused to bend to the march of time, whether due to unbounded ambition, vanity, or the lure of profit. They cannot, or do not want to, forget the secret, as did the others, who have long ceased to pose a threat. They violate the past. This idea, which runs throughout all adventure stories, plays a prominent role in this one. The inquiry is no longer a method of narration, as in *Citizen Kane,* but is the very subject of the film. My explication does not claim to be complete. I simply want to show that of all his stories, this story especially cannot be taken literally. Who is Arkadin, in fact? One of these adventure figures, a few examples of which exist today? A Basil Zaharoff, a Serge Rubinstein? Probably, but he is different from the usual type. He resembles the god Neptune too much not to represent something more: the incarnation of destiny, a modern and omnipresent god, returning to the sky from which he seemed to come (his death is not shown, the plane crashes empty), a vulnerable god, a cruel, yet just god. Van Stratten saves his skin but loses Raina's love, who condemns him for having chosen his own life instead of her father's. His fault is less moral than metaphysical. The psycholanalysts will quibble endlessly over this story, as they did over *King Lear* or *The Tempest.* But I wanted to propose a meaning that would be less dependent on the director's personal obsessions.

This story is therefore not fantastic but, more precisely, marvelous, a type of marvelous that is all the more rare because it functions without resorting to the aids of modern fairytales: exoticism and science fiction. All symbolism aside, the adventure alone brilliantly illustrates a genre that has deteriorated since Jules Verne and *Fantômas,** or in some cases has become overly intellectual. It builds its novelistic quality on neither anticipation nor displacement, which today is almost an impossible feat. In a century when reporting and memoirs of all types have made us more demanding concerning exact details, we find our familiar Europe in a strange light, and yet we recognize it. This unrealistic tale rings truer than many stories in which verisimilitude is carefully maintained. Although Welles neglects to justify many aspects of his story, whereas he meticulously follows up on others, he doesn't play around with the truth, which is carefully reconstructed. Some say this film "looks poor," and it did not require costly sets and all the technical extras that only specialists notice. The layman will find, in contrast, that this film is very rich, more than any European or American film this year, and he is right. In what way does the billionaire Arkadin interest the man on the street, which we all are, in a sense? His wealth consists not so much of possessions but of the most modern power: the ability to move around, to be somehow pres-

---

* Story by Marcel Allain and Pierre Souvestre (CV).

ent at the same moment all over the world. The life of voyages and palaces charms us in a way that sedentary luxury no longer does. Most of the time, Welles was careful to bring his crew to the very spots where the action is supposed to take place, and the precaution pays off. The actors, who all are excellent, play "character" roles but play even more on their physical, even ethnic, characteristics. The power of money is portrayed with a precision that only Balzac would have no need to envy. All the true elements create an exceptional world, whose existence we believe in all the more because it is presented as an exception.

And then there is the style, the tone, the inimitable magic that stimulates us from the first chords of music by Misraki. Are the low angles, the short focal lenses, the first monstrous shots, merely trademarks, whose excellence crushes its many imitators? Never were these distortions, this delirium, so much in place, so justified: the truth that crumbles into fatal dust in the hands of the detective, these bits of a past that tumble like a sand castle, unable to be approached head-on and forcing us to emphasize both their crushing weight and inconsistency. As if he owned them, had invented them, Welles uses a mechanical system that he alone has been able to understand. Although he was justly praised in the past for his use of the still shot, since *Lady from Shanghai,* and especially in *Othello,* he likes his shooting script to be extremely fragmented, without shocking our modern demand for continuity. André Bazin observed that his favorite figure of speech was the litote, the strong point of the scene remaining in the background before the impassive camera. Here, he multiplies the angles, yet these leaps do not move forward. The camera seems stricken with the same illness as the characters are, who turn and totter. I am thinking of the scene on the yacht, on a stormy sea, when the drunken Mily tells Arkadin the secrets that will cost him his life. At every instant, everything seems carried off by the surge of a great wave. Even if it rarely appears, the sea continues its low rumble. I bet that the resemblance between Arkadin and "the god who shakes the earth" is not coincidental.

It is not the first time in the history of cinema that a effervescent genius, traveling on ordinary paths, so royally misused the technical or human material that fell into his lap. Orson Welles's case reminds us in many ways of Stroheim's. But I prefer to compare the director of *Citizen Kane* with Eisenstein. In both we find the same opinionatedness, though more didactic in the first, the same skill at using the *primary* power of the camera, of transfiguring reality by manipulating camera shots, the same confidence in the effects of *editing*, whether material or ideal (on the contrary, the use of ellipsis and camera movement, *shooting script* techniques, characterize Hitchcock). Yet, thanks to implicit or explicit *attractions,* we find the same ability to express more than a sentiment, to express an *idea.* We are compelled to place them among the greats, even if we refuse to be hypnotized by their brilliant examples. Both, too attentive to their own music, did not try to discover the lyricism that comes from things alone and that a camera "placed at a man's height," like that of Hawks, but also of Renoir and Rossellini, is more apt to bring out. Cinema's mission is more to direct us toward the aspects of the world that we didn't see than to place us before a distorting mirror, as good quality as it may be. Personally, I prefer the first school, but one must recognize that genius is still genius, no matter what form it takes.[*]

(*Cahiers du cinéma* 61, July 1956)

Nicholas Ray: *Bigger Than Life*

Nicholas Ray has enough partisans among our readers for me to venture praising him without preliminaries. Yet I can easily see how his last film might be shocking in the eyes of those who demand a certain literary *content* in a cinematic work. *Bigger Than Life* is not a melodrama. If it were, defending it to certain people would be easier. I will therefore limit myself to pleading guilty; I will consider the style, and only incidentally mention the conventions inherent in the genre.

We may fear an attack on this film on two counts. The first is precisely that it mixes genres that have nothing in common with the academic categories of the comical and the serious, nor with those of the philosophical fable or popular tale. Quietly accompanying the tone of psychological realism and theatrical solemnity are a certain intellectual distance and undisguised pathos. This combination leads us to feel definitely ill at ease, which is not the way we are used to feeling when reading Sartre or Faulkner.

But let us hold back our response and go on to the second count, which is that it seems difficult to base an entire tragedy on the properties of a medicine. I say the properties, for although the remedy is abused, it is not this abuse, and the weakness implied, that forms the subject of the drama. Ed Avery, a teacher in a small American town, is attacked by a formerly fatal disease, an inflammation of the arteries. Only cortisone can save him, but taking this still little known hormone has its dangers. Nervous, even mental disorders, are to be feared: We then are faced with what appears to be a pure drama of medical science, devoid of any moral or psychological content.

Would it therefore be so audacious to speak of tragedy once again, as we did in regard to *Rebel Without a Cause?* Tragedy understood in

---

[*] This article was entitled *Une fable du XXème siècle* (JN).

James Mason, Barbara Rush, and Christopher Olsen in *Bigger Than Life* by Nicholas Ray.

its full, noble sense, and not that considered in the evening papers: a child dying of a vaccine inoculation is "tragic" only if aesthetics are involved, if science, for example, plays the role of a modern fate, a mysterious goddess who dispenses good and evil, in the manner of ancient fate. Now this idea is merely suggested in the film. Even if the directors claim it is there, the setting does not emphasize it.

What it does make clear are the symptoms of the illness, of the delirium, which is not just any delirium. Hardly has the treatment begun, even before he has surpassed the prescribed dosage, Avery starts to seem larger; he feels his confidence and ambition grow. He spouts theories that, taken out of context, are perfectly logical, too perfectly. He is literally "possessed" by a kind of demon of lucidity: There are no contradictions in his text. At school, he rises up against the new educational methods, and even his choice of words to denounce certain popular pedagogical concepts shows that the director, or directors, did not wish to defend them. This lunatic, then, possesses a certain wisdom, even if we perceive in the end that this wisdom is madness.

Cortisone does not play the role of a deus ex machina but, rather, of a catalyst. Let us admit that it would have been more compelling, from a literary viewpoint, for this madness to have come from a cause, from an excess, for example, of logic, or from the rage common in Nicholas Ray's characters, or even from the monotony of modern life, the impatience with the yoke of machines and the rationalization of work and pleasure. But we understand that as opposed to a novelist, a filmmaker is interested less in the genesis of madness than in its effects. These are presented to us one after the next, without a very marked progression, like different variations on a theme. Avery shows signs of his delusions of grandeur later at his home. He shows his wife and young son how mediocre they are: If not for his duties as a father, he would abandon his family in pursuit of a more noble task, that of transforming the world through education.

As the film progresses, the internal logic of Avery's madness becomes apparent, to the point that we disregard its original cause. And besides, this drug – which is a true "stimulant" – only augmented an already-present tendency, whose symptoms we noticed before the treatment began. Avery had already said "we are mediocre" the very evening he fell, overwhelmed by his first attack. Then, under the influence of cortisone, he gives way to a temptation that is not just vanity, tyranny, or cruelty. It is a more universal temptation, in that it expresses this desire, which is present in each of us, to bend the order of things in accordance with our will. We could say this temptation is *aesthetic,* because this controlling delirium aims to substitute for morals, and far from affirming a will to power, it refuses to consider both the special nature of the individual and the generality of ethics.

If I use – very freely – a terminology dear to Kierkegaard, it is not because I think that *Bigger Than Life* illustrates the theory of tragedy that Abraham's sacrifice inspired in the Danish philosopher. But one need not have read *Fear and Trembling* to detect the symbol of paradox and faith in this biblical scene. And this reference to the *most paradoxical moral act possible* naturally fits in at the end of this series of paradoxes. Avery, betraying the spirit of the Holy Scriptures in favor of its literal meaning, decides to cut the throat of his rowdy and apathetic son whom he has, in addition, caught hiding the precious violet bottle of cortisone.

This biblical reference would be pedantic (it even is common in America) if it were not justified by this pedant's madness. Just as O'Neill's *Electra* leaves us cold, so this reference, even if it is a bit arbitrary, seems to belong to the family of liberties that the last century's great painters were able to take with ease. Even in the most realist context, Nicolas Ray's works always contain – and I return without transition to the first of the two counts against the film, for form, here, cannot be dissociated from content – certain simplifications or salient features foreign to the ordinary rhetoric of the screen. True, he is more of an architect (which was his first profession) than a painter, if we consider a painter to be someone who fiddles with images. He is highly adept at the art of playing with the totality of the set, and although his frames are rather compact, he is able to avoid making them heavy. But he is still a painter, not only because he uses the power of color well – which is more expressive than decorative (Barbara Rush's orange-colored dress, the violet of the bottle, the red of the child's blouse, accentuated by a mostly beige harmony and by the skill of cameraman Joe McDonald) – but because by slightly slowing the pace or by accelerating it a bit too much, by inserting a pause that lasts perhaps not more than a fraction of a second, he is able to give the simplest gesture an eternal quality, thereby making it as expressive as it is handsome. He is able to make his film's most important shots: a woman filling a bathtub with a kettle or standing stiffly in her new dress, a child holding a football or digging through a pile of shirts, or again, kneeling on his bed, handing the football to his father who is entering the room.

Outside their dramatic context, these gestures undoubtedly lose some of their expression and beauty, but to try to detach them is as senseless as separating the arabesque from a Raphaël painting. I am making this preposterous comparison on purpose, in order to warn against a comparison that is easy to make between film and painting:

James Mason and Christopher Olsen in *Bigger Than Life*.

The filmmaker works his material by using researched, slightly unreal, artificial gestures, just as the painter outlines the elements of his composition. And it is in arbitrary situations, or more specifically in situations dependent on a contingent fact, that such gestures find their moment to bloom. Note how many close-ups are made possible by the very existence of the little bottle of cortisone. A purely psychological motive would not have afforded these finds.

We are free to see these things as easy ways out (as for me, I have reservations only about the fight scene, which is too acrobatic, and the scenes in the hospital) and to turn to filmmakers who do not disdain other, sterile ways out. We are free to detect the presence of America's own banalities: In Sophocles' theater (one of his tragedies, *Ajax*, has a madman as its hero) one finds many more truisms familiar to fifth-century Athens. There is something naive in the way Hollywood speaks about things of the mind, which shocks New York no less than it does Paris. But to continue my comparison with painting, would we ever think of taking offense at the Renaissance painters' customary anachronisms. Would we condemn them for not dressing biblical characters like true Hebrews, and didn't the achievement of local color come at the expense of art in the centuries that followed?

This story would surely furnish the subject matter for a very mediocre novel, leagues away from, say, *Moby-Dick*. But aren't we at the movies? The tragedy, the depth, the beauty of this film come from relationships that literature would be hard pressed to describe, if it were even capable of it. The true subject of *Bigger Than Life* is perhaps neither medicine nor madness but *life*, everyday life, this uneventful life whose story can be told only by a story as extraordinary as this one. Evoked by art, the mediocrity of daily existence hardly interests us, but at the same time, it is what affects us, what concerns us most in the world. For without this mediocrity in which we all participate more or less, in one way or another, we would not be able to gauge the extraordinary. The greatest literary works were able to paint this zone, this borderline fringe between life and drama. But the camera, like a microscope, detects a wide surface where we saw only a line. I say that because Ray shows us a woman in the kitchen, a man in the bathroom, a child in front of the television, all things that many others have done before him – and most succeeded only in boring us. What counts is the *tone* he uses to show them, a tone that is not without evoking, mutatis mutandis, that of *Viaggio in Italia (Strangers)*, the ever-so-precise attention to small things and the refusal to enjoy only their picturesque qualities, the glances that betray the concerns of love, rather than curiosity, fear, or any other sentiment, this strong sense of both man's earthly attachments and his freedom. In this combat, which materialism seems to have won in advance, the soul is the victor, not so much because of the providential dizziness that holds back Avery's arm, as because of the particular air one breathes, from the very beginning right to the last shot, an air of the same quality, in that it is graceful without pathos, as the final images of *Ordet (The Word)* or *Europa 51*. Also because of the *faith* one can read in the eyes of Barbara Rush or of the child, a faith tainted with doubt and yet always present "by virtue of absurdity."

Perhaps I am going too far in making Avery's wife the receptacle of this faith (faith in healing, faith in love, faith with no well-defined object), this faith without which Abraham is no more than a common murderer. Just the same, the connection one can make with Nicholas Ray's other films permit this conjecture. There is too much unity among his subjects, too much kinship among his characters for him not to have something to say other than just the facts.

This is why, with all due respect to François Vinneuil, I believe it is legitimate to "look beyond" the description of the medical case and, in judging *Bigger Than Life,* to consider the contribution of a mise-en-scène conceived not as a simple means of emphasis but as a veritable creation. *Either* there is "something" in this film, that indescribable quality that we find, despite the diversity of subjects and style, in the greatest works of the screen, *or* we were perhaps wrong about these great works as well. *Or* the paradox is such that a story of this kind, technical, with no explicitly tragic quality, is particularly apt to reveal the very essence of cinema, that world *beyond* which I mentioned in my critique of *Moby Dick, or else* all of cinema is merely Saturday evening entertainment.*

(*Cahiers du cinéma* 69, March 1957)

Luis Buñuel: *The Criminal Life of Archibaldo de la Cruz* (*Ensayo de un crimen*)

Archibaldo de la Cruz has the good fortune to see someone else commit the crimes that an equally fortunate fate prevents him from committing himself. In a word, this is the story of the film that Luis Buñuel shot in Mexico three years ago.

Like all well-told tales, this one leaves a respectably wide margin for interpretation. Are we to understand, very simply, as the author suggests in a brief passage – whose naiveté is equaled only by the splendor of its unraveling – that it is not worth trying to complicate life, that one should send scruples and casuistry to the devil? Or, to push the text a bit further, is it important to consider the female victims of these murders as different symbols of bourgeois or religious taboos, which every self-respecting man must quickly discard?

Finally, in this apologue, must we see a Buñuelian addition to the famous work by Thomas de Quincey, *Murder, Considered as One of the Fine Arts,* so dear to diehard surrealists? Because we are in doubt, let us stick to appearances, that is, to the images, which are fascinating enough, although they lack the cynicism that a Hitchcock or a Stroheim would have given them. But let us leave Buñuel his own world, especially when we are lucky enough to find it better constructed than usual. I just used the word *naive.* I did not mean it pejoratively. Our hero is cruel in the way that children are, when they torture animals or mistreat toys. In fact, the object of his cruelty actually is a toy, a mannequin. Sadism? We are nowhere near it. Death (that is, melting in the potter's kiln) seems to bring life to a dead face: The eye shines and shifts, the flesh palpitates and softens more than it decomposes, and from this second on we understand that Archibaldo, with a purer heart than he himself knows, has fallen in love with the

---

* This article was originally entitled *Ou bien ... Ou bien* (JN).

The Criminal Life of Archibaldo de la Cruz by Luis Buñuel.

woman who served as a model for the wax figure. Similarly, the doll-like face of the young bride is animated for one second: when her ex-lover points the revolver at her, and fires...

I am insisting on these details because with Buñuel, whose social or philosophical pet subjects often irritate me because of their narrow scope of vision, I am always looking for the moment when the stroke surpasses the intentions of the hand drawing it. I regretted the absence of these choice instants in his last two films (especially in *Cela s'appelle l'aurore*) so much that in return, I must admit to being satisfied beyond all hopes with this film. And I am all the more certain of this because a preview of *Archibaldo de la Cruz* had legitimized my expectations and demands.

Everything right down to the satire is of better quality than usual. As one might expect, the clergy and police are right on target. The shot is mischievous, but lively, elegant, with no oratorical precautions. The caricatures of the American tourists are also well developed, with no, or almost no, excess.

There is more to be praised. The slightly affected allure of the characters is in keeping with their ethnic background and social milieu. The static quality common in Buñuel's work is only slightly noticeable, even in the most artificial effects, the most plastically orchestrated movements. Just as Buñuel frees the hero, the mannequin frees the author from his immobility complex. She is the sacrificial victim for the greatest outrage against cinema, which is to consider beauty in film according to the norms of Baudelaire.

Which is why I will quickly gloss over the film's most obvious merits, the pictorial ones. And yet this modern set, with its unctuous blacks and whites, its baroque knickknacks, its sophisticated dresses, and magnificent undergrowth in the final scene, counts for a great deal in the fascination, with which the display of imaginary or real, sumptuous and scintillating murders attracts us, like a jeweler's window display. After all, who cares about the symbol's significance? What we see satisfies a hunger that is essentially too delicate to be unhealthy. Therein, I believe, lies the true moral of the fable.

One will have guessed that of all of Buñuel's films, old or new, I consider *Archibaldo de la Cruz* to be the most agreeable and most accomplished one. I even prefer it to *El,* in which the general atmosphere did not have the same crystal clarity. The entomologist hid the poet. I perceived a bit too much disdain for the characters, regardless of what anyone says. Here Buñuel is the lovable accomplice of his lovable hero, in fact, if not by intention. And we know very well that in film, intentions are not what count.

(*Arts* 638, October 1957)

The art of caricature: Frank Tashlin's
Will Success Spoil Rock Hunter?

For a certain time, we considered Frank Tashlin's work as the culmination of the trend toward the *new* American comedy, as opposed to that of *classical* comedy illustrated by people like Capra, Lubitsch, McCarey, and La Cava, the many *remakes* of which persist in flowering the grave, only to make its death more apparent. Tashlin is new, yes, and even slightly decadent, or if one prefers, baroque. He enriches the arabesque of grimaces with a thousand spirals, grimaces that in the works of Hawks or Cukor still maintain a very classical serenity. Jerry Lewis's contortions, Tom Ewell's prominent shoulders, Jayne Mansfield's bust, rock 'n' roll saxophones, allow us to explore a universe dominated by the curve, far from the straight, puritanical, and rationalist America of yesteryear that we so loved.

In *Will Success Spoil Rock Hunter?* has this ornamental craziness calmed down? At first glance, there are fewer embellishments, but perhaps we have grown accustomed to the curve of this space, which is more Euclidian than we first believed. In any case, we would significantly reduce Tashlin's contribution by seeing only a simple deviation from a comical doctrine, a doctrine to which we would have gladly adhered for a few more years. *Nihil fit ex nihilo,* and especially not comedy, which needs a solid infrastructure and in which the individual genius is in danger of never showing its capabilities if the genius of the genre is not there to back it up. This film, inspired by a play by George Axelrod (author of *The Seven-Year Itch*) of which almost nothing remains, is very similar in its dramatic structure, its love of caricature, and its antisentimentalism, to *Born Yesterday* or to *Inside Daisy Clover.* But to really understand its originality, I believe it is necessary to look farther than its brothers, or even its father and mother; so far back that we can finally believe that the gap that until now separated the silent and talking periods of the comical American genre has been bridged.

Not that I detect a hint of archaism in Tashlin's work. This return to the primitive echoes the return that has been discerned for some time in cinema as a whole, which is more and more conscious of its *visual* value. This is why I will not go further into what *Will Success Spoil Rock Hunter?* owes to circumstances, to allusions, to keys that open doors to the intimate chronicle of Hollywood, doors that skimming through a magazine will allow the reader to open without the help of a critic. I will not mention the modernity of the work either, except as proof, among others, of its endurance, for what is in vogue does not go out of vogue as much as its imitations do. To be up-to-date is the minimum requirement for the comic director, the necessary condition, if not a sufficient one (as *A pied, à cheval, en voiture* and *Lavandières du Portugal* fully prove). I will not even mention satire, or more specifically, in place of this term too loaded with literary references, I prefer to substitute the word *caricature,* which conforms better with the pictorial genius of cinema.

Tashlin's greatest asset, his great originality, is that he is the first caricaturist of the screen, in the proper sense of the word. We know why: He was a cartoonist. But what is very ordinary, almost obligatory in cartoons, becomes a difficult exception when working with living material. And we should note that it is not a question of an intended caricature, the stumbling block of the mediocre, but of an absolutely real caricature, *written* into the film with the freedom, if not the means, of a McLaren. The actors here are truly made of flesh and blood and possess, at the same time, the malleability of Emile Cohl characters. What matters is the means by which this second graphic nature is achieved. It may be done by simple special effects: the deformation of Tony Randall's face on the television screen, the remodeling of Jayne Mansfield's body by use of the appropriate clothes and under-

Jayne Mansfield in *Will Success Spoil Rock Hunter?*

clothes. It may be, more simply, an expression that simplifies, purifies, one might say, a face or a silhouette. Henry Jones and Tony
Randall give us perhaps one hundred of these pictures, pure and
clean, reduced to a few essential lines. Plastic invention is no longer
based on the juxtaposition of inalterable elements, but on the grinding
up of these very elements. The image of Rock Hunter, worn out, leaning over the handrail will remain clearer in our memory than that of
Charlie at the beginning of *The Immigrant.*

It works on the screen, which is not easy. This is the only rule of an
art that prides itself in frustrating all grammatical and stylistic rules.
It may seem, beforehand, that such an enterprise would risk becoming
rather fixed, and this would have happened if it had been done by a
less able hand. In general, nothing repulses me more in a film than
when a man starts to resemble a puppet. But here, expression is far
from stifled; the deformation of caricature enriches it with infinite nuances. A kind of beauty flows from this continual battle between the

ideal line and the reality of human anatomy, between the flesh and geometry, a struggle in which both are victorious. The *contemplation* of this represents half, if not three-fourths, of our pleasure. For can we speak of "gags"? No, if we only look for their dramatic function, based on waiting or surprise. The plot is skillfully worked, but not more than in other good American comedies. As for the purely comedic effects (the gurgling of the water reservoir, the bursting of the popcorn bag), they have the musty odor of an aesthetic that no longer exactly fits this film. Gags in *Will Success Spoil Rock Hunter?* are something to contemplate – and not only to understand, or, one might say, "collect" – the length of this contemplation not exceeding one or two seconds. Tashlin's comic universe allows for movement: Instead of presenting it at a single stretch, however, he presents it as a passage from one immobile state to another, thus restoring, in an entirely modern way, the discontinuous nature that it had when silent films were young. This discontinuity is perhaps secretly due – as it is not directly perceived by the spectator – to the film's undergoing twenty-four pauses per second.

Finally, we should add that these "states" are not at all stable (as is the case in classical ballet, for example). Rather, they correspond to a tension; the feeling that they are destined to be prolonged stimulates the eye instead of allowing it to rest, as do Betsy Drake's arms, hardened by gymnastic exercise. In this respect, we can compare Tashlin with Buster Keaton, in whose work the comic quality is also contemplated and who is indifferent to suspense. In these situations, he grants a distinct privilege to the axis of space, as opposed to that of time.

Of all the cinematic genres, comedy offers the most lessons. Which is why, in conclusion, I will permit myself to continue the discussion on a higher plane. It is true that we can never be too wary of a superficial comparison between cinema and painting, and yet the insights this film provides into the relationship between these arts have nothing in common with those proposed formerly by the theoreticians of the "belle photo." Nearly thirty years of talkies caused us to lose sight of one aspect of cinematic expression, which, for lack of a better word, I can only call *plastic. Will Success Spoil Rock Hunter?* proves that although the cinema is not a "spectacle" (to use Bresson's word), it would still be sad for it to be reduced to a piece of "writing." As for me, I have always preferred what we are shown to what we must decipher. Or, because it is now a question of caricature, I believe I am more sensitive to the persuasion of the cartoon than to its caption, as appealing as it may be in this case.[*]

(*Cahiers du cinéma* 76, November 1957)

[*]This article was originally entitled *L'Art de la caricature* (JN).

The quintessence of the genre: George Cukor's *Les Girls*

There are roughly two kinds of films, just as in the French language there are two ways of forming words: scholarly and popular. Films, of course, do not necessarily have a label attached to their credits. Even if they did, we couldn't accept it as proof of quality. Given our theoretical standpoint – which, as we know, is one that places emphasis on the director – *Cahiers* deliberately ignores social prejudice. We pay no heed to those – and they are numerous – who are annoyed to see the same consideration given to a western and a social drama, or to a musical comedy and a psychological study. But we shall just as firmly resist the snobbery, more prevalent than one thinks, that under the pretext of the love of the bizarre, sells its dadaistic soul for a flop.

It is just as stupid to link the value of a film to the more or less acknowledged presence of an ambition as it is to link it to the more or less deliberate absence of one. Bresson, Renoir, Rossellini, and Ophuls hold their art in great esteem, and it pays off. Walsh, Dwan, Minnelli, Kelly, and Donen display less consideration for their art. In return they receive less in absolute value but proportionately more than the others do. In order to explain the difference, we should speak of a certain *genius of the genre,* to use André Bazin's expression, a notion that is still obscure but whose existence is not in doubt.

Among these genres, the one whose value is the most controversial happens to be the *musical comedy* because of its double character as both entertainment and reproduction. Let's skip over the first aspect; it is the second one especially that is prone to alarm the cinephile, convinced that the goal of cinema can never be, in any way, simply to record what lives an autonomous and perfect existence before the camera is put in place. And yet even when the director's task is reduced to a minimum, because the choreographer or the photographer has taken the reins (which is not at all the case in Cukor's current film), the cinema has something to say, something that seems to be important.

The musical comedy is cinema, because, very simply, the cinema is musical comedy. The cinema is also cabaret, circus, fashion, and decoration, or at least it is the enormous river into which these innumerable streams of so-called minor arts wind up flowing, thereby attaining, if not actual existence, at least a version of it. In short, they reach eternity. I know that a reel of film is fragile, that this eternity is also relative. What does it matter? The definitions of cinematic specificity up until now have been so incomplete that I am suggesting this one, which has the advantage of embracing all cases without exception: The greatest advantage of the camera is that it *freezes the instant.*

Simply because it permits what is unique to be reproduced indefinitely, the cinema transforms the pure event into art, a minor art into a major art.

It is, of course, a paradox, whose sole justification is not to furnish a starting point for defending Guitry. I am far from wanting the transformation of the motion picture industry into an enormous canning factory. I would especially like to insist on an aspect of the Seventh Art that its theoreticians have been content to tackle in a roundabout way: its importance as a *total art.* It is the expression of life – modern life especially – in all its manifestations, including its artistic ones. And in fact, its smallest manifestations are artistic: A moving automobile, a man firing a shot, a woman going to her window all are art. You doubt it? Cinema is there to show you.

Which is why my argument would be quite fragile if the cinema did not return more to the arts that give it its material than they provided. The camera films dance, something that is much less photogenic than are the movements of a waiter in a café, or the handshake of two businessmen. It films without much conviction, a coolness that many failures seem to justify. But behold: The dance transforms itself, not so much in front of the camera as outside it. It "thinks" cinema, just as, more and more, the theater, the circus, the music hall, and photography do, because these days, especially on American soil, no art that stays in touch with the times can avoid thinking cinema. And thus, before the first turn of the crank, the Hollywood director knows that his work, thanks to the location and the times he lives in, is half, even three-fourths, finished.

One more argument. It is false to compare the camera with a perfect recording box. Or at least, if everything seems to point to that conclusion, certain privileged moments show us the chink in the armor, the channel by which art likes to sweep through full sail. In the days when film proceeded at a pace of sixteen images per second, the accuracy of certain rapid movements was automatically destroyed, and the art of the great silent comics was to use this inaccuracy to their advantage. Certain of Chaplin's pirouettes give a much livelier impression on the screen (even projected at shooting speed) than they would seem live. At the current rhythm of twenty-four images, this distortion is most often imperceptible, but theoretically it exists and contributes significantly to give the actors' movements a drier, squarer character, especially when the film uses a series of soft-focus effects, which in movement are no longer experienced as soft focuses. The secret of the art of the great choreographers and dancers of the screen may be that they instinctively perceive the discontinuous nature of cinematic reproduction and always instinctively bend the norms of their movements in accordance with it. Thus, as André Martin – to whom I owe the basis of this explanation – loves to say, the cinema of live action is an animation cinema without knowing it.

Excuse this preamble, in which I wanted to express some of the ideas that a showing of George Cukor's *A Star Is Born* brought to mind. It is one of the greats. I believe there is no other in which the cinema speaks a more direct language, speaks of things less able to be translated into any other dialect but its own. One can, in a pinch, imagine a novelistic equivalent of *The Rules of the Game* (*La Règle du jeu*), *Viaggio in Italia* (*Strangers*), and *Mr. Arkadin,* but not the equivalent of the scene in which Judy Garland, standing in front of James Mason, mimes the film she is in the process of shooting. It is not so much because the scene is made of pure mime – Griffith can also be transposed into a novel, and Eisenstein into a poem – it is more a question of a unique beauty whose existence, before the birth of film, was entirely unknown.

Cukor fans will undoubtedly have been surprised, a bit baffled, when first viewing his new film, *Les Girls.* This work is cold, inspires little laughter, and nips it in the bud when it does. And it counts more on the power of the dialogue for these effects than on that of pure cinematic gags. Such passivity is surprising to us, coming from a director whose films generally evoke such visceral reactions. But the director probably tried only to make an enjoyable picture while he was busy pursuing the most complete and systematic investigation of the musical comedy genre ever. First the script, with its deliberately factitious nature, forms the backbone of the system. He juxtaposes three versions of the same events, according to the differing perspectives of the three narrators: Sybil (Kay Kendall), a former showgirl bitten by the memoir-writing bug, Angela (Taina Elg), her ex-companion who, libeled, drags her to court, Barry Nichols (Gene Kelly), the ballet instructor, who admits to being too in love with Joy (Mitzi Gaynor), his current wife, to pay attention to the two others. The sandwich man who appears three times carrying a board with the inscription "What is truth?" indicates the moral of the fable. Far from trying to reconstruct the puzzle of facts, Cukor simply paints three pictures or, if one prefers, composes three "movements," each with its own tonality.

What does the storyline matter, one will say! I am not at all convinced but I am persuaded, to the contrary, that the libretto is as important as the music, here as in Mozart's operas. In a film that tries to give us a taste of the quintessence of the musical comedy, the theme of sincerity plays an important role, as the very spirit of the genre is in mixing truth with artifice. This is why Cukor – by instinct, I suppose, rather than by intention – hit the bull's-eye. "What is truth?" We have

Mitzi Gaynor, Kay Kendall, Gene Kelly, and Taina Elg in *Les Girls*.

heard this line somewhere before, and not only in Pirandello. We know at least the admirable variation, Camilla's question in *The Golden Coach* (*La Carosse d'or*): "Where does life end, where does the comedy begin?" As for the interplay of being and appearance, a fundamental cinematic theme, our director improvises an embroidery whose meanderings recall the contorted shapes of the latest Renoirs, *French Cancan* and *Eléna,* which are also deemed musical comedy or fantasy. We witness the same work of synthesis, of recreation in both cases, the same refusal of psychology and comic suspense.

True, there is still a great distance between the director of *Les Girls* and that of *Carosse,* but both assume the same responsibility. The ambition of his project deprives Cukor of the right to claim attentuating circumstances. The genius of the genre – comedy or musical – can no longer come to his defense, because in this reflexive work, the genre is reconsidered, rethought by him, reduced to the role of a point of departure, an element of inspiration. He draws sophistication, dear to the music hall and to fashion photography, from effects very similar to those that Renoir drew from the belle epoque imagery in *Eléna*. If in "depth," the latter clearly wins, Cukor does admirable surface work, although the quality of the photography and sets, and the means used, leaves something to be desired when compared with the luxury of *A Star Is Born*. He has a talent for positioning elements that is perhaps unequaled, even in Hitchcock (for instance, the position of the two partners in the boat during the song "Ça, c'est l'amour"). Better still, he is one of the few filmmakers who can legitimately be called a painter, if it is true that his actors do not perform a single gesture that he does not control as surely as if he had drawn it himself. This firmness in "directing the actors" for which he is praised should therefore be credited not so much to the interpretation of the role as to its pure creation. The advances made just in the mise-en-scène earn him, in our eyes, the envied rank of auteur.

Such films show us how the cinema can gain maturity, wisdom, and reflection without losing the spontaneous valor of its heroic age. If it sometimes gets lost, it is not because of an excess of understanding but, on the contrary, because it lacks an understanding of its own nature, its own vocation. Cinema should not look to literature, theater, or painting, but to itself. It is important for it to bring to a clear, acknowledged, definitive existence a thousand precious elements, still shown only in their embryonic state, obscured and confused by the magma of everyday production. It is fitting for cinema to do this without the affected disdain, the taste for facile parody, that too many intellectuals on both continents still consider to be the finest of fine art. It is to Cukor's credit that we cannot find in his work – as in that of Hawks – the slightest shadow of disdain for the popular form by which it is inspired, without this respect prohibiting him – on the contrary – from keeping a desirable distance.[*]

(*Cahiers du cinéma* 83, May 1958)

Politics against destiny: Joseph L. Mankiewicz's *The Quiet American*

This is an admirable film and is well worth a change of opinion. He who says *politique des auteurs,* says loyalty, and it is certainly easier and more appealing to maintain faith in a man than in a system. This is why one should not be too surprised to see me take the opposite view of the one I expressed here earlier, concerning *Les Girls.* No film caused more ink to flow at *Cahiers* than *The Barefoot Contessa,* and yet

*This article was originally entitled *La Quintessence du genre* (JN).

the films that we ordinarily defend in this review, films of spatial construction or of corporeal expression, as our friend André Martin would
say, bear hardly any resemblance to the film Mankiewicz now proposes. Even Bergman, whose *All These Women* reminds us a bit of *A
Letter to Three Wives,* is a far cry from Mankiewicz. We like *our* directors, which does not stop us from being critical when they go astray.
And what more monumental mistake than the director of *All About
Eve* trying his hand at *Guys and Dolls!* Musical comedy requires talents that he lacks and scorns those that he possesses to such a high
degree. In short, we have here a filmmaker whose strong point is neither theater nor "shows," nor perhaps "writing" either, in the sense
that Bresson uses the word.

I am therefore obliged to return to a former pet subject, which was
prevalent at the time of Objectif 49 and which is probably less outdated than we had thought since the CinemaScope era. At that time,
you may remember, the conquest of cinema by a certain "novelistic
depth" was a much-debated topic. This film is not seen: *It is read.* The
audience forgets that it is an audience, and its silence is not so much
reminiscent of the tense attention of an auditorium as it is of the
peace of libraries. We have not heard the hum of this prose, which is
not at all oratorical, for a few years: since *The Barefoot Contessa,* to
be exact. We are free to have partly forgotten its appeal and to have
replaced it with the poetry of twenty other engaging films. But why
wouldn't there be enough room in our hearts for *both* one *and* the
other?

The craze for adaptations has never been so great as it is now. And
almost all have been failures. It is undoubtedly just as stupid for a
filmmaker to remake *Moby-Dick* or *The Brothers Karamazov* as it is for
a sculptor to recreate the Mona Lisa in marble. These crazy projects
risk compromising both the script and the sculpture.

But in posing the question in such a way, are we not oversimplify-
ing it? Can we really impose any other limitation on the filmmaker
than that of producing something *better* than his model? If he succeeds, bravo, but we may be skeptical when faced with the pretensions
of an Autant-Lara or of the team Aurenche–Bost to improve Dostoyevski's *The Gambler!* On the other hand, when it is a question of a modern novel, we need not be as humble, not so much because our century
is inferior to past centuries, but because our literature owes so much
to cinema that it is only fair if cinema ransacks it.

Before talking about what Mankiewicz adds to Graham Greene's
novel, let us begin by noting all that he *cuts out.* Roughly, he eliminates all that seemed "cinematic," the pointillism of descriptions, the
ellipses, the sudden changes of subject, the behaviorism, the physical,
carnal atmosphere. This is what Nicholas Ray did, in cutting out René

Michael Redgrave and Giorgia Moll in *The Quiet American*.

Hardy's flashbacks, or Preminger when he took it upon himself to eliminate all of Sagan's impressionist discoveries [in *Bonjour tristesse*]. Rather than a film that was already there, they all preferred to offer us a new
one, one that is their own, not that of the public domain. Mankiewicz
is talkative, and so his film will be so: But why should he be silent if
his dialogue works majestically on the screen? An admirable dialogue,
worthy of comparison with those of Giraudoux, Meredith, and *tutti
quanti* but that does not in the least irritate the actors' palates.

Let's just say, if an explanation is necessary – with the understanding that it is entirely provisional – that film loves extremes. Either it is
leery of words or it cherishes them. It is true that before anything else,
it gives us something to see, but when it provides an opening onto a
world of brilliant chatterers, they must be as eloquent as possible. To
restrain their prolixity would be to betray the fundamental realism of
the cinematic work. And that is why Mankiewicz *adds* to it.

He covers the sentences cut out by Greene's scissors with a kind of
sociability that every conversation possesses, at least among people
who are gifted with words, and his characters, each in his domain, are

definitely members of that class. They talk, always saying something, but never saying too much, whether to their conversation partner or to us, the audience. Each reply is realistic, each reply is necessary. There are lines in many films that burn the actors' lips, a bit the way that "The marquise departed at five o'clock" pierced Valéry's eardrums: allusions, for example, to an excessively recent literary or political event. But here, Fowler or Pyle or Phuong or Vigot can go from the Marshall Plan to Shakespeare, from Commissioner Maigret to Chinese cuisine without making us wince in the least, because it is guaranteed in the first minutes of the film that their conversation will be part of this continuing and full duration which is that of life more than fiction, that of the novel more than drama.

We are now compelled to bring up that dangerous word *psychology*, which we may have spoken ill of following Jean Renoir's comments (must we always take him literally?) but whose virtues are not unpleasant to discover following as subtle a leader as Mankiewicz. Or if one prefers, let us propose the word *intelligence*, for these characters "analyze themselves" much less than do those in any Freudian drama on Broadway, and when they do, it is for tactical reasons. Let us define this term *intelligence* more precisely, a term that could lead us to believe that we are witnessing a bout of intellectuals – which they are more or less. A different kind of intelligence accounts for their worth here, that of *connoisseurs.* They are deceived by one another, but in a championship contest. Too many films – whether they treat the world of gangsters, love, sports, politics, or fishing – succeed only in making specialists laugh. For the first time in cinema since *Julius Caesar,* by the same Mankiewicz, we listen to a story of adult espionage, and perhaps to one of the great *political* films that the history of cinema has known.

You may say that this value can be partly attributed to Graham Greene, and that is true. It is no less true that in giving this intrigue an ending of his own invention, the filmmaker transforms the golden subject matter into the most precious of diamonds, whose facets with their thousand inextinguishable sparkling lights haunt us long after the film's ending.[*] On the one hand, we have the story of an English journalist who out of jealousy collaborates with the Vietnamese to assassinate a naive American. The American, a partisan of the Third Force, delivers bombs to dissidents and turns out to be responsible for some horrible attacks: This latter circumstance does not excuse the Englishman, but it saves him from appearing too odious. The film itself is enriched by a new chapter. Pyle, the American, was really an

---

[*] For nothing forces us to think that the final explanation given by Commissioner Vigot furnishes the definitive key.

Audie Murphy in *The Quiet American*.

idealist. He never delivered ammunition. The story was entirely forged by Vietnamese agents desirous, among other things, of obtaining from a British journalist evidence of violent American activities in Indochina.

Yes, I know, it is an American film, and it was important not to present Uncle Sam's nephew in too bad a light. But we have a similar situation here as in the end of the *Last Laugh* which, though added on, still is one of Murnau's most brilliant sequences. To consider this dramatic twist as a concession means forgetting *The Barefoot Contessa, All About Eve,* and all of Mankiewicz's works, which are constantly constructed around a *plot.*

In the past, we looked to Stendhal to help explain *The Barefoot Contessa;* I would now like to speak of Balzac, a good half of whose work – the best and the last – is a catalogue of more or less complex machinations, starting with *Une Ténébreuse Affaire,* the most beautiful spy and adventure novel of all time. I hope that this comparison will compensate for more ample proof. Truthfully, how can one prove, if not with examples, that "politics," in the broadest sense of the word, should rightfully take the place of "destiny," especially of a destiny in which we barely believe, a destiny for which a vague sense of "failure" or of "absurdity" is generally offered as a substitute.

If World War I, and even World War II, were connected by a tragic stopwatch – at least in the works that they inspired – I do not believe that the explanation of our most recent times by means of *fate* (I am of course speaking as a pure aesthete, as "disengaged" as possible) is the most profound, or the most attractive for art. Isn't the West's current and immense error that it makes sacrifices to this defunct god, that it places faith in the ineluctable march of history, a faith that is allotted more sparingly by those whose profession it is to fight in its name? No doctrinal position, I repeat, dictates my judgment: This sermon is even more in honor of the Vietnamese, sly enough to play on something as subtle as the confusion of words on the part of the conceited Englishman, between "plastic" – the material – and "plastic" explosives.* Every good communist owes it to himself, it seems to me, to approve of the ending, just as Karl Marx did not hide his admiration for the antirevolutionary fresco the *Peasants*, whereas our neutral press was outraged.

There is nothing more disappointing than the last pages of an adventure story: "My God, that was it!" Here, with no break in tone, with a simple "dialogue detour," as Luc Moullet astutely noted on Radio-Cinéma, this dispute between meaning and shaken pride suddenly takes its place in the immense prism of history, and we need not stop at the White House to appreciate the same perspective that Balzac gives us in the admirable last scene of his novel, in the office of the minister from Marsay. "This is a story, not a piece of history," says Greene in his preface. Mankiewicz does the same, but we can still feel that the echo of history, which serves as a backdrop to this little sentimental chronicle, has a better ring in the film than in the novel. The fragment of this enormous plot conforms better with the truth of our time, and every new day offers us a word-for-word rendition of the collusion between an American sophist and a Bellounis Indochinese.

The other change made by Mankiewicz, the relationship between Fowler the journalist and his mistress Phuong, strikes me, in the same way, as enriching the literary work, and not as impoverishing it, as many people say. In fact, this change flows from the first one, and vice versa. From the moment that human will is established as a major part of the intrigue, the heroes must no longer be the vegetables defined by unchangeable coordinates that they are in the novel: Outbursts, changes, become natural to them. It is important that the Vietnamese woman learn about love in the arms of the American, so that her resigned disdain for the Englishman in the book can become deep hatred in the film. Fowler had to be made to look ridiculous, not only from a romantic viewpoint, but also from that of his Western

---

* We know that a similar mistake in interpretation – blé [wheat] was translated as *maïs*, which means corn in American – resulted in yellow bread for quite a while after the war.

pride, so that his shame would transform the vague "regrets," mentioned in Graham Greene's last sentence, into self-disgust.

There are many lovers of ambiguity who deplore these supplementary chisel marks that the filmmaker added to the characters' traits. But I do not think anything has been erased from Graham Greene's work, which subsists like the pencil strokes under a painting. The definitive state, far from destroying the sketch, enriches it. Do we have the right to confuse the vague with the complex, to say that the emotional tumult of a novel's hero was his richness, a tumult that did not resist being put in order or being confronted by events? The novel's characters are only one aspect of the personality of those in the film. Pyle does not seem any larger in our eyes because of his innocence; Fowler's treachery takes on more relief as soon as he allows himself to be stupidly fooled; and Phuong, finally, abandons her abstract Far Eastern hieratic manner. In regard to the characters' psychology, and adventure or political intrigues, the novel is very much the rough draft of the film.

"And the mise-en-scène?" This question troubled me, I admit, given that personally I hardly noticed the mise-en-scène, as one does immediately in the films of Kazan, Visconti, Ophuls, Hitchcock, and so on. Then I realized that the rapt attention that I never ceased to give the story right from the first seconds, the unique feeling of comfort that up until then I had experienced only when reading a novel, was the surest guarantee of the mise-en-scène's existence. Isn't the work Mankiewicz put into adapting the film already the mise-en-scène, which actually means mise-en-film, and isn't his rendering called *production* in movie studio jargon? The worst mistake on our part would be to define a notion, one that is justifiably important to us, in too simplistic a fashion: a simplification that, for example, made our initial approaches to Bergman more severe than they should have been. True, in Mankiewicz, especially in this work, which was photographed in the English style by Robert Krasker, we hardly find the decorative improvements that Minnelli's last two films used – not to mention Welles's films, of course! But can we be sure that *The Quiet American* extracts its fascination only from the grace of its dialogue? Would it work so well on the screen, spoken by actors who were less firmly directed? Don't they find, at every moment, the right silences, the right glances, to serve them as supports? And even supposing the text were touching when spewed out quickly – which is not the case – wouldn't that be the greatest miracle? For why should the means count, in this art or in others, more than the result?

The purist may rest assured. Mankiewicz is certainly not the most prolix in purely cinematic finds. But even if there is only one per film,

I wouldn't give it up for a hundred others back to back. In *The Barefoot Contessa,* we had the astonishing flashback that took us beyond the point where we had left the characters, as well as the only emotion, I believe, in all the history of cinema (for neither *Rashomon* nor *Les Girls* really plays the game) at the approach of the famous slap, shown from a new angle. In this film we have the mixture of languages, sketched out in the novel, but that the cinema uses more subtly and effectively. The method is not new, it is true, but until now it was only ornamental, whereas it constitutes the basis of this story of plastic and plastic explosives. Let us beware of hasty definitions: Would we have believed, for example, that one day, our old friend, the mise-en-scène, would hide beneath the cloak of a play on words?[*]
(*Cahiers du cinéma* 86, August 1958)

Ingmar Bergman's *Dreams* (*Kvinnodröm*)

Cahiers now will be a subscriber to Ingmar Bergman for a good long while, as *Dreams* inaugurates a series of more or less varied releases to take place over the coming months. We will certainly not complain about this, nor will the reader, whether provincial or Parisian. The year 1958 will be the year of Bergman for French audiences, just as 1953 was the year of CinemaScope. These two events have nothing in common, except their equal ability to enhance our reflections, which we know to be bulemic: If one awakened hopes that were mostly fulfilled, the other comes just in time to throw the necessary wrench into a critical machine believed by some to be excessively greased.

Some of us have been led to reconsider our somewhat hasty rejection of a cinema that is indifferent to trends. There is something old-fashioned about Bergman and even, we might say, resolutely provincial. The artistic capitals are no more stable than the outer reaches, and even if they were, it would not be the first time in the history of art that a voice has been heard the world over that cared little about being heard beyond its own borders. Therefore, while continuing to love America and also being a bit nomadic these days, let us pay tribute to the greatest Swedish filmmaker for his avowed loyalty to his little country: Freedom flourishes there, a freedom whose benefits almost everywhere in the world had seemed questionable to us until now.

We do not admire Bergman solely because he benefits from the same independence as a New York or Parisian playwright does, but we also will not refuse to breathe the air of freedom found in his films. We might say, to conclude a debate that had to be mentioned to avoid our being accused of faulty logic, that we praise him less for using

---

[*] This article was originally entitled *Politique contre destin* (JN).

this freedom to a good end than we do others – Hawks or Hitchcock – for having dealt with their constraints. Just as the lion is carnivorous and the deer herbivorous, one painter is validated by the violence of his colors and another by his rejection of color, our new idol can adopt the glorious titles that meant little when applied to his contemporaries.

Nevertheless, there is one quality that all filmmakers concerned with being included in our Olympus must have. No one works for *Cahiers* if his is not a *metteur en scène*: This is not a truism, as flexible as the term may be for us. Bergman has no reason to be alarmed at the chaos with which his films are appearing in Paris. Of all his works that we have seen, *Dreams* is truly the one in which the portion of what we have agreed to call the *production* (shooting script, editing, directing) is the easiest to see. On paper, the plot is very thin, often almost beyond words, in any case incapable of hinting at its depth. It seems that the director thought in terms of pure cinema right from the start, before imposing on it, as he often does, the primary form of a theatrical piece.

Although the second episode is the most talkative one, I bet that even before deciding what the characters would say, the director had the idea of filming it as a close-up with an almost fixed camera. In addition, this film's mise-en-scène, by virtue of its diversity, presents the greatest homogeneity. It is the film in which the mise-en-scène seems to be based most fully on a *formal postulate* whose consequences are carried through with the utmost rigor.

The film starts off being "silent," or more exactly, with sound, just as a hundred others have done, are doing, and will do. But this sort of introduction, though serving an ornamental purpose in other films, sets the tone of the work. It is not so much that we are subsequently led to consider the protagonists' words as epiphenomena. The fact that the characters do not talk is not important. Their silence is "appropriate": The model poses, the photographer looks, annoyed by the boorish impatience of the fashion director, who taps the table with his fat fingers. On the one hand, this raw feeling of irritation foreshadows the complexities to come, in which the physical aspect, though it does not take precedence over the moral aspect of the story, serves as a guide and a springboard. On the other hand, the depiction of the physical aspect by using editing closer in style to that of silent films than to that of talkies, gives the film a more concentrated symbolic color than is customary these days. We might mention in passing that we forgive Bergman for this archaism – which is more apparent than real – for in our preamble, we gave him the right to do as he likes.

These two women's dreams are shown each time in the form of an

Gunnar Björnstrand and Harriet Andersson in *Dreams* (*Kvinnodröm*).

intoxication in which, through the exaltation of images and sounds, the director wants us to participate. The photographer (Eva Dahlbeck) leaves for a shooting session with her model and heads to a city where the man she loves – would like to leave but cannot resist seeing again – lives. In the train corridor she is overcome by desperation. Using a few parallel shots of the fogged-up window, the door handle, the rails, and the moving train, Bergman communicates the fascination so well that we forget his method has been used a thousand times and that we had legitimately found it to be heavy and arbitrary in others' works. No musical partition (from start to finish, the film has none) could serve better, as either an accompaniment or an interpreter of the heroine's thoughts.

In Gothenburg, while the photographer calls her lover, the model

(Harriet Andersson) is accosted in front of a shop window by an old playboy (Gunnar Björnstrand). Once again we have a portrayal of various states of drunkenness: that of the young girl intoxicated by her seducer's various gifts: a dress, a necklace, a bracelet, cake, and champagne; and that of the man in his fifties, moved by the beautiful girl and the amusement park rides. Both will have a more or less nauseating awakening: he, upon leaving the amusement park, when he falls sick in the middle of the street, and she, when the old-timer's daughter arrives, slaps her, and snatches the bracelet given to her by her father. It is, of course, a golden situation for a filmmaker, especially if he has at his disposal actors as extraordinary as Gunnar Björnstrand or Harriet Andersson, both of them at their finest, seemingly improvising their lines and facial expressions. But the goldsmiths in this material can be counted on one hand, and Bergman is a match for the two greatest that ever were: the Renoir of *Nana* and the Stroheim of *Queen Kelly*.

There is probably not more here, if there truly isn't less, than in the aforementioned films. But it would be a mistake to consider this and the next chapter as two separate sketches. Although we may forget the model's misfortunes in the scene that immediately follows, between the photographer and her lover who has come to her hotel room, these misfortunes can be read between the lines. This, by both analogy with and in contrast to the second situation (two people return to their solitude after being dazzled by a semblance of love, just as the two others had been by a glint desire), and also, because after the *fortissimi* and the *prestissimi* of the preceding passage, the film, in which the soul's effervescence always finds lyrical expression, requires a slower, more muffled movement, just as in a symphony the *andante* follows the *allegro*. Here the actors' faces are glued to one another, and the impassive camera lets them pour forth a wave of words that would have constituted what we call in the slang of the profession "a tunnel" if the formal system adopted by the filmmaker throughout the sequence (which is to put us in the position of a spectator with binoculars at the theater) did not give the scene a color, or if one prefers, a tonality that it could not have found solely in the dialogue. Not that we read fresh nuances in the facial expressions, which are destined to corroborate or contradict the meaning of the words. The "plus" that the proximity of the profiles of this forty-year-old man and woman contributes – to which the cheated wife's profile, surprising the couple, will be added – is not, I believe, in the realm of expression. These faces, smooth and clear as cameos, exert a charm that is essentially less dramatic than poetic: They distract us from the words more than they help us understand them, but the medal-like forms with which they haunt us are the means by which we can break through their fundamental opacity, the same opacity that, at the beginning of the film, the noise of the train was enough to dissipate, like a puff of smoke.

Let's admit that, here, Bergman is traveling roads as thorny as the ones before were rosy. But at least this time we cannot accuse him of not being absolutely modern. His refusal to dramatize is followed with such rigor, such efficacy, that until now, Rossellini aside, we have hardly seen the likes of it. But as we said, this film has a lyrical composition, and this scene of constrained progress – even in the three-way explanation – leads to an admirable *appassionato,* developing in counterpoint the work's two themes, which had been isolated until then. First, once the door is closed, we have Eva Dahlbeck's unexpected outburst, an explosion that is more real, more *cinematic* in its theatrical affectation than are the close-ups of searching eyes by which so many inept filmmakers confirm their inability to find the right expression to communicate a certain distress of the soul, confident that some all-purpose ambiguity will come to their rescue. Then, we have Harriet Andersson's sobbing to the photographer, as she expresses a desperation that she believes she is alone in feeling. Here we have an example of the kind of sentimental transfers by which the great filmmakers like to show us all the breadth of their genius, a scene very similar to the one in *Bonjour tristesse* in which Anne, discovering Raymond's infidelity, seems to express her sorrow by her rival's burst of laughter.

May this reference to the most beautiful film ever shot in Cinema-Scope bring an additional contribution to the appeasement of the aforementioned quarrel.*

(*Cahiers du cinéma* 89, November 1958)

Alfred Hitchcock's *Vertigo*

Itself, by itself, solely ONE everlastingly,
and single.

                – Plato

We would have gladly pardoned Alfred Hitchcock for following the austere *Wrong Man* with a lighter work, more of a crowd pleaser. Such was perhaps his intention when he decided to bring the novel by Boileau and Narcejac, *D'entre les morts,* to the screen. Now, the esoteric nature of *Vertigo,* so they say, repelled Americans. French critics, on the contrary, seem to be giving it a warm welcome. Our colleagues have now given Hitchcock the place we [at *Cahiers*] have always reserved for him. As a result, we are now deprived of the pleasurable task of defending him.

* This article was originally entitled *Pourvu qu'on ait l'ivresse* (JN).

There is therefore no reason to measure his genius according to someone else's standards. Hitchcock is sufficiently renowned to merit comparison with no one other than himself. I used as a preface to this critique a sentence by Plato, which Edgar Poe used at the beginning of "Morella" and whose argument, in certain respects, resembles that of *Vertigo*. I did this not because I mean to put our filmmaker on equal footing with Plato, nor even with Poe, but simply to propose a key that, in my opinion, is capable of opening more doors than others can. Too bad if it seems somewhat pretentious. We are not trying to make Hitchcock into a metaphysician. The commentator alone is responsible for the metaphysics, but he believes it to be both suitable and useful.

Vertigo seems to be the third panel of a triptych, the first two being *Rear Window* and *The Man Who Knew Too Much*. These three films are architectural films, first, because of the abundance of architectural motifs, in the proper meaning of the word, which we find in all three. In this case, the first half hour is even a kind of documentary on the urban setting of San Francisco. The backdrop is furnished by a number of turn-of-the-century homes, on which the camera lens likes to rest, just as it rested before in *To Catch a Thief* on the Côte d'Azur. Their immediate, pragmatic reason for existence is to create an impression of disorientation in time. They symbolize the past toward which the detective turns, at the same time as does the supposed madwoman.

In the course of the film, we find an older architecture, that of an eighteenth-century Spanish monastery, which is linked, this time very directly, by the tower above it, to the major theme of the story, vertigo. And here we are one step further in the analogy with the two films mentioned. In each one, the heroes are victims of a *paralysis* relative to movement in a certain milieu. The reporter in *Rear Window* is in a situation of forced immobility, the milieu being space. In *The Man Who Knew Too Much,* the doctor and his wife, in conforming with the title, knew too much about the future but, at the same time, too little: Their paralysis is ignorance, and the field is no longer that of space, but of time. In this film, the detective, once again acted by James Stewart (who in his corset, reminds us of the photographer in *Rear Window*), is also a victim of paralysis, that of vertigo. The milieu in this instance is constructed by time, but not that of premonition, oriented toward the future. Rather, it is directed toward the past: reminiscence.

Like the two others, *Vertigo* is a film of pure "suspense," that is, it is a constructed film. The motive for the action is no longer the march of passions or some tragic moral (as in *Under Capricorn, I Confess,* or *The Wrong Man*), but a process that is abstract, mechanical, artificial,

Hitchcock's *Vertigo*.

and external, at least in appearance. In these three films, man is not the driving element. It is not fate, either, in the meaning that the Greeks gave it, but, rather, the very shapes that the formal entities space and time acquire. We can, of course, quibble indefinitely about whether or not Hitchcock's films contain "suspense." In the general sense of the word – the ability to keep the audience breathless – we will always agree that they do, especially in this film, even though the detective's key (which closes the novel) is revealed to us a half hour before the end. We already knew that Hitchcock's secret passageways did not open onto the secrets of police machinations, clever as they may be. We wanted to know more and more, as we learned more of the truth. The important thing is always that the solution to the enigma not burst the whole of the intrigue, which up until the last minute was busy expanding, like a soap bubble (a criticism we could have made, for example, about *To Catch a Thief*). Here, the suspense has a double effect: It not only sensitizes us to the future, but it also makes us reappraise the past. For the past in this case is not a mass of unknowns, which an author has the divine right to keep in reserve and which, when exposed, will untangle all the knots. When it reappears, the past tightens these knots even more. As the smoke of the story clears, a new figure appears whom we did not know as such but who was always present: the Madeleine believed to be real, yet whom we never really knew, who was, in any case, a real phantom, because she existed only in the mind of the detective, because she was only an *idea*.

Just like *Rear Window* and *The Man Who Knew Too Much*, *Vertigo* is a kind of parable of knowledge. In the first, the photographer turned his back on the true sun (meaning life) and saw only the shadows on the wall of the cavern (the courtyard). In the second, the doctor, who had too much faith in the police's deduction, also missed his mark, although feminine intuition succeeded. Here, the detective, fascinated from the start by the past (represented by the portrait of Carlotta Valdes, with whom the phony Madeleine pretends to identify) is continually sent from one set of appearances to the next: in love not with a woman but with the idea of a woman. But at the same time, just as in the two other parts of the trilogy, outside this intellectual meaning (I mean relative to knowledge) we can distinguish another one, a moral one this time. Here once again, Stewart is not only wretched and deceived but also guilty, "falsely guilty" as Hitchcock says, that is, falsely innocent. A tribunal accuses him of being guilty, by his blunder, for the woman's death. But although he did not in any way cause Madeleine's death, this time, because of his perspicacity and his recaptured dexterity, he will certainly be responsible for Judy's death, whom he falsely accused of complicity.

In using the term *parable*, I do not mean to accuse *Vertigo* of dryness or unreality. In no way is it a tale. At most, one discerns here and there, as in all of Hitchcock's films, small distortions of verisimilitude – one might say the disdain for certain "justifications" – that in the past often disturbed some people. If *Vertigo* is bathed in a fairytale atmosphere, the fogginess and blurriness are in the mind of the hero, not of the director, and do not affect the ordinary realism of the tone. On the contrary, we should admire the artistry with which the filmmaker creates this fantastical impression by the most indirect and discreet means, and especially how much, in a subject close to that of *Les Diaboliques*, he is reluctant to play on our nerves. The impression of strangeness is produced not by hyperbole, but by attenuation: Thus, the first part is almost entirely filmed in wide shots. The distracting satirical episode (the relationship between the detective and the designer) is treated with a no less subtle humor and prevents our feet from ever leaving the ground. These casual asides are not simply meant as a balancing act: They help us better understand the character, by making his madness more familiar, changing it from a state of madness to a certain deviation of the mind, a mind whose nature may be to turn in circles. The passage in which Stewart becomes Pygmalion is admirable, to the point that we almost lose the thread of the story itself. All of Hitchcock's depth is in his form, that is, in the "rendering." Like Ingrid Bergman's gaze in *Under Capricorn,* this removal of makeup – which is in fact an application – can be seen and not told.

Finally, in this silent, glossy film, which is actually a love story, more than the burning kiss between the detective and the woman he tries in vain to bring back from the dead, Stewart's breathless final speech introduces a dimension that until then is curiously absent: passion. It is not a rhetorical sermon in the least, but a digression to discourse, as is Bergman's monologue in *Under Capricorn.* So what if this outburst comes late, as this film is characterized by an alternating current: Future and past incessantly switch positions. In the light of this vibrant act of accusation, the entire film takes on a new color: What was sleeping awakens, and what was living simultaneously dies, and the hero, conquering his vertigo, but *for nothing,* once again finds only emptiness at his feet.

Of course, comparisons other than the ones I suggested can be made with the two films starring James Stewart. Allow me one more comparison, this time with *Strangers on a Train.* We know how much this film owed, not just in severity, but in lyricism, to the obsessive presence of a double geometrical motif, that of the straight line and the circle. In this case, the figure – Saul Bass draws it for us in the credits – is that of the spiral, or more specifically, the helix. The straight line and the circle are married by the intermediary of a third dimension: depth. Strictly speaking, we find only two spirals materially figured in all the film, that of the lock of hair at the nape of Madeleine's neck, a copy of the one worn by Carlotta Valdes that, one must not forget, arouses the detective's desire, and that of the stairway that leads up the tower. For the rest, the helix is suggested, by its revolving cylinder, which is represented by Stewart's field of vision while following Novak's car, by the arch of the trees over the road, by the trunks of the sequoias, or by the corridor mentioned by Madeleine and that Scottie finds in his dream (a dream, I admit, whose flashy designs clash with the somber grace of the real landscapes), and many other motifs that can be detected only after several viewings. The shape of the thousand-year-old sequoia and the traveling shot that pivots (in fact, the subject is pivoting) around the kiss still belong to the same family of ideas. It is a vast family that counts many relatives by marriage. Geometry is one thing, art is another. It is not a question of finding a spiral in each of the film's shots, like the men's heads proposed as a guessing game in sketches of leaves, or even like the crosses in *Scar-*

face (a bet magnificently kept, but a bet nonetheless). These mathematics must leave a door open to freedom. Poetry and geometry, far from crushing each other, travel together. We travel in space in the same way we travel in time, as our thoughts and the characters' thoughts also travel. They are only probing, or more exactly, spiraling into the past. Everything forms a circle, but the loop never closes, the revolution carries us ever deeper into reminiscence. Shadows follow shadows, illusions follow illusions, not like the walls that slide away or mirrors that reflect to infinity, but by a kind of movement more worrisome still because it is without a gap or break and possesses both the softness of a circle and the knife edge of a straight line. Ideas and forms follow the same road, and it is because the form is pure, beautiful, rigorous, astonishingly rich, and free that we can say that Hitchcock's films, with *Vertigo* at their head, are about − aside from the objects that captivate us − *ideas,* in the noble, platonic sense of the word.*

(*Cahiers du cinéma* 93, March 1959)

* This article was entitled *L'Hélice et l'idée* (JN).

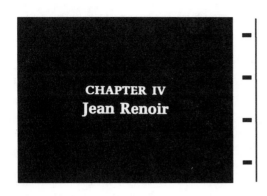

CHAPTER IV
Jean Renoir

The American Renoir

Though the sign of a genius may be that he owes recognition to posterity, our times also seem so good at rushing the day of judgment, formerly reserved for succeeding or future generations, that it is probably ridiculous for a critic, born one hundred years after Baudelaire, to take it upon himself to dig up the concept of the *misunderstood* from the romantic ashes and to apply it to the work of a man universally recognized as excellent in his art and, what is more, a man who has chosen the medium the least apt to be affected by the posthumous approval of a few pious connoisseurs. And yet the respectful indifference with which France welcomed Renoir's last films – an indifference that is still very much alive, as was apparent during the recent showing of *The Woman on the Beach* and *The Southerner* before the veteran audience of the two Parisian film clubs, the same clubs from which they turn people away for *Potemkin, Blood of a Poet (Le Sang d'un poète)* or *The Rules of the Game (La Règle du jeu)* – forces the critic to perform the disagreeable task, no longer of defending, but now of provoking a battle, only at the cost of which the evolution of the greatest French filmmaker can be seen in its true light. For as far as I know, Renoir had no reason to "complain" about the judgments of the American period of his work – of judgments passed by most of our journalists, who were more than fair with *The Southerner,* among others, and were very good at emphasizing everything in this film that bore the mark of the director of *Toni* or of *A Day in the Country (Une Partie de campagne).* But with one or two exceptions, as enthusiastic as their praise was, it implicitly inferred that if Renoir had occasionally succeeded in doing "as well" as he did before, he was nevertheless unable to "do better," and they slyly invited a public that loves novelty to refuse to have anything to do with films that they were led, at most, to consider as well-constructed replicas of earlier works – works that a distance of ten or fifteen years and the very difficulty one has in seeing them again glorified with an unassailable charm. No one went so far as to speak of a drying up or a decline but, more cleverly, the disappointment was blamed on the effects of new working conditions, on the demands of different audiences or less liberal producers, and other good reasons in which, my word, a quite understandable patriotism played a part.

One has to think that Renoir's interviews with the press, in which he was careful to specify that in Hollywood he was completely free to choose his subjects, actors, collaborators, or means, were only skimmed. Has he a devious enough mind for us to explain such declarations by the most elementary need for prudence, just as we think that fear of Richelieu or Louis XIV equally deprived us of the republican or libertine ideas of Corneille or Molière? For those who believe that, I will add that these so-called commissioned works had very modest success in the United States, and André Bazin himself said that the most recent one, *The Woman on the Beach,* far from being the result of a producer's whim, as is believed, is among those for which Renoir assumed the most responsibility, even though he did not finish it himself (but Welles did not finish the *Ambersons,* or Stroheim *Queen Kelly,* either). Here we are, far from the myth of a Renoir polluted by the dictates of a large firm, crushed by the wheels of the overwhelming Yankee machine: I know of no films that exhibit a more complete freedom to improvise on the set than does *Swamp Water* or *The Southerner.* It seems, moreover, that far from leading to a rigidity in the shooting script that some people lament, the use of more refined technical means must instead have facilitated the task of the French director most adept at manipulating the traveling crane shots.

One cannot prove the beauty of a work, and I admit to being sufficiently unimpressed by the false truths of reasoning by analogy not to practice it much myself. But the stakes here are such that no weapon, even the most devious, is to be completely rejected. In any case, as a token of my admiration for Renoir's last films, I would like to show the extent of their greatness by reminding us of the most esteemed masterpieces of certain great musicians, writers, or painters. To admit a possible decadence on the part of their creators – all extenuating circumstances aside – would be to recognize that their evolution follows the laws of those with ordinary talents; for as far as I know, the history of art offers us no example of an authentic genius who, at the end of his career, had a period of real decline. Rather, beneath the seemingly unrefined or meager appearance of the aforementioned films, we are prompted to seek evidence of the desire for simplicity that characterized the final works of a Titian, a Rembrandt, a Beethoven or, closer to us, a Bonnard, a Matisse, or a Stravinsky. Having mentioned these

great names, I would now like to propose a critical approach that will
focus neither on "beauties" nor on "faults" but that has its roots in the
internal reasoning of an evolution whose path evaded us. This critical
approach will help us discover the virtues beneath these pseudofaults,
which the poorly trained eye has been unable to appreciate. Such an
idea reverses certain commonly admitted values, but I believe our
times are better prepared to recognize that the nature of a masterpiece
is to suggest a new definition of beauty. Given the reputation that today's intellectuals have for being nonconformists, I am always surprised when they are quick to copy the canons of their own aesthetic
from that of a work declared sacrosanct by the very fact that it was, in
its time, revolutionary. To invite them one day to adore what they
burned is enough to make those most practiced in the subtleties of dialectical reasoning jump with indignation. I am tempted by this prospect. However, the works I am speaking of deserve better than the
ever-so-tempting response that their good parts are those that are considered *bad,* that if *Nana* is usually appreciated because we see a fifty-
year-old on all fours, or *The Crime of Monsieur Lange (Le Crime de
Monsieur Lange)* because it is anticlerical, most of the pleasure I had
in seeing *The Southerner* for a second time was in admiring a man
who loves his wife and believes in God. Don't misunderstand me: It is
not by redoing Poussin that we can surpass Picasso, and I am as leery
of all neoclassicism as I am of belated surrealism. This return to good
feelings, to the traditional concept of art, to the values of order and
harmony, would indicate defeat only if it didn't correspond to the evolution of cinema as a whole. It is important to note that the director
whose career is already one of the longest, has, by a secret instinct, or
simply because of destiny, found his "personal philosophy" constantly
adapted to the trends of his art. On the level of pure expression, he
never ceased being an innovator. The originality of the best films of
these past ten years owes very little, all things considered, to the use
of new techniques. Rather, it is characterized, as Bresson said, by a
heightened consciousness of film's ability to explore "interior life."
This spirituality that underlies most of the greatest and, yes, the most
misunderstood recent films, from *Les Dames du Bois de Boulogne (Ladies of the Park)* to *Under Capricorn* and *Flowers of St. Francis,* pro-
claims the brilliant revenge of an art that, earlier lowered to the level
of a serial story, now strives to find the best of its inspiration in the
belief in the *soul.*

In all honesty, therefore, we cannot say that Renoir is behind the
times. I remember watching a projection of *Miss Julie,* astonished at
not being moved by a story signed by one of the greatest dramaturgists
of the beginning of the century. During this projection, the image of

Zachary Scott (right) in *The Southerner* by Jean Renoir.

Francis Lederer, who, as we know, played the part of the valet in *Diary of a Chambermaid,* insisted on superimposing itself on the Strindberg character so much that the idea of a comparison, which was not to the advantage of the Swedish film, naturally came to mind. I will say right away that the very ordinary talent of Alf Sjöberg, the director, was not so much in question but, rather, the content of the dialogues, the characters, and the situation: in short, all that they had most faithfully preserved from the play. I found that this story of masters and servants was based on ethics that were *out,* to use today's terminology, perhaps because it preached the "free" morals in which we no longer have the pleasure of believing, whereas the other film, Renoir's (so freely adapted from Mirbeau that I can mistake the adapter for the author), far from troubling in any way the hierarchy of bourgeois values, led us both to hate and to admire the efforts of a man clever enough to exploit the cynical mentality of servants for his own best interests. Not that I don't believe in personal tragedy, but every real tragedy always begins with an acceptance of the established order, as difficult as it shows the constraints to be. Some people may be surprised that I am presenting as a conservative the director who shot *La Marseillaise* for the Popular Front and who is said to have exposed the faults of a certain French high society so well in *The Rules of the Game*. I will answer that in all of his works (except for *The Crime of Monsieur Lange*, in which one senses too much Prévert for my tastes), the satire is pushed to a point that allows us to see some true tenderness for the vices it claims to portray. We should leave to the literary manuals the belief in an art that condemns. I find it significant that our greatest novelist, Balzac, whom many well-meaning people want at all costs to portray as a censor of his time, and consequently an apostle of socialism, was an ardent legitimist (cf. certain pages of *Curé du village*). I would not like to make out Renoir to be something he may not be, but sensing how much his current "conformity" bothers some of his former admirers, instead of proving – as they would like – that this is only superficial, I prefer to give in to the wicked pleasure of detecting aspects of our filmmaker's past work that can be seen to foreshadow his present orientation.

If it is true that art is above all the search for beauty, it is hard to imagine an artist condemned to paint what he dislikes. In response, one can object that the realism to which Renoir formerly subscribed rebels precisely against the naive idea of an art in love with "nature's beauty." To this I would reply that the logic of cinema's basic realism, which I readily admit to be its seminal principle, is, starting with a truer, more severe look at things, to inspire a keener respect in the creator for his model, which he only aspires to reproduce exactly. It has often been said that the screen transfigures: On the contrary, I see the camera as a mechanical instrument able, at most, to bring out only the most sordid aspects of nature, that is, the flattest. Therefore the lyricism, whose dangers we might warn of elsewhere, appears here as the exclusive privilege of a few great works by those who are able to bring nature out of its shell. There is poetry in cinema only when it surpasses realism (isn't it interesting that Renoir said *poetry* had become his only goal!). When I said at a film club, at the end of a showing of *Tabu*, that Murnau was the greatest man of our time, I sensed that the audience had trouble believing I was serious. I want someone to dare take me at my word; yes, the most beautiful poems of this century are not, I repeat, those of Lorca, Eluard, Mayakovski, Eliot – or whoever else – but the documentary films (one of which was paid for by the advertising agency of an oil company, and fragments of some others are part of an educational film series) entitled *Tabu, Que Viva Mex-*

ico!, and *Louisiana Story.* Once this idea is accepted, one will grant that it is easier to add *The Southerner* to the list than the unduly famous and contorted *A Day in the Country,* which some insist on making one of the high points of Renoir's art. This is what I wanted to show.

Do we need supporting texts? I will not abuse this type of proof, and whoever knows Renoir knows that he is not a man to be bothered by his own contradictions. But I noticed, in what I have read of him since his departure from France, that he insists on combating the idea of a naive realism so much that it seems difficult not to repeat some of his statements:

Less improvised, less intuitive, such will be, I presume, the film of tomorrow. But to arrive at this new form of expression, we must avoid a great danger: that of the current idea we have created of realism, the faith in the photographic representation of a reality chosen at random. To want things to "seem real" is a colossal mistake. Art must be artificial and constantly recreated. This facility to recreate was cinema's reason for existence, and if we forget it, we will lose it. The root of cinema's fatal sin is in forgetting that it must remain fictional.

Another text, same language:

Since man exists, he confuses art with the imitation of reality. In the primitive periods, either limited technical means or certain religious rules formulated by well-advised prophets prohibited artists from following this unfortunate tendency. In our day of so-called progress, there are no more limitations, no more rules, and we are witnessing a kind of debauchery. Individual artists, painters, writers, sculptors can still avoid it. Nothing prohibits them from digesting nature as they please and from giving it back to us in the most unexpected forms. But in making a film, the artist brings many people together, and even if one of them vaguely senses that one of art's characteristics is to be artificial, even if he manages to communicate this point of view to his co-workers, the odious voice of reason is quickly heard. By "reason," I mean the necessity to make a commercial film and not to shock an audience whom we suppose to be composed of experts on this wonderful reality. And in fact, it is composed of experts, and how could it not be after twenty-five years of imbecilic perfection in photographic reproduction. As a result, we have today's canons.

An actor becomes a star because he resembles many of the people that one can meet on the street. That way, they think, these people will be happy to see themselves on the screen, with just a few improvements: better-tailored outfits, clearer skin, and no little hairs in their nose. Once in a while, a filmmaker tries to be innovative, by putting the little hairs back in the nose or by using a young star with rotted teeth. As for me, if I see the same people at the cinema that I can meet in a café, I don't see why I shouldn't just go to a café instead of to the cinema. It's more comfortable and you can order something. Those who came before us were lucky: orthochromatic film prohibited all nuance and forced the most timid cameraman to accept violent contrasts; no sound, which led the least imaginative actor and the most vulgar director to use involuntarily simplified means of expression. (*Ciné-Club,* May 1948)

Robert Ryan and Joan Bennett in *The Woman on the Beach* by Jean Renoir.

This deliberate effort toward "simplified means of expression" can be followed throughout all of Renoir's American works, from *Swamp Water*, in which the technique, as Jacques Rivette pointed out (*Gazette du cinéma,* June 1950), still reminds us of that used in *The Rules of the Game*, right down to the simple style of *The Woman on the Beach*, in which one can count the camera's movements and in which one feels, beneath the apparent casualness of the script, a firmness in the directing, the likes of which we rarely find in talkies. This return to its original sources, far from indicating a renunciation, is, as history proves, characteristic of the final phases of a creator sure enough of his personality and his inventiveness to appropriate what he likes.

But back to *Diary of a Chambermaid,* for which I will not hide my secret preference and which I consider (with all due respect to its director, but must we take him literally?) as one of Renoir's most personal films (because if need be, Flaherty could have done *The Southerner,* and Stroheim, *Nana*). I see the grouping together of a thousand motifs from earlier films, and the expert on cruelty, who is nevertheless sufficiently refined not to be satisfied with entirely superficial violence, will find what he is looking for here. It is true, there is not a rape in sight, nor a tortured rabbit, but the knife that Francis Lederer brandishes toward the goose's neck shines with such sinister brilliancy that the normal mind will not be sorry that the neck in question is out of the field of vision. More importantly, as perfect as *Nana, La Chienne, Madame Bovary,* or *The Rules of the Game* were, they do not tell us any more about the power of cinema than we already knew – they treat the outward relationships among human beings: the human comedy and its many faces. *Diary of a Chambermaid* is perhaps the only film, to my knowledge (quite honestly, *The Last Laugh* is the only one I see to equal it), that depicts the kinds of feelings we like to bury in the depths of our soul – not just feelings of repressed humiliation, but even the distaste or weariness we feel toward ourselves – and depicts them so limpidly, without the help of commentary or other artifice, that the boldness of such a subject becomes apparent only after some thought. Renoir, as we know, said he regretted that this film was not shot in France. But we should be happy that the problems of reconstruction forced him to give up pursuing the picturesque, of which he has given us enough examples, but gave him in exchange the freedom to pursue his attempt at interior exploration and to transfer the film's interest to the enigmatic, clear face of the valet, an interest that more faithfully portrayed supporting roles would have diverted for their own benefit. I'll stop here, for fear that an excess of subtlety will make my demonstration, which I wanted to be directly convincing, seem specious. I will remind those of my readers who had the good fortune to see *Diary of a Chambermaid* to remember what they felt at the "strong" points of the work (admitting that there were "weak" ones): for example, the lady of the house's slap, the fight with the son in the conservatory, or the wonderful shot in which the crowd backs away from the whip. Name a less gratuitous example of violence or one that is more soberly fascinating. One of the reasons I place this film even higher than *The Southerner* is that the fight scenes that stand out in the latter, poignant as they are, seem too much like school exercises when compared with the savage clash between the robust servant and the consumptive master, that show us, in a flash, a world of secrets that until then had only been glimpsed. It is true, especially at this moment, that we are still shown only this world, and no one rejects the "allusive" style, so dear to our lazy filmmakers, more than Renoir. But what makes a film such as this so worthwhile is that the transparency of gesture comes from an initial opacity, suggesting the mystery of interior life that three centuries of novelistic investigation have still left us unable to penetrate.

I have not yet seen *The River.* What I have heard of this film makes me fear, as enthusiastically as it is praised, that it may incur the same criticisms of blandness, conformity, or meagerness. I will feel I have done something useful if this rapid plea succeeds in fostering, among those who are impatiently awaiting the opening, not indulgence, which Renoir does not need, but the demanding severity without which, uninformed of his project's ambition, we may be deceived by the voluntarily modest appearances behind which every authentic masterpiece maliciously likes to hide.*

(*Cahiers du cinéma* 8, January 1952)

Paris Does Strange Things (*Eléna et les hommes*): Venus and the apes

French Cancan generally disappointed Renoir's fervent admirers. Not that the film seemed a failure, but it was somewhat below the director's usual caliber. And this was even more apparent because it adopted – simplifying it to an extreme – one of the themes of *The Golden Coach* (*La Carrosse d'or*): show biz.

Italian comedy is one thing, Theater with a capital T, but the cancan? In making a plea for cabaret, Gabin also made a plea for Renoir, who had no other concern than that of making a "commercial" work. Popular, easy, but nonetheless worthy of its predecessors, capable of appealing to both the uncultured and the refined, and for the same reasons.

---

* This article was signed Maurice Scherer (JN).

This arrogant and simple project was merely the result of an evolution whose significance, since *The Rules of the Game (La Règle du jeu)*, we have not yet been able to grasp. Renoir, who at the start of his career declared war on clichés and opposed the public's tastes, left his conquests to others and returned to aesthetic or moral conformity. The cinema, no longer a springboard to bounce off new ideas, became a particularly good place to play with clichés, which a paradoxical mind such as his loves to nurture. Renoir loves cinema too much not to accept it as it is, with its vulgarity and, to be honest, its foolishness. Such is the "message" of *French Cancan,* if there is one to speak of.

Eléna is more ambitious, but this ambition must pass through an initial simplicity, a simplicity that is as complacently prevalent as in the preceding work. Conceived in the form of a fable, it has a moral that seems much more simplistic than the one expressed in *Boudu Saved from Drowning (Boudu sauvé des eaux)* or *The Rules of the Game.* It therefore obliges us, if only out of love for these films, not to stick to the initial appearances. Didn't Renoir himself warn us that cinema was a difficult art and that "in a large theater like the Gaumont-Palace, there may not be three people capable of understanding the film showing on the screen."

What does *Eléna* prove, then, for once again according to Renoir, "a film proves nothing but proves something just the same"? That nothing in life counts but love and eating well and that laziness is better than any action? This rule of life has its respectable patrons, Diogenes and Epicurus. What is more surprising is the brutal and linear form that Renoir gives it. By condemning Rollan, the puppet general, he condemns not only shoddy dictators but politics altogether. In mocking Eléna, the new Philaminte* or Madame de Chevreuse, he only thickens, with a fat pencil mark, the caricature that a particularly misogynous tradition, from Horace to La Fontaine, passing through the fables of the Middle Ages, has displayed to us in a thousand diverse forms. I know: "Eléna is Venus," but do we still believe in Venus?

Is Renoir merely rehashing the same truisms? If so, this must be a necessary exercise. Our century, though hardly prudish, has its taboos just the same. *Work* is one of them. "But really," one might say, "what sense does it make to preach idleness?" – "It shocked you," he will answer, "That's a start." After all, a film is not a catechism; this word *lazy* is, of course, symbolic. We smile when a bum says it, but now the director seems to be saying it: That is what bothers us. To be lazy is still to preserve, in these hurried times, some taste for contemplation, for pleasure. Look at our classics, on which we expound so well but essentially forget to put into practice.

---

* One of Molière's *Femmes savantes* (CV).

Mel Ferrer (horizontal) in *Paris Does Strange Things* (*Eléna et les hommes*) by Jean Renoir.

It is therefore not the least merit of this film to reinforce the meaning of some clichés. The proof that this is not a useless exercise is that we are suddenly surprised by maxims that were familiar to us when we analyzed Epicurus and Montaigne.

Everyone is free to use another key. I am adopting the one furnished by Renoir, when he uses the word *classicism.* He is trying to refer us to classical wisdom, rather than to the Hindu *nirvana.* The peasants, the bohemians of the last act, become a chorus of good ancestral sense, earth bound, as opposed to the glitter of an artificial civilization. This is not a materialistic film but, more precisely, a *pagan* one. And pagan, as we know, signifies peasant.

Let's go a step further, at the risk of being imprudent. There is always something reckless about explaining symbols. That is why I will limit myself to asking questions. Why does our blond and fair Venus, in order to be adored and to discover herself, need a black priestess surrounded by sad, dirty children who evoke the rituals of some free-

masonry less open to "enlightenment" than that of *The Magic Flute?**
Why do all the masculine characters, including the "young" stars Jean
Marais and Mel Ferrer, have an apish quality? In mentioning the word
ape, we evoke an animal but also, at the same time, a puppet. Renoir
is interested in both our most superficial crust and our deepest attachments to the earth. The soul is not rejected but finds shelter where it
can. Man is perhaps merely an animal who apes man. The idea is
both reassuring and terrifying.

Optimism and pessimism rub elbows with each other in Renoir's
work, as do grimaces and gracefulness, masks and truth. You remember the film by Hawks in which a chimpanzee was not the most repel-
ling actor? I am comparing on purpose the subtle Renoir to the least
intellectual of American filmmakers. Both of them, traveling on different roads, one carried by the genius of his art, the other fully conscious of the genius of his art and his own genius, arrive at the same
evident conclusion, one that cinema is best able to show. We live in
both the best and the worst of all worlds, the most beautiful and the
ugliest possible. That is why Renoir, more and more, is getting away
from the picturesque, which easily offers him both ugliness and
beauty. He prefers to reveal the animal beneath the tailcoat or uni-
form, the satyr beneath Adonis.

I am not trying to suggest that our director is a puritan. The Ancients had reason to couple Venus with Vulcan, the nymphs with the
fauns. There is probably an admission of an obsession close to his
heart here, which we constantly discover in the course of his work, but
he never ceases to give it a more universal significance.

According to the seventeenth-century classical canons, the art of
burlesque is to speak "of little things in a noble fashion." It seems
that in this farce, Renoir does exactly the opposite, as he treats the
most serious actions mockingly. But in truth, he works less with a noble reality than with the caricature that it inspires. Without dulling it,
he embellishes a portrait in the Caran d'Ache style, heightens the tone
of an Epinal imagery that is its true subject matter. Such is, I believe,
his secret here. Far from simplifying, he portrays life's liberty in a
schematic style from the start. Nothing is easier for a mediocre filmmaker than to move a marionette, and nothing is more contrary to the
genius of cinema than mime. Renoir knows this better than anyone,

---

* Nothing is less Manichaean than Renoir's world. The number *three* rules, as in the
masonic opera by Mozart, whose libretto Hegel admired so much. Far from leaning toward renunciation, the director of *The River* searches for reconciliation. That is why
there is always a *mediating* event or character in his works. A provisional mediation
that could be considered Christian spiritualism (*The Southerner, Orvet*), as well as the
spiritualism of the religion of Rabelais's Messer Gaster or that of the black masses. But
listen to the song by Gréco...

but his mastery is such – he did such a long and brilliant internship at the realist school – that he plays with the difficulty on which others stumble.

In this case, the art must not be grasped in great chunks, but in its embellishments, which is why a second, even a third, viewing is necessary. Little by little the puppets lose their mechanical gait, and we become sensitive to a thousand nuances in their acting that had at first escaped us and that explain the rather rough, angular dialogue. It is not that the characters take on more depth. Once again, Renoir tells us, still in regard to *Eléna,* "that he did not want to use psychology." We should interpret psychology in the meaning given it by nineteenth-century writers. His characters have reactions that are as predictable as, let's say, those of the Wolf and the Sheep in La Fontaine's *Fables.* Like the fabulist, Renoir considers no genre to be deserving of disdain, provided one can bring "novelty and gaiety" to it and, of course, elegance.

This comparison will perhaps shock the admirers of each of these men, especially, I believe, those of the filmmaker. But remember that Valéry restored the poet of *Adonis* in a rather majestic fashion, and in any case, why not grab the rope Renoir has thrown us, even if it is a tiny bit treacherous? His classicism is not spontaneous, like that of the Ancients or the Americans in Hollywood, but voluntary, like that of our French writers, and yet not at all pedantic. Like Molière, who brought the farce from the scaffolds of the Tabarin to the Théâtre français, he aims to "make men of honor" and commoners laugh with the same-sounding laughter. Cinema, one will say, had accomplished this difficult task since the work of Chaplin and Mack Sennett. Renoir has, in addition, a clear picture of what he is doing, which does not make his task any easier. He is unfamiliar with the disdainful humor beneath which so many others, less inventive and bitter, hide. He wants others to forget that he knows his classics so well, those of the cinema and the others, and the strange thing is that he succeeds.

Let us not be fooled by his aristocratic nonchalance or by the current simplicity of his style. Having mastered the traveling shot and depth of field, he now enjoys presenting us with a flat, choppy, discontinuous image, as if to evoke his own kaleidoscopic action. Don't you be fooled. One question, for example. What kind of shot is most common in *Eléna?* The master shot, you unhesitatingly answer. Well, the detail images are much more numerous than those of the whole, but by using the correct proportion, the director is able to give us the impression that we are seeing all of the set at each moment and that at the same time the characters are as close to our eyes as we would like.

One more example: Try to recreate the arm movement at the very end, by which, before sitting down to eat, Pierre Bertin expresses the moral – one of the morals – of the fable, and in such a savory manner. Try, and you will understand why Renoir cannot be imitated, and what a thankless task the critic has, who, using only words, must celebrate the merits of an art able to turn mime into something more subtle and eloquent than the most beautiful prose in the world.

(*Cahiers du cinéma* 64, November 1956)

Renoir's youth

There was much talk this year of young cinema. In 1959 we saw more new French names listed on credits than during the preceding decade. Some members of the team at *Cahiers* are part of the class. They rejoice in their luck. They thank the public for the attention it was kind enough to show their first attempts. They are pleased to lead their mission, only whose negative aspects we were able to see, into a constructive era. Until now, all efforts were limited to spreading the grains of sand destined to impede the wheels of a decrepit but sturdy machine: the sacrosanct monster of "quality cinema."

But our current good fortune does not make us ungrateful to the masters who entertained and educated us. Now that we have moved into action, the distance that separates our productions from theirs seems even greater. The year of the New Wave is 1959, but this fact may concern only the local press. The great history of cinema will forever remember a date particularly prolific in masterpieces. I am not even speaking of the two films that are being released late, *Ivan the Terrible* and *Ugetsu* (*Ugetsu monogatari*), works that are already covered by a definite patina and that are on our list of the twelve best films of all time. It happens that we saw – or will see – in the next several months, two Hitchcocks, one Hawks, two Rossellinis, and two Renoirs, directors that we have always, as you know, elected as our guiding lights. *Vertigo* or *North by Northwest, Rio Bravo, India,* and even *Il Generale della Rovere, Dr. Cordelier, Picnic on the Grass* (*Le Déjeuner sur l'herbe*) are striking not so much because of their perfection as because of their novelty, novelty that in relation not so much to the individual evolution of their directors as to the future of film as a whole. The breath of fresh air that these films offer will perhaps be noticed only by true connoisseurs. It is not easily reduced to a concept or formula. These films remain, of course, very visibly attached to tradition, but that is not what interests us. What is important is the way they extend certain of the camera's powers, the way they force us to reconsider the art itself, to enrich our knowledge of it. Truthfully, they offer nothing new in the way of substance or style. But they do better:

Paul Meurisse and Catherine Rouvel in *Picnic on the Grass* by Jean Renoir.

They suggest an idea, until now inconceivable, of the relationship between substance and style.

Just the same, from among these four names, it is appropriate to consider Jean Renoir's evolution separately. The novelty of *Picnic on the Grass*, without being the least bit ostentatious, is immediately apparent, even to the layman. It is *technical* in nature. On this point, one must read the director's own ideas, published in *Cahiers* no. 100.* It is both very easy and very difficult to speak of Renoir, and for the same reason: He has said everything about his art, and better than anyone else could say it. It is not enough for him to be the greatest filmmaker in the history of talking films, he is also film's most intelligent theoretician. Others have been able to speak of themselves and their problems with precision and subtlety: He alone possesses the distance of

* *Cahiers du cinéma* 100, October 1959, *Pourquoi ai-je tourné Cordelier?* (JN).

which only professional critics are capable, or so we thought. Let us therefore merely repeat after him that the importance of shooting with several cameras is that it replaces the notion of the *shot* with that of the *scene*.

A method is worth only the use made of it. I do not know what the future of this one will be. What I am certain of, on the other hand, is that it will force us, for better or worse, to look at the films of tomorrow with a different eye than we did before. *Dr. Cordelier* and *Picnic on the Grass* begin a new chapter, just as *Citizen Kane, Rope,* or *The Robe* did. They appear deceptively simple. Just as the anamorphic lens existed some twenty-five years before Fox bought it, and the spirit of the wide-screen already animated the best films of the 1940s, so the method of multiple camera shots has always been used on television, but it helps us better distinguish the originality of all of Renoir's works. We undoubtedly perceived its rare quality but were never able to figure out the reason for it. Perhaps it is simply – but this is no small thing – that it was able to scorn superbly a condition of cinematic expression as necessary to other directors as the sentence is to the writer, the canvas to the painter, the bar to the musician. True, there are beautiful, admirable shots in Renoir, but their spatial or temporal borders do not exert the same tyranny over the material they enclose as do others. The double limitation of the frame and the splice was considered, for good reason, to be the necessary foundation for all cinematic language. Time and time again, it has been said that encircling a piece of reality in space and in time (whether these limitations were static or mobile, near or far) ennobled that piece of reality and bestowed the prestige of an art on a pure instrument of reproduction. Renoir, like everyone else, obeyed this essential rule, that not the depth of field, or the long take, or the wide screen have been able to dethrone, but at the same time, he has never stopped showing us glimpses of what could be an extreme case, the possibility of a cinema freed of its master, disdainful of the benefits of cinematography and editing.

If he likes to use the term *cinematography,* it is perhaps not, as it is for others, because he wants to be a purist but because "cinema" does not exist for him. The instrument interests him, an instrument with infinite possibilities, but not the finished product, the established religion, the official art. His films always in some way break up the ceremony of a cult to which others constantly make sacrifices, though they may pretend to be iconoclastic. In Renoir's work, people, sets, objects, and landscapes are shown in their true state, full of sudden starts, unpredictable reactions, drunk with freedom. In comparison, all other films, without exception, even the supposedly realist ones, evoke only the murky light and muted life of an aquarium. Before the

shooting, a preliminary transmutation takes place from the natural order of things to the cinematic order, even if the second means to reproduce accurately the first. The grain of the skin, seized by a filterless
lens closed as far as possible, may replace the unctuous glow of
makeup beneath diffused lights: Nothing changes. The acting may become less theatrical; the man on the street may replace the actor; and
the links may go from noticeable to invisible, but this does not have
much effect, either. In some indirect way, the camera will always proclaim its existence. Thanks to this profession of faith, it will mark
with a more or less noble stamp all it captures. And we will go to our
dark temples to admire things whose originals we would ignore in the
light of day.

Renoir is not ignorant of any of the camera's and the recorder's powers, either. He does not look to turn them off but refuses all the ways
offered by his art's inability to reproduce exact reality. If he is sensitive to the unfaithful splendor of orthochromatic film, it is really an
indication that the day is past when one could rely solely on the
charm of the film itself. Unlike the majority of his colleagues who are
often modern against their will, Renoir was able to be ahead of his
time on many occasions and to match the line of his personal evolution to that of cinema as a whole, an art always more in love with
truth, although over the years, truth is never defined in the same way
(sometimes by realism, sometimes by a rightful reaction against the
banalities of realism). The others, on the contrary, eager as they may
have been to use technical innovations, found them mostly to be an
additional constraint, apt to awaken their vitality.

This point deserves some consideration. I do not mean to say that
Jean Renoir is more realist than another. It is something else. In fact,
Picnic on the Grass is one of the most unrealistic films ever shot.
There is an avant-garde, popular theater side to this film: the simplicity, the intentional naïveté, the didacticism, right down to this famous
distancing that makes, say, [Brecht's] *Herr Puntilla und sein Knecht
Matti (Puntilla and His Servant Matti)* the absolute archetype of antici-
nema. But hasn't cinema's goal always been to include everything in
nature or human creation that seemed most foreign to it? Renoir's
films teach us to avoid taking what is accidental for what is part of
the substance, from confusing the true beauty of the cinematic work
with the kind of charm that, without sounding too ridiculous, we could
call "reelistic" – after all, even the prudent Sorbonne was not afraid of
creating barbarous neologisms. Just as the weave of the canvas forms
an integral part of the pleasure derived by the lover of paintings, the
cinephile is fascinated – even if he only indirectly realizes it – by the

very material of the *backing* or the *emulsion*. This is why the television screen throws him off and irritates him.

The great works of the screen get better with age, contrary to what might have been said before. Just like a painting or a sculpture, they acquire a patina, unstated in most cases, but the discomfort of the theater, the scratches on the film, the slipups in the projection – to the extent that they give substance to this patina – contribute, if need be, to fortifying the respect inspired. A Renoir film does not grow old in this fashion: It does not evoke nostalgia for the past but seems still newer in the eyes of its contemporaries. It has nothing of the herbarium's dried flower: It is a fruit that was picked a bit too early and that ripens slowly on the shelf. A process of enrichment, not of purification, takes place. Many beauties, drowned at the first showing in a somewhat disorganized mass, rise to the surface. Nuances, formerly confused, become distinct and form the guiding colors. We are surprised not to have noticed them earlier.

I know this parallel between Renoir and the other filmmakers has its share of simplifications. There are many films that, because of their perfection, have extended the limits not only of their genre but also of their art. But what is an exception elsewhere is the rule here. Renoir never wanted to get comfortable with cinema. If he likes to keep his distance, it is because he knows the cinema better than anyone else. He knows that the art's main asset is not that it adds a new interpretation of nature to those already furnished by the painter or the writer, that what is special about it are not only its means, its perspective, its writing, but also the original relationship it reveals between nature and the artist. He knows that it is apt to capture the most wayward aspects of *nature,* those aspects that are least able to be reduced to the canons of aesthetics, its *freest* aspects.

This is why Renoir has paid special attention to the fundamental relationship between appearances and beings, between freedom and rules, especially in those of his works that I would gladly call *reflexive* (even though they all are, in a sense) and in which he gives us his own version of [Horace's] *Ars poetica: Madame Bovary, The Golden Coach,* and now *Picnic on the Grass.* We have been struck many times by the similarities between his comic vein and that of Howard Hawks, the head of what we could call the *instinctive* school of cinema – as intelligent and united as it may be – that is, a school born of its own works and exempt from all reference to other art forms. The resemblance to *Monkey Business,* which we pointed out in regard to *Eléna,* is quite apparent here. And I do not think there are notions more worthy of cinema's interest – and consequently, more apt to stimulate its ridicule – than those of *science* and *nature,* one a symbol of its methods, the other a symbol of its object. The fable in *Déjeuner sur l'herbe* can be taken as an aesthetic as well as a moral parable. I am not making anything up: I will simply quote a paragraph from the interview published here two years ago:*

Simplicity is absolutely essential to creation. People who make love while saying: "We're going to conceive a magnificent child," well, they might not conceive any child at all that evening. The magnificent child comes unpredictably, one day after a good laugh, a picnic, fun in the woods, a roll in the grass, then a magnificent child is born!

I admit that we can stop at this interpretation of the film and enjoy it without taking too seriously the satire on science. Renoir is above all an artist, not a philosopher, or even a moralist. Yet as far as I am concerned, I give this satire the greatest credit, even though, like all satires, it proves nothing. *Picnic on the Grass* refutes the practical scientism of the twentieth century no more than "Le Souris et le chat-huant"[†] refutes the Cartesian system. But we cannot hold a grudge against the filmmaker for contenting himself with moralities in his recent works, any more than we can against the fabulist for doing the same in his last books, the most beautiful in the eyes of adults, if not of schoolchildren. I do not believe that didacticism is less acceptable in cinema than in poetry. In the beginning, like poetry, the Lumière brothers' invention was didactic, and in many ways it has remained so. Yes, like a document, one might say, because of the evidence that the image provides. Why only in this way? Why compare cinema with theater, if in turn we praise only cinema's love of the concrete by comparing it with the novel? The novel and film are close relatives, no doubt, but we may also find that the former exerts too great a tyranny over the latter, to the point that we often speak of cinematic quality when the word *novelistic* would be more appropriate. Long live fables, even if they seem to introduce a grain of impurity! This type of impurity is certainly less dangerous than many others are, which are more subtly disguised.

    This film saves us from one other danger: that of the *confession*. During its existence, cinema has been able to maintain a definite objectivity, owing to its own powers and also its limitations. The conquest of subjectivity, if it cannot be condemned in advance, may represent only a kind of suicidal victory. For here, film can do nothing less than conform to the models provided by the other arts, arts that are better equipped in this regard. Even if cinema manages to beat them in this area, will it avoid being contaminated by the illness that

---

* *Cahiers du cinéma* 78, 1957.
† "The Mouse and the Screech Owl" by La Fontaine (CV).

today plagues almost all of them? We should therefore praise Renoir for declaring war, in his interviews and conferences, on the mirages of *subjectivity,* just as he did on those of *psychology.* If throughout his works, we are able to see the man behind them, it is because the rose, as he says, is the best portrait of the artist. We should not blame our director for preferring to confide his ideas, rather than his heart, in us, as the art he practices is still the only one in which ideas can express themselves clearly and simply, even if at times we find their ingenuousness too simple.

Whoever has read Renoir or heard him speak could not have helped being struck by the extraordinary understanding this likable, eloquent man has of the problems not only of his art but also of his time. This is not to say that he is a master of thought or a prophet. But his remarks or anecdotes often open more appropriate and lucid perspectives on the spirit of the modern world than do the dissertations of specialists in the social sciences. God save us from a didactic cinema, but in the case at hand, the director's temperament is the best antidote to pedanticism. I believe that the artist has the right to look around him without, as they say, getting involved. He remains faithful to his vocation while speaking his piece on the great problems of today, which our masters of philosophy have overly politicized. One of these problems, a major one, concerns him directly, for by definition it comes from aesthetics: that of happiness, that is, *l'art de vivre.* Although specialists in dialectics, slaves of polemics, see only conflicts among men, it is more the great combat waged between our species and nature that gets Renoir's attention.

What I have said here proves nothing, of course, about the value of *Picnic on the Grass.* Yet, I believed it to be more useful to paraphrase some of Renoir's ideas than to make a detailed analysis, which is certainly necessary to highlight the many perfections of the film but which would risk losing sight of its great novelty. Let it simply be known that I consider *Picnic on the Grass* to be superior to *Eléna,* in whose vein it continues, in that the subject seems more vast and its expression less checked by commercial realities. It would be useless to rank Renoir's last period and the American period, or the first French period. Let's just say that our director has had the same fruitful old age as had a Titian, a Beethoven, or a Goethe, or even a Cézanne, a Matisse, or his father Auguste Renoir. These artists did not win the hearts of the contemporary or futures masses with their last works; these final creations are not only the delight of connoisseurs but banish any doubts about the flashier works of these artists. They may lack the gracefulness of youth or middle age, but I believe their merits to be more certain, better marked by the seal of eternity, less subject to the vagaries of fashion. This is also why they throw us off at first by their aridness, their asceticism, even the blurriness of certain passages, their apparent disorder. They seem to lack some flesh, whereas once the years have passed, it is mostly their rich sensuality that touches us, to the point of making the earlier works seem poor and thin in contrast. And as one can imagine in the case of Renoir, this is no small feat.

(*Cahiers du cinéma* 102, December 1959)

The Little Theater of Jean Renoir (*Le Petit Théâtre de Jean Renoir*)

Paradox: After this *Little Theater,* all other films seem theatrical. The initial theatrical project permits Renoir to escape from cinematic convention. This film is a long stroll through the different forms of theatrical convention,* toward the direct, (hyper)realistic expression of life, which is, at the same time, pure fantasy, an overflow of emotion that goes beyond the necessities of expression, liberates the sign from its function as a sign, is the ultimate last laugh.

This laughter is an audience's laughter, but it begins only when the hero himself decides to laugh. As is often the case with Renoir, there is a give-and-take between the audience and the film. In the three main sketches, there is a film (and an audience) inside a film. In "Le Dernier Réveillon," the rich people look at the poor person who looks at the rich people; in "La Cireuse électrique," the chorus of employees looks at the couple, and then the neighbor spies. In "Le Roi d'Yvetot" the role of the chorus is played by both the people of the village, and the maid.

The ordinary *realism* of the cinema is no longer used here. Since his American period, Renoir has declared war against it. He refuses to employ the reproductive powers of the camera, even if he means to use it later on, once he has acquired the right. He affirms the artificial quality of his universe by means of the set in "Le Dernier Réveillon" and by the lyrical convention in "La Cireuse." In "Le Roi d'Yvetot," we think we have rediscovered the prewar "realist" (was he?) Renoir, but the extravagance of the acting quickly reveals our mistake.

But *excess* and comedy quickly stop at certain moments in the three sketches, giving way to a sudden seriousness. Almost all of Renoir's films do this. This break in tone has nothing to do with affected expression. It is the thing itself, not the way it is said, that seems to

---

* *The Little Theater of Jean Renoir,* filmed in 1969, is composed of four sketches: "Le Dernier Réveillon" ("The Last Midnight Supper"), a Christmas story; "La Cireuse électrique" ("The Electric Polisher"), a musical comedy; "Quand l'amour se meure" ("When Love Dies"), a filmed song; and "Le Roi d'Yvetot" ("The King of Yvetot"), a comedy set in Provence.

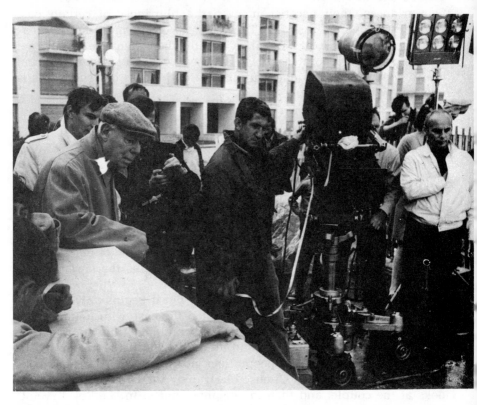

Jean Renoir during the shooting of *The Little Theater of Jean Renoir* (*Le Petit théâtre de Jean Renoir*).

change. Reality splits in two and looks at itself, in an attempt to capture the things in life that cannot be reduced to a performance. To capture nature, one must first dress it in artifice. We must aim for truth by means of falsity.

And yet it is cinema's *prerogative* to go from truth to truth without passing through the falsity of performance. The camera "records"; it presents more than it represents. In the end, however, this is true only for hard-core documentary, for the ingenuous age of *La Sortie des usines* (Lumière). As soon as film becomes fiction, it loses its innocence and its radical originality – even Lumière lost his, in *L'Arroseur arrosé* [*Le Jardinier*], which was drawn from a cartoon. Cinema must then bend to the traditional forms of performance or discourse: the comedy, the tragedy, the lyric, and the epic. In this sense, all cinema is impure as soon as it tells a story, *The Gold Rush* just as much as *Monsieur Verdoux*. The space and the time that it presents are fake. Mixing genres is one way of evoking, now and then – in the time it takes to pass from one to the next – that fleeting purity. The great moments in cinema, in Chaplin and in Keaton, are perhaps those when the comical and the serious, which are constantly running alongside each other, meet each other, intersect each other. The same is true in Renoir, but with more surprise and more violence.

The least original *example* (but it is a nostalgic tale) is in "Le Dernier Réveillon." The passage from the amusing to the pathetic is right in the tradition of Chaplin – and the beggar behind the window reminds us of a scene in *The Gold Rush.* But in "La Cireuse," the burlesque, exaggerated side of the situation kills all emotion. The characters are treated too much like puppets for their fate to move us at all. The machine's fate is almost more touching. Dislocated, splintered, lying helplessly on the ground, it is pitiable, contrary to the stated moral of the fable.

The break in tone here resides not only in the passage from one dramatic tonality to the other (from the comical to the serious), but in the passage from fantasy to normality. In almost all of Renoir's films, one can see the acting, starting with an excess sometimes giving the impression of awkwardness, suddenly give way to a very natural moment. Paradoxically, the sight of the broken machine sends us back to an untouched reality. This story is representative of all Renoir's directing: When the mechanical nature of the acting goes awry, the natural side springs forth.

Since *Paris Does Strange Things,* the acting has been systematically overstated, but this exaggeration sometimes stops, as if the actor, tired of "pretending,"* is catching his breath. He does this not by becoming himself again (the actor) but by identifying with the character. In this way his credibility is reinforced: The character who plays his character becomes the character when he isn't acting, whereas the actor who plays the character becomes only the actor. This is how Renoir's most discussed actors function, and yet they present the most fascinating characters: Georges Flamant (Dédé) in *La Chienne,* Valentine Tessier in *Madame Bovary,* Max Dalban (Albert) in *Toni,* Dalio (criticized in his day) in *The Rules of the Game (La Règle du jeu).*

If Michel Simon, in *Boudu Saved from Drowning (Boudu sauvé des eaux)* and Jules Berry in *The Crime of Monsieur Lange (Le Crime de Monsieur Lange)* are more easily accepted in their split acting, it is not so much because they are more "skillful" but because their characters belong to a social type (hobo, crook) for which ham acting is accepted as a natural attribute. Let's admit it: There may be some awkwardness among the first group, and Renoir, wanting to counter it,

---

* Renoir's own term, in admiring the burlesque Lumières and the Auto-Mabouls.

sometimes provoked it.* But only the result counts, and it is the same as in the postwar films, in which the dialectic skillfulness/awkwardness is replaced by that of elaboration/carelessness. In this case the blame is attributed to the director and no longer to his actors: He asks too much of them, or not enough.

This passage, in Renoir, from the comical to the serious, from the fantastic to the natural, from skillfulness to awkwardness, or vice versa, provokes a particular anxiety in us, which fits into no other known dramatic category. It is not "tragic." It is really a fear of what is going to happen, or is happening, but not to the characters. What is feared is sometimes not even an event: It does not happen on the level of events but on that of morality, of professional morality, of the consideration that the director owes his audience – in whom violent reactions are sometimes aroused. It is not so much a catastrophe as it is trickery. We are shocked; the rules of the game have been violated. It is as if we were having fun playing with a pistol and found that it was loaded.

In Fellini's *Satyricon,* we witness the theatrical representation of the punishment of a slave, and we believe it is rigged (as it is in the photography). But the character of the executioner is really supposed to cut off the slave's hand. The uncomfortable feeling one gets in this situation is often felt in Renoir, with less horror but with no less force. We go from behavior fit for a "comedy" (in the sense which Balzac, for example, gives to "human comedy") – the habitual behavior of the civilized person, to what we believe to be our natural state. But this natural state is just another costume for Renoir. The real man can be distinguished only while he is changing costumes. At that moment, we have a very strong sense of indiscretion. The cinema of today has made indiscretion its cardinal virtue, but the indiscretion is broadcast right from the start and so holds no surprises for us. Renoir, on the other hand, leads us to the heart of man's secret, a man shocked by the glance he casts at himself, at his own indiscretion concerning himself. "Le Roi d'Yvetot" holds in store for us a moment of prodigious intensity when Duvallier learns through the maid's embarrassment that his wife is in the bedroom with his rival. The exaggerated and comical acting of Dominique Labourier does not lessen, but reinforces, the pathos of the scene. We are not disturbed by the incident, which is a common one, but by the way it happens, which is all the more disconcerting, as the situation is almost that of a *boulevard* play. All Renoir lies in this "almost."

One word as to the morality or, if one prefers, the "ideology." These

---

* In retrospect, Jean Gabin's acting, which "cinematically" is the most irreproachable, seems less appropriate to the filmmaker's universe.

Dominique Labourier and Fernand Sardou in "The King of Yvetot" (the last
sketch in *The Little Theater of Jean Renoir*).

sketches are dramas of ideas, and they are presented as such each
time by a director's preamble. All of Renoir's later films, from *Paris
Does Strange Things* on, except for *The Elusive Corporal (Le Caporal
épinglé)*, take the form of fables. In "Le Dernier Réveillon," more interesting than the relationship between poor and rich is that between
viewer and viewed. The gaze is something that is troubling: It devours.
One thinks of Chaplin, but also of Nosferatu, the sad and pathetic
vampire. The face of the actor (the Italian Nino Fornicola) makes an
unforgettable impression on us. The morality here seems to be very
"idealistic," as Brecht* would say, even mystical: One can be happy

* Renoir and Brecht have some common ground. In each one's work, the actor distances
himself from the character, and each of them denounces "illusionist theater" and travels
the slippery roads of didacticism. The difference is that Brecht's irony, which is an irony
of combat, strikes only its adversaries, whereas Renoir's irony, petrified with doubt, is
not afraid to work on itself.

even in poverty and in death. This fable has a resolutely outmoded quality. Renoir expresses his nostalgia for an age that has gone and also for a way of thinking taught to him by childhood tales. It is almost the negative of his usual work. Death, immobility, and coldness (already seen in *The Little Match Girl* and *The Elusive Corporal*) are celebrated.

The subject of "La Cireuse" is the idea of revolution against the machine. (Its first title was *It's the Revolution!*) After his return to France, Renoir was constantly called reactionary. No one noticed that he was ahead of his time, preaching idleness and the rejection of industrial civilization. In *Paris...*, we had the first hippy, in *Picnic on the Grass (Le Déjeuner sur l'herbe)*, the first ecologist. But what is the main idea in this film? For the most engaging character is without a doubt...the machine. It is unlikely that Renoir wanted to trap the audience into a worthless sympathy, for the trap would be poorly laid! The machine is like the little rabbit in *The Rules of the Game (La Règle du jeu)*. It is cruel and deserves to die, but its death is painful, nonetheless.

This is the story in which Renoir took cynicism the furthest, especially when the chorus sings "Humans reproduce, their death is not as serious as the death of a machine." And this sentence does not have an absolutely negative (ironic) ring to it, as it would have had in Brecht, for the image seems to agree with it.

Renoir's *thought,* even if he proposes a certain wisdom, is above all nihilistic. He admits all ways of thinking, even the most shocking: shocking for bourgeois morality but also for the more "advanced" minds that constituted his prewar audience. Unlike many others, he is not being an instigator but, rather, sympathizes with humans, sometimes whole and passionate (and doomed to misfortune in the tragedies of the thirties), sometimes hiding from the vicissitudes of the world in their cocoon of indifference (Boudu, the vagabonds of Gorki, the pious workers of the South), sometimes even becoming the puppets of his last comedies, devoid of "psychology" but not of humanity. This is why it is perfectly natural for the final sketch, the filmmaker's ultimate work, to preach tolerance, "a virtue," Renoir tells us, "that is rare these days."

After this preamble, we expect a political epilogue. In reality, we have the story of a husband who tolerates his wife's having a lover. But after all, a fable is a fable, and one must generalize. Here, we rediscover one of the themes in *Toni* and *The Rules of the Game*. Faced with a rival, the character steps aside in the interest of the one he loves. But this self-effacement is not in the least heroic; it is presented in a ridiculous, shameful light.

If I had to keep just one film to give future generations the idea of what the art of cinema was in the twentieth century, I would choose *The Little Theater*, because all of Renoir is contained in it, and because Renoir contains all of cinema.

(*Cinéma 79*, no. 244, April 1979)

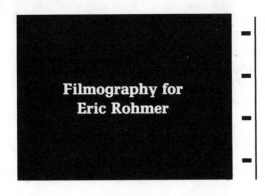

Filmography for Eric Rohmer

Films are listed chronologically by year of production (not of release). American release titles are given in parentheses.

1950

Journal d'un scélérat
Screenplay: Eric Rohmer
Director: Eric Rohmer
Editing: Eric Rohmer
Cast: Paul Gégauff

1951

Présentation or *Charlotte et son steak* (*Charlotte and Her Steak*)
Screenplay: Eric Rohmer
Director: Eric Rohmer
Editing: Agnes Guillemaut
Music: Maurice le Roux
Producer: Guy de Ray
Cast: Jean-Luc Godard, André Bertrand, Anne Coudret

1952

Les Petites Filles modèles (unfinished)
Screenplay: Eric Rohmer, after the story by Mme la Comtesse de Ségur
Directors: Eric Rohmer and Pierre Guilbard
Producers: Guy de Ray, Joseph Kéké

1954

Bérénice
Screenplay: Eric Rohmer, after the story by Edgar Allan Poe
Director: Eric Rohmer
Director of photography: Jacques Rivette

200

Editing: Eric Rohmer
Cast: Eric Rohmer, Teresa Gratia

1956

La Sonate à Kreutzer (*The Kreutzer Sonata*)
Screenplay: Eric Rohmer, after the story by Leo Tolstoy
Director: Eric Rohmer
Editing: Eric Rohmer
Producer: Jean-Luc Godard
Cast: Jean-Claude Brialy, Eric Rohmer, Françoise Martinelli

1957

Tous les garçons s'appellent Patrick or **Charlotte et Véronique**
Screenplay: Eric Rohmer
Director: Jean-Luc Godard
Director of photography: Michel Latouche
Editing: Cécile Decugis
Music: P. Monsigny
Production company: Les Films de la Pléiade
Producer: P. Braunberger
Cast: Jean-Claude Brialy, Anne Colette, Nicole Berger

1958

Véronique et son cancre
Screenplay: Eric Rohmer
Director: Eric Rohmer
Director of photography: Charles Bisch
Editing: Eric Rohmer
Production company: AJYM Films
Producer: Jean-Luc Godard
Cast: Nicole Berger, Stella Dassas, Alain Debrieu

1959

Le Signe du lion (*Sign of the Lion*)
Screenplay: Eric Rohmer
Dialogue: Eric Rohmer and Paul Gegauff*
Director: Eric Rohmer
Director of photography: Nicolas Hayer
Editing: Anne-Marie Cotret
Music: Louis Ségur
Production company: AJYM Films

* Paul Gegauff claims to have been credited for the dialogue without having truly collaborated on it.

Producer: Claude Chabrol
Cast: Jess Hahn, Van Doude, Michèle Girardon, Jean le Poulain, Paul Basciglia, Jill Olivier, Gilbert Edard, Christian Alers, Paul Crauchet, Sophie Perrault, Stéphane Audran, Malka Ribowska, Jean-Luc Godard, Macha Meril, Françoise Prévost, Jean Domarchi, Fareydoun Hoveyda, Jose Varela, Vera Valmont

1962

La Boulangère de Monceau
First of "Six contes moraux" (Six Moral Tales)
Screenplay: Eric Rohmer
Director: Eric Rohmer
Directors of photography: Jean-Michel Meurice, Bruno Barbey
Editing: Eric Rohmer
Production companies: Studios Africa, Les Films du Losange
Producers: G. Derocles, Barbet Schroeder
Cast: Barbet Schroeder, Michèle Girardon, Claudine Soubrier, Michel Mardore

1963

La Carrière de Suzanne (*Suzanne's Profession*)
Second of "Six contes moraux" (Six Moral Tales)
Screenplay: Eric Rohmer
Director: Eric Rohmer
Director of photography: Daniel Lacambre
Editing: Eric Rohmer
Production company: Les Films du Losange
Producer: Barbet Schroeder
Cast: Catherine Sée, Philippe Beuzin, Christian Charrière, Diane Wilkinson, Jean-Claude Biette, Patrick Bauchau, Pierre Cotrell, Jean-Louis Comolli

1964

Nadja à Paris
Screenplay: Eric Rohmer, after text by Nadja Tesich
Director: Eric Rohmer
Director of photography: Nestor Almendros
Editing: Jacqueline Raynal
Production company: Les Films du Losange
Producer: Barbet Schroeder
Cast: Nadja Tesich

1964–9

For "En Profil dans le texte" (educational TV series):
Les Cabinets de physique au XVII siècle
Les Métamorphoses du paysage industriel

Perceval or *Le conte du graal*
Don Quichotte
Les Histoires extraordinaires d'Edgar Poe
Les Caractères de la Bruyère
Le Béton dans la ville
Pascal
Victor Hugo
Les Contemplations
Mallarmé
Hugo architecte
Louis Lumière

1965

"Place de l'etoile"
Fourth short film comprising *Paris vu par six* (*Paris by Six*)
Screenplay: Eric Rohmer
Director: Eric Rohmer
Director of photography: Alain Levant, Nestor Almendros
Editing: Jacqueline Raynal
Production company: Les Films du Losange
Producer: Barbet Schroeder
Cast: Jean-Michel Rouzière, Marcel Gallon, Jean Douchet, Philippe Sollers, Sarah Georges-Picot, Georges Bez, Maya Josse
For "Cinéastes de notre temps" (TV series):
Carl Dreyer
Le Celluloid et le marbre

1966

Une Etudiante d'aujourd'hui
Screenplay: Eric Rohmer, after text by Denise Basdevant
Director: Pierre Cotrell
Director of photography: Nestor Almendros
Editing: Jacqueline Raynal
Production company: Les Films du Losange
Producer: Pierre Cotrell

1967

La Collectionneuse
Fourth* of "Six contes moraux" (Six Moral Tales)
Screenplay: Eric Rohmer
Director: Eric Rohmer

---

* Nonsequential numbering is Rohmer's: The third in the series (*Ma Nuit chez Maud*) was postponed until Trintignant became available.

Director of photography: Nestor Almendros
Editing: Jacqueline Raynal
Music: Blossom Toes, Giorgio Gobelsky, La Voix de l'Eternal
Production companies: Les Films du Losange, Rome – Paris Films
Producers: Barbet Schroeder, Georges de Beauregard
Cast: Patrick Bauchau, Haydée Politoff, Daniel Pommereulle, Alain Jouffroy, Mijanou Bardot, Annik Morice, Denis Berry, Seymour Hertzberg, Brian Belshaw, Donald Cammell, Alfred de Graaff, Pierre-Richard Bré, Patrice de Bailliencourt

1968

Fermière à Montfaucon
Screenplay: Eric Rohmer
Director: Eric Rohmer
Production company: Les Films du Losange
Producer: Barbet Schroeder

1969

Ma Nuit chez Maud (*My Night at Maud's*)
Third of "Six contes moraux" (Six Moral Tales)
Screenplay: Eric Rohmer
Director: Eric Rohmer
Director of photography: Nestor Almendros
Editing: Cécile Decugis
Production companies: Les Films du Losange, FFF, Les Films du Carrosse, Les Productions de la Guéville, Renn Productions, Les Films de la Pléiade, Les Films des Deux Rondes
Producers: Barbet Schroeder, Pierre Cotrell
Cast: Jean-Louis Trintignant, Françoise Fabian, Marie-Christine Barrault, Antoine Vitez, Léonide Kogan, Anne Dubot, P. Guy Léger, Marie Becker

1970

Le Genou de Claire (*Claire's Knee*)
Fifth of six *Contes moraux* (Moral Tales)
Screenplay: Eric Rohmer
Director: Eric Rohmer
Director of photography: Nestor Almendros
Editing: Cécile Decugis
Production company: Les Films du Losange
Producer: Pierre Cotrell
Cast: Jean-Claude Brialy, Aurora Cornu, Béatrice Romand, Laurence de Monaghan, Michèle Montel, Gérard Falconetti, Fabrice Luchini

1972

L'Amour l'après-midi (*Chloe in the Afternoon*)
Fifth of six *Contes moraux* (Moral Tales)

Screenplay: Eric Rohmer
Director: Eric Rohmer
Director of photography: Nestor Almendros
Editing: Cécile Decugis
Music: Arie Dzierlatka
Production company: Les Films du Losange
Producer: Barbet Schroeder
Cast: Bernard Verley, Zouzou, Françoise Verley, Daniel Ceccaldi, Malvina
Penne, Babette Ferrier, Françoise Fabian, Marie-Christine Barrault, Haydée
Politoff, Aurora Cornu, Laurence de Monaghan, Béatrice Romand

1975

Die Marquise von O (*The Marquise of O*)
Screenplay: Eric Rohmer, after the novella by Heinrich von Kleist
Director: Eric Rohmer
Director of photography: Nestor Almendros
Editing: Cécile Decugis
Production companies: Les Films du Losange/Gaumont, Janus Film
Produktion/Artemis
Producers: Margaret Menegoz, Jochen Girsch
Cast: Edith Clever, Bruno Ganz, Peter Luhn, Edda Seippel, Otto Sander, Ruth
Drexel, Eric Rohmer, Edward Linkers, Bernhard Frey, Ezzo Huber, Erich
Schachinger
Ville nouvelle (four TV programs on architecture)

1978

Perceval le Gallois (*Perceval*)
Screenplay: Eric Rohmer, after the romance by Chrétien de Troyes

1979

Catherine de Heilbronn (for TV)
Based on the play by Heinrich von Kleist
Director: Eric Rohmer
Director of photography: Nestor Almendros
Editing: Cécile Decugis
Music: Guy Roberts
Production companies: Les Films du Losange, FR3, Gaumont, ARD, SSR, RAI
Producers: Margaret Menegoz, Barbet Schroeder
Cast: Fabrice Luchini, André Dussolier, Pascale de Boysson, Clémentine
Amoureux, Jacque le Carpentier, Antoine Bard, Jocelyne Boisseau, Marc
Eyraud, Gérard Falconetti, Raoul Billerey, Arielle Dombasle, Sylvain Levignac,
Guy Delorme, Michel Etcheverry, Coco Ducados, Gilles Racek, Marie-Christine
Barrault, Claude Jaeger, Frédérique Cerbonnet, Anne-Laue Meury, Catherine
Schroeder, Francisco Orozco, Deborah Nathan

1980

La Femme de l'aviateur (*The Aviator's Wife*)
First in the series "Comédies et proverbes" (Comedies and Proverbs)
Screenplay: Eric Rohmer
Director: Eric Rohmer
Directors of photography: Bernard Lutic, Romain Windig
Editing: Cécile Decugis
Production company: Les Films du Losange
Producer: Margaret Menegoz
Cast: Philippe Marland, Marie Rivière, Anne-Laure Meury, Mathieu Carrière, Philippe Caroit, Caroline Clément, Lise Hérédia, Haydée Caillot, Mary Stephen, Neil Chan, Rosette, Fabrice Luchini

Le Beau Mariage
Second in the series "Comédies et proverbes" (Comedies and Proverbs)
Screenplay: Eric Rohmer
Director: Eric Rohmer
Directors of photography: Bernard Lutic, Romain Windig
Editing: Cécile Decugis, Lise Hérédia
Music: Romain Girre, Simon des Innocents
Production companies: Les Films du Losange, Les Films du Carrosse
Producer: Margaret Menegoz
Cast: Béatrice Romand, André Dussolier, Feodor Atkine, Huguette Faget, Arielle Dombasle, Thamila Mezbah, Sophie Renoir, Herve Duhamel, Pascal Greggory, Virginie Thévenet, Denise Pailly, Vincent Gauthier, Anne Mercier, Catherine Rethi, Patrick Lambert

1982

Pauline à la Plage (*Pauline at the Beach*)
Third in the series "Comédies et proverbes" (Comedies and Proverbs)
Screenplay: Eric Rohmer
Director: Eric Rohmer
Director of photography: Nestor Almendros
Editing: Cécile Decugis
Music: Jean-Louis Valero
Production company: Les Films du Losange, Les Films Ariane
Producer: Margaret Menegoz
Cast: Amanda Langlet, Arielle Dombasle, Pascal Greggory, Feodor Atkine, Simone de la Brosse, Rosette

1983

Les Nuits de la pleine lune (*Full Moon in Paris*)
Fourth in the series "Comédies et proverbes" (Comedies and Proverbs)
Screenplay: Eric Rohmer
Director: Eric Rohmer

Director of photography: Renato Berta
Editing: Cécile Decugis
Music: Elli and Jacno
Production companies: Les Films du Losange, Les Films Ariane
Producer: Margaret Menegoz
Cast: Pascale Ogier, Fabrice Luchini, Tcheky Kario, Christian Vadim, Virginie Thévenet, Laszlo Szabo, Anne-Sévérine Liotard

1986

Le Rayon vert *(Summer)*
Fifth in the series "Comédies et proverbes" (Comedies and Proverbs)
Screenplay: Eric Rohmer
Director: Eric Rohmer
Director of photography: Sophie Maintigneux
Editing: Maria-Luisa Garcia
Music: Jean-Louis Valero
Production company: Les Films du Losange
Cast: Marie Rivière, Amira Chemakhi, Sylvie Richez, Lisa Heredia, Béatrice Roman, Rosette, Eric Hamm, Gérard Quéré, Maria Couto-Palos, Isa Bonnet, Yve Doyhamboure, Dr. Friedrich Gunther Christlein, Paulette Christlein, Vincent Gauthier

1987

L'Ami de mon amie *(Boyfriends and Girlfriends)*
Sixth in the series "Comédies et proverbes" (Comedies and Proverbs)
Screenplay: Eric Rohmer
Director: Eric Rohmer
Directors of photography: Bernard Lutic, Sabine Lancelin
Editing: Luisa Garcia
Music: Jean-Louis Valero
Producer: Margaret Menegoz
Cast: Emmanuelle Chaulet, Sophie Renoir, Eric Viellard, François-Eric Gendron, Anne-Laure Meury

Quatre aventures de Reinette et Mirabelle
Screenplay: Eric Rohmer
Director: Eric Rohmer
Director of photography: Sophie Maintigneux
Editing: Maria-Luisa Garcia
Music: Romain Girre, Jean-Louis Valero
Production companies: CER, Les Films du Losange
Cast: Joëlle Miquel, Jessica Forde, Philippe, Laudenbach, François-Marie Banier, Jean-Claude Brisseau, Yasmine Maury, Marie Rivière, Béatrice Roman, Gérard Courant, David Rocksavage, Jacques Auffray, Haydée Caillot, Fabrice Luchini, Marie Bouteloup, Françoise Valier

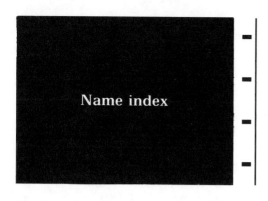

Name index

This index lists people, periodicals, organizations, studios, and so on. Abbreviations: f, photo; n, note.

Title index

This index lists works cited in the text. Abbreviations: f, photo; n, note.